Off The Shelf COOKING

Meredith® Books
Des Moines, Iowa

BETTER HOMES AND GARDENS® OFF THE SHELF COOKING
Editor: Carrie E. Holcomb
Contributing Project Editor: Mary Williams
Contributing Writer: Cynthia Pearson
Contributing Graphic Designer: The Design Office of Jerry J. Rank
Copy Chief: Terri Fredrickson
Publishing Operations Manager: Karen Schirm
Senior Editor, Asset & Information Management: Phillip Morgan
Edit and Design Production Coordinator: Mary Lee Gavin
Editorial Assistant: Cheryl Eckert
Book Production Managers: Pam Kvitne, Marjorie J. Schenkelberg,
    Rick von Holdt, Mark Weaver
Contributing Copy Editor: Lisa Bailey
Contributing Proofreaders: Alison Crouch, Karen Fraley, Gretchen Kauffman
Contributing Indexer: Elizabeth Parson
Test Kitchen Director: Lynn Blanchard
Test Kitchen Product Supervisor: Marilyn Cornelius
Test Kitchen Home Economists: Elizabeth Burt, R.D., L.D.; Juliana Hale;
    Maryellyn Krantz; Greg Luna; Laura Marzen, R.D.; Jill Moberly;
    Dianna Nolin; Colleen Weeden; Lori Wilson; Charles Worthington

MEREDITH® BOOKS
Executive Director, Editorial: Gregory H. Kayko
Executive Director, Design: Matt Strelecki
Managing Editor: Amy Tincher-Durik
Senior Editor/Group Manager: Jan Miller
Senior Associate Design Director: Ken Carlson
Marketing Product Manager: Gina Rickert

Publisher and Editor in Chief: James D. Blume
Editorial Director: Linda Raglan Cunningham
Executive Director, Marketing: Steve Malone
Executive Director, New Business Development: Todd M. Davis
Executive Director, Sales: Ken Zagor
Director, Operations: George A. Susral
Director, Production: Douglas M. Johnston
Director, Marketing: Amy Nichols
Business Director: Jim Leonard

Vice President and General Manager: Douglas J. Guendel

BETTER HOMES AND GARDENS® MAGAZINE
Deputy Editor, Food and Entertaining: Nancy Hopkins

MEREDITH PUBLISHING GROUP
President: Jack Griffin
Executive Vice President: Bob Mate

MEREDITH CORPORATION
Chairman and Chief Executive Officer: William T. Kerr
President and Chief Operating Officer: Stephen M. Lacy

In Memoriam: E.T. Meredith III (1933–2003)

All of us at Meredith® Books are dedicated to providing you
with the information and ideas you need to create delicious
foods. We welcome your comments and suggestions.
Write to us at: Meredith Books, Cookbook Editorial Department,
1716 Locust St., Des Moines, IA 50309-3023.

Our seal assures you that every recipe
in *Off The Shelf Cooking* has been
tested in the Better Homes and
Gardens® Test Kitchen. This means
that each recipe is practical and
reliable, and meets our high standards
of taste appeal. We guarantee
your satisfaction with this book for
as long as you own it.

Contents

Appetizers   5

Soups & Stews   27

Meats   57

Poultry   105

Fish & Seafood   155

Meatless Meals   185

Side Dishes   205

Desserts   229

Index   250

Homemade Meals in Little Time

Do you and your family crave a home-cooked meal, but you can't find the time to make one? With a few shortcuts in the kitchen, that homemade meal can be a reality, even for time-strapped families.

The recipes in this book are designed to **make your life easier and your meals more satisfying and delicious**. By using a combination of **ready-made convenience foods** along with a few fresh ingredients, these recipes cut your prep time so you get dinner on the table faster than ever. **With everything from classic family favorites to meals for entertaining**, this book will soon become your go-to cookbook for every occasion. You'll find recipes for appetizers, meat, poultry, seafood, meatless dishes, soups, sides, and desserts.

The secret ingredient to turning out delicious, mouthwatering dishes that don't require a day in the kitchen is using the good stuff that's on your grocer's shelves.

Look for these icons throughout this book: **LOW FAT** = less than 12 grams of fat per serving. **FAST** = start to finish in 30 minutes or less. **EASY** = prep time of 15 minutes or less. **NO FAT** and **SLOW COOKER**

Why cut, chop, and mix everything from scratch when the work is done for you with high-quality, easy-to-find products from the shelves of your local supermarket? **Make it simple and make it scrumptious. Make it Off the Shelf!**

Appetizers

French Onion Dip

PREP
25 MINUTES

CHILL
1 TO 24 HOURS

MAKES
6 SERVINGS

1½ cups chopped sweet onion (such as Vidalia, Maui, or Walla Walla) (3 medium)
2   tablespoons butter or margarine
1   10.75-ounce can condensed cream of onion soup
¼   teaspoon coarsely ground black pepper
⅛   teaspoon cayenne pepper
4   teaspoons snipped fresh chives
    Assorted dippers (such as potato chips, tortilla chips, and/or baby carrots)

OFF THE SHELF TIP Grab a can from the soup section. Just make sure your choice is condensed, not ready-to-serve.

STEP 1   In a large skillet cook onion in hot butter over medium heat, for 10 to 15 minutes or until tender and golden, stirring occasionally. Cool.

STEP 2   In a blender or food processor combine cooked onion, soup, black pepper, and cayenne pepper. Cover and blend or process until nearly smooth.

STEP 3   Transfer dip to a small bowl. Stir in chives. Cover and refrigerate for at least 1 hour or up to 24 hours. Serve with assorted dippers.

PER ¼ CUP DIP: 96 cal., 6 g total fat (3 g sat. fat), 17 mg chol., 429 mg sodium, 9 g carbo., 1 g fiber, 2 g pro.
EXCHANGES: ½ Other Carbo., 1 Fat

Garbanzo Bean Dip

Mild garbanzo beans join intensely flavored olives and crushed red peppers for a thick, hummus-style dip that's terrific served with crackers or crispy vegetable dippers.

EASY

START TO FINISH
15 MINUTES
MAKES
6 SERVINGS

1   15-ounce can garbanzo beans (chickpeas), drained
½   cup plain low-fat yogurt
¼   cup bottled buttermilk salad dressing
2   tablespoons seasoned fine dry bread crumbs
2   teaspoons lemon juice
½   teaspoon crushed red pepper
2   tablespoons chopped pitted, ripe olives
        Assorted crackers or vegetable dippers

OFF THE SHELF TIP Find seasoned bread crumbs in the packaged goods section of your supermarket, near stuffing mixes and pastas.

STEP 1   In a food processor or blender combine garbanzo beans, yogurt, salad dressing, bread crumbs, lemon juice, and crushed red pepper. Cover and process or blend until smooth. Stir in olives. If desired, cover and refrigerate at least 1 hour before serving. Serve with crackers or vegetable dippers.

MAKE-AHEAD DIRECTIONS: Prepare as directed, except cover and refrigerate for up to 24 hours.

PER ¼ CUP DIP: 164 cal., 6 g total fat (2 g sat. fat), 4 mg chol., 396 mg sodium, 20 g carbo., 4 g fiber, 4 g pro.
EXCHANGES: ½ Starch, 1 Fat

Hot Artichoke & Roasted Pepper Dip

Use your food processor to combine this dip until smooth, then bake it to serve warm for a full melding of flavors.

PREP
15 MINUTES
BAKE
25 MINUTES
OVEN
350°F
MAKES
12 TO 14 SERVINGS

RECIPE PICTURED ON PAGE 142.

1   **8-ounce package cream cheese, softened**
1   **cup shredded Parmesan or Asiago cheese (4 ounces)**
1   **teaspoon bottled minced garlic (2 cloves)**
1   **13- to 14-ounce can artichoke hearts, drained**
1   **cup bottled roasted red sweet peppers, drained**
1   **cup sliced fresh mushrooms**
½   **cup sliced green onion (4)**
    Thinly sliced baguette-style French bread or pita wedges, toasted
    Chopped bottled roasted red sweet peppers (optional)
    Fresh parsley (optional)

STEP 1   Preheat oven to 350°F. In a food processor combine cream cheese, Parmesan cheese, and garlic. Cover and process until well mixed. Add drained artichoke hearts, the 1 cup roasted peppers, the mushrooms, and green onion. Cover and process with on/off turns until finely chopped.

STEP 2   Transfer cheese mixture to an 8-inch quiche dish or 9-inch pie plate, spreading evenly.

STEP 3   Bake, covered, in the preheated oven about 25 minutes or until heated through. Serve warm with thinly sliced French bread or pita wedges. If desired, garnish with additional roasted pepper and parsley.

ELECTRIC MIXER METHOD   In a medium mixing bowl beat cream cheese, Parmesan cheese, and garlic with an electric mixer on medium to high speed until well mixed. Finely chop drained artichoke hearts, the 1 cup roasted peppers, the mushrooms, and green onion. Stir into beaten cheese mixture. Transfer mixture to an 8-inch quiche dish or 9-inch pie plate, spreading evenly. Bake and serve as directed in Step 3.

MICROWAVE DIRECTIONS   Prepare as directed through Step 2, making sure to use a microwave-safe quiche dish or pie plate. Microwave on 70% power (medium-high) for 6 to 8 minutes or until heated through, stirring the dip and turning the dish halfway through cooking time.

PER ¼ CUP: 126 cal., 10 g total fat (7 g sat. fat), 31 mg chol., 271 mg sodium, 4 g carbo., 2 g fiber, 5 g pro.
EXCHANGES: 1 Medium-Fat Meat, 1 Fat

OFF THE SHELF TIP   Save tons of time by using bottled minced garlic instead of mincing your own. Look for jars near the spices or in the produce section of your supermarket. Be sure to refrigerate after opening.

Creamy Spinach Dip

LOW FAT

PREP
15 MINUTES

CHILL
2 TO 24 HOURS

MAKES
16 SERVINGS

2   cups plain low-fat yogurt
1   8-ounce carton light dairy sour cream
1   1.4-ounce envelope vegetable soup mix
1   10-ounce package frozen chopped spinach, thawed
½   cup finely chopped jicama or ½ cup sliced water chestnuts, drained and finely chopped
¼   cup finely chopped onion
        Dash cayenne pepper
        Assorted vegetable dippers (such as carrot sticks, sweet pepper strips, zucchini slices, and/or broccoli florets) and/or assorted crackers

STEP 1   In a large bowl stir together yogurt, sour cream, and dry vegetable soup mix. Squeeze excess liquid from spinach. Finely chop spinach. Stir spinach, jicama, onion, and cayenne pepper into yogurt mixture.

STEP 2   Cover and refrigerate for at least 2 hours or up to 24 hours. Serve with assorted vegetable dippers and/or assorted crackers.

PER ¼ CUP DIP: 50 cal., 2 g total fat (1 g sat. fat), 6 mg chol., 220 mg sodium, 6 g carbo., 1 g fiber, 3 g pro.
EXCHANGES: ½ Milk, ½ Fat

OFF THE SHELF TIP Vegetable soup mix is sold in a packet or a bag. You'll spot it on shelves near soups. Be sure to use within 6 months of purchase. **FRIENDS OVER FOR DINNER?** Underplan the menu. Yes, you heard right. Offer a simple menu with just a single starring attraction—maybe dessert—that's otherwise straightforward and tasty but not complex. With so many people trying desperately to develop healthier eating habits, they'll love you for making it easier to succeed in social settings. Take this approach and your guests will leave refueled and comfortable on the high note of a lovely meal in good company, rather than feeling overstuffed and off course.

No-Fail Swiss Fondue

START TO FINISH
25 MINUTES

MAKES
12 SERVINGS

1   10.75-ounce can condensed cream of onion soup
¼   cup dry white wine
¼   cup milk
3   cups shredded process Swiss cheese (12 ounces)
⅛   teaspoon ground nutmeg
⅛   teaspoon ground white pepper
6   to 8 cups assorted dippers (such as toasted French bread cubes, precooked broccoli and/or cauliflower florets, and/or sweet pepper pieces)

OFF THE SHELF TIP Grab a can from the soup section. Just make sure your choice is condensed, not ready-to-serve.

STEP 1   In a large saucepan stir together soup, wine, and milk; cook and stir over medium heat until bubbly. Add the cheese, a little at a time, stirring constantly and making sure the cheese is melted before adding more. Stir until the cheese is completely melted.

STEP 2   Stir in nutmeg and white pepper. Transfer cheese mixture to a fondue pot. Keep warm over a fondue burner. (If mixture becomes too thick, stir in a little more milk.) Serve immediately with assorted dippers.

PER ¼ CUP FONDUE WITH FRENCH BREAD CUBES: 135 cal., 9 g total fat (5 g sat. fat), 29 mg chol., 609 mg sodium, 6 g carbo., 0 g fiber, 8 g pro.
EXCHANGES: ½ Starch, 1 Medium-Fat Meat, ½ Fat

Smoky Chipotle Fondue

Canned chipotle peppers in adobo sauce spike an irresistible creamy fondue. Soft bread cubes or crisp tortilla chips make excellent dippers.

START TO FINISH
15 MINUTES
MAKES
8 SERVINGS

8	ounces American cheese, cubed
2	tablespoons dry white wine
2	teaspoons Dijon-style mustard
½	teaspoon Worcestershire sauce
1	to 2 canned chipotle chile peppers in adobo sauce, chopped
2	to 4 tablespoons milk
	Crusty French bread cubes or tortilla chips

STEP 1 In a heavy medium saucepan combine cheese, wine, mustard, Worcestershire sauce, and chipotle peppers. Cook and stir over medium-low heat until melted and smooth. Stir in enough of the milk to reach desired consistency. Transfer to a fondue pot; keep warm over a fondue burner.

STEP 2 Serve fondue immediately with bread cubes or tortilla chips. If the fondue mixture thickens, stir in additional milk.

PER 2 TABLESPOONS FONDUE: 114 cal., 9 g total fat (6 g sat. fat), 27 mg chol., 427 mg sodium, 1 g carbo., 0 g fiber, 6 g pro.
EXCHANGES: 1 High-Fat Meat

OFF THE SHELF TIP Fetch cans of chipotle peppers in adobo sauce—dried and smoked jalapeño peppers in a tangy sauce of vinegar, pepper, and chiles—from the ethnic section of your supermarket. Take care when chopping them because they contain volatile oils that can burn your skin and eyes.

Chipotle con Queso Dip

SLOW COOKER

PREP
10 MINUTES
COOK
3 TO 3½ HOURS (LOW) OR
1½ TO 1¾ HOURS (HIGH)
MAKES
16 SERVINGS

2   pounds packaged process cheese spread, cubed
1   10-ounce can chopped tomatoes and green chile peppers, undrained
1   to 3 chipotle peppers in adobo sauce, chopped
1   tablespoon Worcestershire sauce
      Tortilla chips

STEP 1 In a 3½- or 4-quart slow cooker combine the cheese spread, undrained tomatoes, chipotle peppers in adobo sauce, and Worcestershire sauce.

STEP 2 Cover and cook on low-heat setting for 3 to 3½ hours or on high-heat setting for 1½ to 1¾ hours. Whisk before serving. Serve warm with tortilla chips. Keep warm on low-heat setting up to 2 hours.

PER ¼ CUP DIP: 352 cal., 22 g total fat (11 g sat. fat), 47 mg chol., 1,030 mg sodium, 24 g carbo., 2 g fiber, 15 g pro.
EXCHANGES: 1½ Other Carbo., 2 Medium-Fat Meat, 2½ Fat

OFF THE SHELF TIP Fetch cans of chipotle peppers in adobo sauce—dried and smoked jalapeño peppers in a tangy sauce of vinegar, pepper, and chiles—from the ethnic section of your supermarket. Take care when chopping them because they contain volatile oils that can burn your skin and eyes.

Blue Cheese Walnut Spread

Soft, piquant cheese and crunchy walnuts characterize this quickly prepared, elegant cheese dip. Serve with crackers, of course, or sliced apples and pears tossed with lemon juice.

FAST

START TO FINISH
10 MINUTES

MAKES
8 SERVINGS

1	3-ounce package cream cheese, softened
2	ounces blue cheese, crumbled
¼	cup dairy sour cream
½	teaspoon Worcestershire sauce
¼	cup chopped walnuts, toasted
1	tablespoon snipped fresh chives
	Assorted crackers, apple slices, and/or pear slices

STEP 1 In a small bowl stir together cream cheese, blue cheese, sour cream, and Worcestershire sauce. Stir in walnuts and chives. Serve with assorted crackers and/or fruit.

PER 2 TABLESPOONS SPREAD: 100 cal., 9 g total fat (5 g sat. fat), 20 mg chol., 138 mg sodium, 1 g carbo., 0 g fiber, 3 g pro. **EXCHANGES:** ½ High-Fat Meat, 1 Fat

OFF THE SHELF TIP Packaged cream cheese is used in so many ways in convenience cooking. It comes in a variety of sizes and flavors. Whipped cream cheese (called spreadable cream cheese) is often combined with other flavors such as herbs or fruits. Use cream cheese within a week of opening.

Hot Crab Spread

Bring this herbed, cream-cheese-based spread to a party and you're sure to return with an empty dish. Serve with a selection of crackers.

FAST

START TO FINISH
15 MINUTES

MAKES
8 SERVINGS

½   of an 8-ounce tub cream cheese spread with garden vegetables
1   6- to 6.5-ounce can crabmeat, drained, flaked, and cartilage removed
2   tablespoons sliced green onion (1)
1   teaspoon lemon juice
½   teaspoon dried dill
      Several dashes bottled hot pepper sauce
      Assorted crackers

STEP 1   In a small saucepan heat cream cheese over medium-low heat until softened. Stir in crabmeat, green onion, lemon juice, dill, and hot pepper sauce. Cook and stir for 3 to 4 minutes more or until heated through. Serve warm with crackers.

PER 2 TABLESPOONS SPREAD: 72 cal., 5 g total fat (3 g sat. fat), 31 mg chol., 151 mg sodium, 1 g carbo., 0 g fiber, 5 g pro.
EXCHANGES: 1 Very Lean Meat, 1 Fat

OFF THE SHELF TIP Packaged cream cheese is used in so many ways in convenience cooking. It comes in a variety of sizes and flavors. Whipped cream cheese (called spreadable cream cheese) is often combined with other flavors such as herbs, vegetables, or fruits. Use cream cheese within a week of opening.

Five-Spice Pecans

SLOW COOKER

PREP
10 MINUTES
COOK
2 HOURS (LOW)
COOL
1 HOUR
MAKES
16 SERVINGS

1   pound pecan halves, toasted (4 cups)
¼   cup butter or margarine, melted
2   tablespoons soy sauce
1   teaspoon five-spice powder
½   teaspoon garlic powder
½   teaspoon ground ginger
¼   teaspoon cayenne pepper

STEP 1   Place toasted pecans in a 3½- or 4-quart slow cooker. In a small bowl combine butter, soy sauce, five-spice powder, garlic powder, ginger, and cayenne pepper. Pour over nuts; stir to coat.

STEP 2   Cover and cook on low-heat setting for 2 hours. Stir nuts. Spread in a single layer on waxed paper to cool. (Nuts appear soft after cooking but will crisp upon cooling.) Store in a tightly covered container.

PER ¼ CUP: 225 cal., 23 g total fat (4 g sat. fat), 8 mg chol., 146 mg sodium, 4 g carbo., 3 g fiber, 3 g pro.
EXCHANGES: 5 Fat

OFF THE SHELF TIP You'll find all sorts of salted and unsalted nuts in the baking aisle or chips section.

Cajun Peanuts

Bake honey-roasted peanuts with a toss of Cajun spice and cayenne pepper for a sassy nibble before a meal of red beans and rice or a shrimp dish.

EASY

PREP
10 MINUTES

BAKE
12 MINUTES

COOL
2 HOURS

OVEN
350°F

MAKES
8 SERVINGS

1	egg white
4	teaspoons salt-free Cajun seasoning
⅛	teaspoon cayenne pepper
2¼	cups honey-roasted peanuts (12 ounces)

STEP 1   Preheat oven to 350°F. Line a 15×10×1-inch baking pan with foil; grease foil. Set aside.

STEP 2   In a medium bowl beat egg white with rotary beater until frothy. Stir in Cajun seasoning and cayenne pepper. Add peanuts; toss to coat. Spread peanuts in a single layer in prepared baking pan.

STEP 3   Bake in the preheated oven for 12 minutes, stirring once halfway through baking. Cool completely. Break up any large clusters of peanuts.

PER ¼ CUP: 182 cal., 16 g total fat (3 g sat. fat), 0 mg chol., 142 mg sodium, 8 g carbo., 1 g fiber, 7 g pro.
EXCHANGES: ½ Starch, ½ Very Lean Meat, 3 Fat

OFF THE SHELF TIP Simple flavor enhancers for a variety of foods, spices should be stored in cool, dark locations.

Sweet 'n' Sour Ham Balls

SLOW COOKER

PREP
35 MINUTES

BAKE
18 MINUTES

COOK
3 TO 4 HOURS (LOW) OR
1½ TO 2 HOURS (HIGH)

OVEN
375°F

MAKES
20 SERVINGS

2	eggs, slightly beaten
1	cup graham cracker crumbs
¼	cup milk
1	pound ground cooked ham
1	pound lean ground raw pork
	Nonstick cooking spray
2	9- or 10-ounce jars sweet and sour sauce (1½ cups)
⅔	cup unsweetened pineapple juice
⅔	cup packed brown sugar
½	teaspoon ground ginger

PER 3 MEATBALLS: 128 cal., 5 g total fat (2 g sat. fat), 45 mg chol., 468 mg sodium, 18 g carbo., 0 g fiber, 9 g pro.
EXCHANGES: 1 Other Carbo., 1 Medium-Fat Meat

OFF THE SHELF TIP Find bottled sweet (the sugar) and sour (the vinegar) sauce in the Oriental aisle of your supermarket near the soy sauce.

STEP 1 Preheat oven to 375°F. For meatballs, in a large bowl combine eggs, graham cracker crumbs, and milk. Add ground ham and ground pork; mix well. Shape into sixty 1-inch meatballs. Lightly coat a 15×10×1-inch baking pan with cooking spray. Arrange meatballs in a single layer in prepared pan. Bake, uncovered, in the preheated oven for 18 to 20 minutes or until an instant-read thermometer registers 160°F when inserted in the center of a meatball.

STEP 2 Meanwhile, in a 3½- or 4-quart slow cooker stir together sweet and sour sauce, pineapple juice, brown sugar, and ginger.

STEP 3 Add cooked meatballs to the pineapple mixture in cooker; stir to coat with sauce. Cover and cook on low-heat setting for 3 to 4 hours or on high-heat setting for 1½ to 2 hours. Serve immediately or keep warm on low-heat setting for up to 2 hours.

Cranberry-Sauced Franks

Sauced cocktail wieners get a little sweet tang with the addition of cranberry sauce. Try dividing the sauce in two small cookers with wieners in one, sausage links in the other.

EASY SLOW COOKER

PREP
10 MINUTES

COOK
4 TO 5 HOURS (LOW) OR
2 TO 2½ HOURS (HIGH)

MAKES
32 SERVINGS

1   16-ounce can jellied cranberry sauce
1   cup bottled barbecue sauce
2   1-pound packages cocktail wieners and/or small cooked smoked sausage links

STEP 1   In a 3½- or 4-quart slow cooker stir together cranberry sauce and barbecue sauce until combined. Stir in the wieners.

STEP 2   Cover and cook on low-heat setting for 4 to 5 hours or on high-heat setting for 2 to 2½ hours. Serve warm with a slotted spoon or toothpicks. Keep warm on low-heat setting up to 2 hours.

PER 3 PIECES: 118 cal., 8 g total fat (4 g sat. fat), 15 mg chol., 275 mg sodium, 8 g carbo., 0 g fiber, 3 g pro.
EXCHANGES: ½ Other Carbo., ½ High-Fat Meat, 1 Fat

OFF THE SHELF TIP Find bottled barbecue sauce in the condiment aisle of your supermarket. Pick your favorite flavor—mild, sassy, or devilishly hot—there are dozens to choose from.

Glazed Ham Balls & Smokies

SLOW COOKER

PREP
30 MINUTES

BAKE
15 MINUTES

COOK
2 TO 3 HOURS (HIGH)

OVEN
350°F

MAKES
25 SERVINGS

1	egg, slightly beaten
½	cup graham cracker crumbs
¼	cup finely chopped onion
2	tablespoons snipped dried cranberries
2	tablespoons milk
	Dash ground cloves
8	ounces ground cooked ham
8	ounces lean ground raw pork
	Nonstick cooking spray
1	16-ounce can jellied cranberry sauce
1	12-ounce bottle chili sauce
1	tablespoon vinegar
½	teaspoon dry mustard
1	16-ounce package small cooked smoked sausage links

STEP 1   Preheat oven to 350°F. For meatballs, in a large bowl combine egg, graham cracker crumbs, onion, dried cranberries, milk, and cloves. Add ground ham and ground pork; mix well. Shape into 50 meatballs.

STEP 2   Lightly coat a 15×10×1-inch baking pan with cooking spray. Arrange meatballs in a single layer in prepared pan. Bake, uncovered, in the preheated oven for 15 minutes. Drain well.

STEP 3   Meanwhile, for sauce, in a medium saucepan stir together cranberry sauce, chili sauce, vinegar, and dry mustard. Cook over medium heat until cranberry sauce is melted, stirring occasionally.

STEP 4   In a 3½- or 4-quart slow cooker combine meatballs and sausage. Pour sauce over meatballs and sausage in cooker. Cover and cook on high-heat setting for 2 to 3 hours. Serve immediately or keep warm on low-heat setting for up to 2 hours. Serve meatballs and sausage with wooden toothpicks.

PER 2 MEATBALLS: 138 cal., 7 g total fat (2 g sat. fat), 29 mg chol., 524 mg sodium, 13 g carbo., 1 g fiber, 6 g pro.
EXCHANGES: 1 Other Carbo., 1 Medium-Fat Meat

OFF THE SHELF TIP Find bottled chili sauce (a spicy tomato blend) in the condiment aisle of the supermarket near the barbecue sauce and ketchup.

Buffalo Chicken Wings

PREP
15 MINUTES
BAKE
1 HOUR
OVEN
350°F
MAKES
10 SERVINGS

1   2- to 2½-pound package frozen chicken wing pieces
1   1.75-ounce package Buffalo chicken wing seasoning mix with cooking bag
1   8-ounce carton dairy sour cream ranch-flavor dip
½   cup crumbled blue cheese (2 ounces)
2   tablespoons milk
      Celery sticks

STEP 1   Preheat oven to 350°F. Place frozen wing pieces in cooking bag. Add seasoning and shake to coat. Close bag with nylon tie. Place bag in a shallow baking pan and arrange pieces in a single layer. Cut 2 slits in the top of the bag to allow steam to escape.

STEP 2   Bake in the preheated oven 1 hour or until chicken pieces are tender and no longer pink, carefully cutting bag open to check doneness.

STEP 3   Meanwhile, for blue cheese dip, in a small bowl stir together ranch dip, blue cheese, and milk. Cover and chill until serving time.

STEP 4   Place wings in a serving dish, spooning some of the cooking liquid over wings to moisten (discard remaining cooking liquid). Serve wings with blue cheese dip and celery sticks.

PER 2 PIECES: 269 cal., 20 g total fat (7 g sat. fat), 114 mg chol., 735 mg sodium, 4 g carbo., 1 g fiber, 18 g pro.
EXCHANGES: ½ Other Carbo., 2½ Lean Meat, 2½ Fat

OFF THE SHELF TIP Look for Buffalo chicken wing seasoning mix in the baking aisle of your supermarket. You'll find this gem of a product near the dried herbs and spices.

Chicken & Rice-Filled Spring Rolls

Invite your children or spouse to help you wrap a simple meat-asparagus-rice mixture in rice papers. Prep's easy but it's fun to share.

PREP
25 MINUTES

CHILL
1 TO 2 HOURS

MAKES
8 SPRING ROLLS

8	8-inch dried rice papers
16	thin asparagus spears, trimmed
1	cup finely chopped cooked chicken
1	cup cooked long grain rice
¾	cup bottled sweet and sour sauce

STEP 1 Place some warm water in a shallow dish. Dip each rice paper in warm water and then place between damp towels for 5 minutes.

STEP 2 Meanwhile, cook the asparagus spears in lightly salted boiling water for 3 minutes. Drain; rinse with cold water. Drain again.

STEP 3 In a medium bowl stir together the chicken, rice, and ¼ cup of the sweet and sour sauce. Place 2 asparagus spears about 1 inch from the bottom edge of one of the rice papers. Place ¼ cup chicken mixture on top of the asparagus. Fold up the bottom edge of the rice paper over the filling. Fold in the sides. Roll up. Repeat with remaining rice papers, asparagus, and chicken mixture.

STEP 4 Cover and refrigerate spring rolls for 1 to 2 hours. Cut each spring roll into thirds. Serve with remaining ½ cup sweet and sour sauce.

PER SPRING ROLL: 56 cal., 1 g total fat (0 g sat. fat), 5 mg chol., 35 mg sodium, 12 g carbo., 1 g fiber, 3 g pro.
EXCHANGES: 1 Starch

OFF THE SHELF TIP Find bottled sweet (the sugar) and sour (the vinegar) sauce in the Oriental aisle of your supermarket near the soy sauce.

Coconut Shrimp with Mango Ginger Dip

A dip in beaten egg whites adheres the coconut breading that dresses this quickly baked shrimp. Gingered juice added to mango chutney makes a tantalizing sauce.

PREP
15 MINUTES

BAKE
10 MINUTES

OVEN
400°F

MAKES
10 SERVINGS

1   pound fresh or frozen peeled and deveined shrimp
1   cup flaked coconut, toasted and chopped
½   cup seasoned fine dry bread crumbs
¾   teaspoon curry powder
2   egg whites, slightly beaten
     Nonstick cooking spray
½   cup mango chutney
¼   cup orange juice
¼   teaspoon ground ginger

OFF THE SHELF TIP Look for flaked coconut in the baking aisle of your supermarket. You'll find it in bags or cans, shredded, flaked—even toasted. Once open, use within six months.

STEP 1 Thaw shrimp, if frozen. Rinse shrimp; pat dry with paper towels.

STEP 2 Preheat oven to 400°F. Generously grease a 15×10×1-inch baking pan; set aside. In a shallow bowl combine coconut, bread crumbs, and curry powder. Place egg whites in another small shallow bowl. Dip shrimp into the egg whites; dip into the coconut mixture, pressing the mixture firmly onto the shrimp. Place in the prepared baking pan. Coat shrimp with nonstick cooking spray.

STEP 3 Bake in the preheated oven about 10 minutes or until shrimp turn opaque. Meanwhile, in a small bowl combine chutney, orange juice, and ginger. Serve with shrimp.

PER 2 SHRIMP WITH SAUCE: 175 cal., 5 g total fat (4 g sat. fat), 69 mg chol., 287 mg sodium, 21 g carbo., 2 g fiber, 12 g pro.
EXCHANGES: 1½ Other Carbo., 2 Very Lean Meat, ½ Fat

Black Bean Nachos

PREP
20 MINUTES
BAKE
21 MINUTES
OVEN
350°F
MAKES
12 SERVINGS

6	7- or 8-inch flour tortillas
	Nonstick cooking spray
2	teaspoons taco seasoning mix
2	cups shredded Monterey Jack cheese or Colby and Monterey Jack cheese or Monterey Jack cheese with jalapeño chile peppers (8 ounces)
¾	cup canned black beans, rinsed and drained
¾	cup bottled chunky salsa
½	cup loose-pack frozen whole kernel corn
	Dairy sour cream (optional)
	Snipped fresh cilantro (optional)

STEP 1 Preheat oven to 350°F. For chips, cut each tortilla into 8 wedges. Place half of the tortilla wedges in a single layer on a large baking sheet. Lightly coat tortilla wedges with nonstick cooking spray; sprinkle with 1 teaspoon of the taco seasoning mix. Bake for 8 to 10 minutes or until dry and crisp; cool. Repeat with the remaining tortilla wedges and taco seasoning mix.

STEP 2 Mound chips on an 11- or 12-inch ovenproof platter or large baking sheet. Sprinkle with cheese. Return to oven for 5 to 7 minutes or until cheese is melted.

STEP 3 Meanwhile, in a small saucepan combine drained beans, salsa, and corn. Cook over medium heat until heated through, stirring occasionally.

STEP 4 To serve, spoon bean mixture over the cheese-topped chips. If desired, spoon sour cream over bean mixture and sprinkle with cilantro.

MAKE-AHEAD DIRECTIONS: Prepare chips as directed in Step 1. Store in an airtight container at room temperature for up to 3 days. Continue as directed.

PER SERVING: 137 cal., 7 g total fat (4 g sat. fat), 17 mg chol., 338 mg sodium, 12 g carbo., 1 g fiber, 7 g pro.
EXCHANGES: 1 Starch, ½ Medium-Fat Meat, 1 Fat

OFF THE SHELF TIP Look for packets of taco seasoning in the Mexican section of your supermarket. How hot? You'll find several heat levels for all tastes.

Toasted Ravioli

PREP
25 MINUTES

BAKE
15 MINUTES

OVEN
425°F

MAKES
10 TO 12 SERVINGS

1   9-ounce package refrigerated cheese-filled ravioli
½   cup Italian-seasoned fine dry bread crumbs
¼   cup milk
1   egg
1½   cups bottled or refrigerated spaghetti sauce

OFF THE SHELF TIP Refrigerated pasta comes in a wide variety of shapes and flavors—from cheese and/or meat-filled ravioli to strands of linguine and fettuccine. It is a fabulous convenience product, but note that its shelf life is shorter than its dried counterpart.

STEP 1   In a large saucepan cook the ravioli in lightly salted boiling water for 3 minutes. Drain well; cool slightly.

STEP 2   Preheat oven to 425°F. Place the bread crumbs in a shallow dish. In another shallow dish beat together the milk and egg. Dip cooked ravioli in egg mixture, allowing excess to drip off; dip in bread crumbs to coat. Place ravioli on a lightly greased baking sheet.

STEP 3   Bake in the preheated oven about 15 minutes or until crisp and golden. Meanwhile, heat sauce in a small saucepan. Serve warm ravioli with spaghetti sauce.

PER 3 PIECES WITH SAUCE: 141 cal., 3 g total fat (1 g sat. fat), 32 mg chol., 391 mg sodium, 22 g carbo., 1 g fiber, 6 g pro.
EXCHANGES: 1½ Starch, ½ Fat

Spinach-Stuffed Mushrooms

Large mushrooms make easy-to-handle packaging for this earthy, sophisticated party treat. The mushrooms are filled with a blend of prepared spinach soufflé, bread crumbs, oregano, and a topper of Parmesan, then baked to bring all the flavors together.

PREP
30 MINUTES

BAKE
15 MINUTES

OVEN
350°F

MAKES
24 SERVINGS

1	12-ounce package frozen spinach soufflé, thawed*
¼	cup Italian-seasoned fine dry bread crumbs
½	teaspoon dried oregano, crushed
24	large fresh mushrooms (1½ to 2 inches in diameter)
2	tablespoons grated Parmesan cheese

STEP 1 Preheat oven to 350°F. In a small saucepan stir together thawed soufflé, bread crumbs, and oregano. Cook and stir spinach mixture over medium-low heat about 10 minutes or until heated through.

STEP 2 Meanwhile, wash and drain mushrooms. Remove stems and discard; reserve caps.

STEP 3 Fill mushroom caps with spinach mixture. Sprinkle with cheese. Place in a 15×10×1-inch baking pan. Bake, covered, in the preheated oven for 15 to 20 minutes or until heated through.

*NOTE: To thaw frozen spinach soufflé, place package in a plastic bag; seal tightly. Place plastic bag in a bowl of hot water for 15 minutes, changing water twice.

PER MUSHROOM: 27 cal., 2 g total fat (1 g sat. fat), 11 mg chol., 98 mg sodium, 3 g carbo., 1 g fiber, 2 g pro.
EXCHANGES: ½ Vegetable, 1 Fat

OFF THE SHELF TIP Don't look for seasoned bread crumbs in the bread section of your supermarket. Instead, try packaged goods, near stuffing mixes and mac 'n' cheese.

Cucumber-Cheese Bites

START TO FINISH
20 MINUTES

MAKES
20 SERVINGS

2	medium cucumbers
½	cup flavored cheese spread (such as Boursin)
	Assorted toppers (such as snipped fresh chives, crumbled crisp-cooked bacon, finely chopped hard-cooked eggs, quartered cherry tomatoes, and/or sliced green onions)

STEP 1 If desired, using a vegetable peeler or zester, remove a few length-wise strips of peel from cucumbers. Cut cucumbers into ½-inch slices. Spread a small amount of the cheese spread onto each cucumber slice; sprinkle with assorted toppers.

MAKE-AHEAD DIRECTIONS: Prepare as directed. Cover with plastic wrap. Chill for up to 4 hours before serving.

PER PIECE: 15 cal., 1 g total fat (1 g sat. fat), 0 mg chol., 17 mg sodium, 1 g carbo., 0 g fiber, 0 g pro.
EXCHANGES: Free

OFF THE SHELF TIP Boursin cheese comes in many flavors: plain, black peppercorn, herb, and garlic.

Soups & Stews

French Onion & Beef Soup

Cooked beef gives this traditional rainy-day favorite a hearty twist.

START TO FINISH
25 MINUTES

MAKES
4 SERVINGS

3 tablespoons butter or margarine
1 medium onion, thinly sliced and separated into rings
2 10.5-ounce cans condensed French onion soup
2½ cups water
2 cups cubed cooked beef (about 10 ounces)
4 1-inch slices baguette-style French bread
½ cup shredded Gruyère or Swiss cheese (2 ounces)

OFF THE SHELF TIP Look for precooked meat in the refrigerated meat section of your supermarket—usually somewhere between the uncooked products and the sandwich meat. You'll find precooked meat in whole pieces or strips, seasoned or unseasoned.

STEP 1 Preheat broiler. In a large skillet melt butter over medium heat. Add onion; cook about 5 minutes or until very tender. Stir in soup, water, and beef. Bring to boiling, stirring occasionally.

STEP 2 Meanwhile, place the bread slices on a baking sheet. Broil 4 inches from the heat about 1 minute or until toasted on one side. Top the toasted sides of bread slices with cheese; broil about 1 minute more or until cheese is melted.

STEP 3 To serve, ladle soup into soup bowls. Top with bread slices, cheese sides up.

PER 1¾ CUPS: 465 cal., 21 g total fat (10 g sat. fat), 82 mg chol., 1,701 mg sodium, 40 g carbo., 3 g fiber, 28 g pro.
EXCHANGES: 2½ Starch, 3 Lean Meat, 2 Fat

Sweet & Sour Beef Stew

LOW FAT   SLOW COOKER

PREP
10 MINUTES

COOK
10 TO 11 HOURS (LOW) OR
5 TO 5½ HOURS (HIGH)

MAKES
6 TO 8 SERVINGS

1½	pounds beef stew meat, cut into ¾- to 1-inch cubes
1	16-ounce package loose-pack frozen stew vegetables (3 cups)
½	cup water
2	11-ounce cans condensed beefy mushroom soup
½	cup bottled sweet and sour sauce
⅛	to ¼ teaspoon cayenne pepper

STEP 1   In a 3½- or 4-quart slow cooker place stew meat and frozen vegetables. Stir in water, soup, sweet and sour sauce, and cayenne pepper.

STEP 2   Cover and cook on low-heat setting for 10 to 11 hours or on high-heat setting for 5 to 5½ hours.

PER 1¼ CUPS: 291 cal., 9 g total fat (3 g sat. fat), 62 mg chol., 1,019 mg sodium, 19 g carbo., 2 g fiber, 30 g pro.
EXCHANGES: ½ Vegetable, 1 Other Carbo., 4 Lean Meat

OFF THE SHELF TIP Grab a can from the soup section. Just make sure your choice is condensed, not ready-to-serve.

Easy Beef & Noodle Soup

Combine cans of beef broth and cream of onion soup to form the base for this quick, satisfying soup. If you have fresh parsley, use 6 tablespoons and stir it in just before serving.

START TO FINISH
25 MINUTES
MAKES
4 SERVINGS

1   pound lean ground beef
2½   cups water
1   10.75-ounce can condensed cream of onion soup
1   10.5-ounce can condensed beef broth
1½   cups dried medium noodles
2   tablespoons dried parsley flakes
     Parmesan cheese (optional)

STEP 1   In a large saucepan or skillet cook meat over medium heat until brown. Drain off fat. Stir in the water, onion soup, broth, dried noodles, and parsley flakes.

STEP 2   Bring to boiling; reduce heat. Cover and simmer about 5 minutes or until noodles are tender, stirring occasionally. If desired, sprinkle each serving with Parmesan cheese.

PER 1½ CUPS: 357 cal., 19 g total fat (7 g sat. fat), 98 mg chol., 1,218 mg sodium, 19 g carbo., 1 g fiber, 27 g pro.
EXCHANGES: 1 Starch, 4 Lean Meat, 1 Fat

OFF THE SHELF TIP Grab cans of condensed soup and broth from the soup section. Make sure your choices are "condensed", not "ready-to-serve."
MENU PLANNING TIPS You're off the hook! No need to make a production of every meal component. Instead, let one dish claim the starring role, then round out the meal with simply presented foods. If a vegetable-grain side dish is getting your attention this evening, serve it with grilled, roasted, or baked meat, a salad, and fresh fruit for dessert.

Chili with Polenta

Polenta—which is cooked cornmeal—is a fresh alternative to corn bread as a match for chili. Here, polenta cooks in the skillet with the chili.

START TO FINISH
25 MINUTES

MAKES
4 SERVINGS

12	ounces lean ground beef
1/2	cup chopped onion (1 medium)
1	15-ounce can hot-style chili beans with chili gravy, undrained
1	15-ounce can black beans, rinsed and drained
1	8-ounce can tomato sauce
1/2	teaspoon ground cumin
1	16-ounce tube refrigerated cooked polenta, crumbled
1/2	cup shredded taco cheese (2 ounces)
	Sliced green onions (optional)
	Dairy sour cream (optional)

OFF THE SHELF TIP Refrigerated tubes of cooked polenta are typically located in the produce section of your supermarket. You can slice and fry it, crumble it, or even follow the package directions to reconstitute it into cornmeal mush.

STEP 1 In a large skillet cook ground beef and onion over medium heat until beef is brown. Drain off fat.

STEP 2 Stir undrained chili beans, drained black beans, tomato sauce, and cumin into beef mixture in skillet. Bring to boiling. Sprinkle the polenta over the beef mixture. Cover and simmer about 5 minutes or until heated through. Sprinkle with cheese. If desired, sprinkle with green onion and serve with sour cream.

PER 1½ CUPS: 497 cal., 15 g total fat (7 g sat. fat), 65 mg chol., 1,464 mg sodium, 58 g carbo., 14 g fiber, 34 g pro.
EXCHANGES: 3 Starch, 1 Other Carbo., 3½ Lean Meat

Taco Chili

SLOW COOKER

PREP
10 MINUTES

COOK
4 TO 6 HOURS (LOW) OR
2 TO 3 HOURS (HIGH)

MAKES
4 TO 6 SERVINGS
(ABOUT 8 CUPS)

1   pound lean ground beef

2   14.5-ounce cans diced tomatoes with chili spices, undrained

1   15-ounce can red kidney beans, undrained

1   15-ounce can whole kernel corn, undrained

1   1.25-ounce package taco seasoning mix

STEP 1   In a large skillet cook beef over medium heat until brown. Drain off fat. In a 3½- or 4-quart slow cooker combine the cooked beef, the undrained tomatoes, undrained beans, undrained corn, and taco seasoning mix.

STEP 2   Cover and cook on low-heat setting for 4 to 6 hours or on high-heat setting for 2 to 3 hours.

PER 2 CUPS: 464 cal., 17 g total fat (6 g sat. fat), 71 mg chol., 2,317 mg sodium, 50 g carbo., 9 g fiber, 33 g pro.
EXCHANGES: 1½ Vegetable, 2½ Starch, 3 Medium-Fat Meat

OFF THE SHELF TIP Cans of Mexican-style tomatoes are a fabulous way to add flavor to recipes without making any extra effort. Located in the canned vegetable aisle of your supermarket, diced and chunky tomatoes come in an abundance of flavor combinations.

White & Green Chili

Green salsa, ground cumin, and snipped fresh cilantro enliven this meat and bean chili. Serve it with sour cream to take the edge off its hot bite.

START TO FINISH
30 MINUTES

MAKES
4 SERVINGS
(ABOUT 6 CUPS)

1   pound unseasoned meat loaf mix (1/3 pound each ground beef, pork, and veal), lean ground beef, or ground pork
1/3   cup chopped onion (1 small)
2   15-ounce cans Great Northern beans or white beans, rinsed and drained
1   16-ounce jar green salsa
1   14-ounce can chicken broth
1 1/2 teaspoons ground cumin
2   tablespoons snipped fresh cilantro
1/4   cup dairy sour cream (optional)

STEP 1   In a 4-quart Dutch oven cook meat and onion over medium heat about 5 minutes or until meat is brown. Drain off fat. Add drained beans, salsa, broth, and cumin. Bring to boiling; reduce heat. Cover and simmer for 15 minutes.

STEP 2   To serve, stir in 1 tablespoon of the cilantro. Divide chili among 4 serving bowls. Sprinkle with remaining 1 tablespoon cilantro. If desired, top with sour cream.

PER 1 1/2 CUPS: 405 cal., 14 g total fat (5 g sat. fat), 81 mg chol., 1,463 mg sodium, 38 g carbo., 11 g fiber, 31 g pro.
EXCHANGES: 2 1/2 Starch, 3 1/2 Lean Meat

OFF THE SHELF TIP   Green salsa—found near the other salsas in the Mexican aisle of your supermarket—typically packs more heat than the red tomato varieties. Look for a mild green version if you don't want a lot of heat.

Reuben Chowder

Process Swiss cheese is the secret to this Reuben-flavored chowder's velvety smooth texture. It's a sure hit if you're a Reuben sandwich fan.

1   tablespoon butter, softened
4   slices rye bread
½   teaspoon caraway seeds
3   cups milk
1   10.75-ounce can condensed cream of celery soup
2   ounces process Swiss cheese slices, torn
1   14- or 16-ounce can sauerkraut, rinsed, drained, and snipped
2   5-ounce packages sliced corned beef, chopped or torn

OFF THE SHELF TIP   Grab a can from the soup section. Just make sure your choice is condensed, not ready-to-serve.

BAKE
15 MINUTES
START TO FINISH
30 MINUTES
OVEN
325°F
MAKES
4 SERVINGS

STEP 1   Preheat oven to 325°F. Butter both sides of each slice of the bread; sprinkle with caraway seeds. Cut into triangles; place on a baking sheet. Bake in the preheated oven about 15 minutes or until toasted.

STEP 2   Meanwhile, in a large saucepan combine milk, soup, and cheese. Cook and stir over medium heat just until bubbly. Stir in sauerkraut and corned beef; heat through. Serve soup in bowls with the toasted bread.

PER 1¾ CUPS: 456 cal., 23 g total fat (11 g sat. fat), 77 mg chol., 2,696 mg sodium, 35 g carbo., 5 g fiber, 27 g pro.
EXCHANGES: 1 Milk, 1 Vegetable, 1 Starch, 2 High-Fat Meat, 1½ Fat

Texas Two-Step Stew

Yes! This is a hearty stew with a fresh flavor you can rave about. This features chorizo sausage, corn, and beans. Serve it with lime wedges, warm tortillas, and beer.

SLOW COOKER

PREP
20 MINUTES

COOK
4 TO 6 HOURS (LOW) OR
2 TO 3 HOURS (HIGH) PLUS
45 MINUTES (HIGH)

MAKES
6 SERVINGS

8	ounces uncooked chorizo sausage
½	cup chopped onion (1 medium)
1	15-ounce can Mexican-style or Tex-Mex–style chili beans, undrained
1	15-ounce can hominy or one 11-ounce can whole kernel corn with sweet peppers, drained
1	6-ounce package regular Spanish-style rice mix
6	cups water

STEP 1 In a medium skillet cook sausage and onion over medium heat until sausage is no longer pink. Drain off fat. Transfer sausage mixture to a 3½- or 4-quart slow cooker. Stir in undrained chili beans, drained hominy, and the seasoning packet contents of the rice mix, if present (set aside remaining rice mix). Pour the water over all.

STEP 2 Cover and cook on low-heat setting for 4 to 6 hours or on high-heat setting for 2 to 3 hours. If using low-heat setting, turn cooker to high-heat setting. Stir in reserved rice mix. Cover and cook for 45 minutes more.

PER 1¾ CUP: 383 cal., 16 g total fat (6 g sat. fat), 33 mg chol., 1,385 mg sodium, 44 g carbo., 6 g fiber, 16 g pro.
EXCHANGES: 3 Starch, 1 High-Fat Meat, 1 Fat

OFF THE SHELF TIP Look for canned chili beans with Mexican seasonings in the canned vegetable aisle of your supermarket.

Sausage-Corn Chowder

PREP
15 MINUTES

COOK
8 TO 10 HOURS (LOW) OR
4 TO 5 HOURS (HIGH)

MAKES
6 SERVINGS

1 pound cooked smoked turkey sausage, halved lengthwise and cut into ½-inch slices
3 cups loose-pack frozen diced hash brown potatoes with onions and peppers
1 cup coarsely chopped carrot (2 medium)
2½ cups water
1 15- to 16.5-ounce can cream-style corn
1 10.75-ounce can condensed golden mushroom soup
Snipped fresh chives or parsley (optional)

STEP 1 Place sausage, frozen potatoes, and carrot in a 3½- or 4-quart slow cooker. In a medium bowl combine water, corn, and soup. Add to sausage mixture in cooker.

STEP 2 Cover and cook on low-heat setting for 8 to 10 hours or on high-heat setting for 4 to 5 hours. Ladle into bowls. If desired, sprinkle with chives.

PER 1½ CUPS: 238 cal., 8 g total fat (2 g sat. fat), 53 mg chol., 1,280 mg sodium, 28 g carbo., 2 g fiber, 15 g pro.
EXCHANGES: 2 Starch, 2 Lean Meat

OFF THE SHELF TIP Pull a bag of diced hash browns with onion and peppers out of the grocer's freezer case. You'll find a number of varieties alongside the diced style.

Quick Pork-Bean Soup

Pork strips get a quick sizzle in a skillet to join beans and seasonings for a hearty soup that's ready to enjoy in just minutes. Crusty rolls and creamy coleslaw make good accompaniments.

PREP
15 MINUTES
COOK
15 MINUTES
MAKES
4 SERVINGS

12   ounces lean boneless pork
2   tablespoons cooking oil
1   cup chopped onion (1 large)
2   cups water
1   11.5-ounce can condensed bean with bacon soup
1½   cups sliced carrot (3 medium)
1   teaspoon Worcestershire sauce
¼   teaspoon dry mustard

STEP 1   Cut pork into thin bite-size strips. In a large skillet heat oil over medium-high heat. Cook the meat and onion in the hot oil for 3 to 4 minutes or until meat is brown. Stir in the water, soup, carrot, Worcestershire sauce, and dry mustard.

STEP 2   Bring to boiling; reduce heat. Cover and simmer for 15 minutes.

PER 1½ CUPS: 312 cal., 13 g total fat (3 g sat. fat), 52 mg chol., 678 mg sodium, 23 g carbo., 6 g fiber, 24 g pro.
EXCHANGES: ½ Vegetable, 1 Starch, 3 Lean Meat, 1 Fat

OFF THE SHELF TIP Grab a can from the soup section. Just make sure your choice is condensed, not ready-to-serve. **STRIKE A BALANCE** Choose your meal round-outs to complement the flavor and texture of your star dish so a plate bears a palate-pleasing variety of textures, forms, and colors.
■ **Hot—Cool (serving temperature and seasoning level)**
■ **Crisp-Crunchy—Soft-Smooth**
■ **Salty—Sweet**
■ **Complex Flavor—Simple Flavor**

Black Bean & Sausage Posole

PREP

15 MINUTES

COOK

30 MINUTES

MAKES

6 SERVINGS

RECIPE PICTURED ON PAGE 132.

1   12-ounce package lean bulk turkey-and-pork sausage

2   14-ounce cans reduced-sodium chicken broth

1   15-ounce can black beans, rinsed and drained

1   14.5-ounce can golden hominy, rinsed and drained

1   14.5-ounce can Mexican-style stewed tomatoes, undrained

1   cup loose-pack frozen diced hash brown potatoes

½   cup chopped green sweet pepper

⅓   cup chopped onion (1 small)

½   teaspoon bottled minced garlic (1 clove)

1   teaspoon dried oregano, crushed

½   teaspoon chili powder

STEP 1   In a large saucepan cook the sausage over medium heat until brown; drain off fat.

STEP 2   Stir in broth, drained black beans, drained hominy, undrained tomatoes, hash brown potatoes, sweet pepper, onion, garlic, oregano, and chili powder. Bring to boiling; reduce heat. Cover and simmer for 30 minutes.

PER 1½ CUPS: 292 cal., 14 g total fat (1 g sat. fat), 45 mg chol., 1,295 mg sodium, 26 g carbo., 4 g fiber, 17 g pro.
EXCHANGES: 2 Starch, 1½ Lean Meat, 1½ Fat

OFF THE SHELF TIP Save tons of time by using bottled minced garlic instead of mincing your own. Look for jars near the spices or in the produce section of your supermarket. Be sure to refrigerate after opening.

Corn-Bacon Chowder

START TO FINISH
25 MINUTES

MAKES
4 TO 6 SERVINGS

5	slices bacon, chopped
1	medium onion, halved and thinly sliced
2	cups milk
2	cups frozen corn
1	10.75-ounce can condensed cream of mushroom soup
1	cup diced cooked potato (1 medium)
¼	teaspoon ground black pepper

OFF THE SHELF TIP Grab a can from the soup section. Just make sure your choice is condensed, not ready-to-serve.

STEP 1 In a large saucepan cook bacon over medium heat until crisp. Remove bacon with a slotted spoon, reserving 2 tablespoons of the drippings in the saucepan; drain bacon on paper towels.

STEP 2 Cook onion slices in reserved drippings over medium heat until tender. Stir in milk, corn, soup, potato, and pepper.

STEP 3 Bring to boiling; reduce heat. Simmer, uncovered, for 2 to 3 minutes. Remove from heat. Top each serving with crumbled bacon.

PER 1½ CUPS: 329 cal., 18 g total fat (7 g sat. fat), 24 mg chol., 750 mg sodium, 34 g carbo., 2 g fiber, 11 g pro.
EXCHANGES: ½ Milk, ½ Vegetable, 1½ Starch, ½ High-Fat Meat, 2 Fat

Quick Asian Chicken Soup

Frozen stir-fry veggie blend, soy sauce, and ginger transform canned chicken with rice soup into a terrific, fresh-tasting light meal that's quicker than fetching takeout.

START TO FINISH
15 MINUTES

MAKES
4 SERVINGS

2½ cups water

2 10.5-ounce cans condensed chicken with rice soup

2 cups frozen broccoli stir-fry vegetables (broccoli, carrots, onions, red peppers, celery, water chestnuts, and mushrooms)

1 tablespoon soy sauce

½ teaspoon ground ginger

2 cups chopped cooked chicken or turkey (about 10 ounces)

STEP 1 In a large saucepan combine water and soup. Bring to boiling.

STEP 2 Stir in frozen vegetables, soy sauce, and ginger. Return to boiling; reduce heat. Cover and simmer for 3 to 5 minutes or until vegetables are tender. Stir in chicken; heat through.

PER 1¾ CUPS: 247 cal., 9 g total fat (3 g sat. fat), 72 mg chol., 1,479 mg sodium, 14 g carbo., 1 g fiber, 27 g pro.
EXCHANGES: 1 Vegetable, ½ Starch, 3½ Very Lean Meat, 1½ Fat

OFF THE SHELF TIP Look in the refrigerated meat section for seasoned or unseasoned strips, cubes, and whole pieces of precooked chicken or turkey.

Curried Chicken & Corn Chowder

Curry powder leads this chicken soup in an exciting direction. Cooked chicken, chopped peanuts, and sweet pepper round out this lively chowder.

LOW FAT **FAST**

START TO FINISH
20 MINUTES

MAKES
4 SERVINGS

1	17-ounce can cream-style corn, undrained
2	cups milk
1	10.75-ounce can condensed cream of chicken soup
¾	cup chopped green or red sweet pepper (1 medium)
1	tablespoon dried minced onion
2	to 3 teaspoons curry powder
1	9.75- or 10-ounce can chunk-style chicken, undrained, or 1½ cups frozen diced cooked chicken, thawed
	Coarsely chopped peanuts (optional)

STEP 1   In a large saucepan stir together undrained corn, milk, soup, sweet pepper, onion, and curry powder. Bring to boiling stirring frequently.

STEP 2   Stir in chicken; cook about 2 minutes more or until heated through. If desired, sprinkle with peanuts.

PER 1½ CUPS: 324 cal., 11 g total fat (4 g sat. fat), 49 mg chol., 1,201 mg sodium, 39 g carbo., 3 g fiber, 24 g pro.
EXCHANGES: ½ Milk, 2 Starch, 2 Lean Meat, 1 Fat

OFF THE SHELF TIP Cans of chicken are perfect for last-minute cooking because they need no thawing. Just add to the recipe and heat through. You can find them near the cans of tuna at the supermarket.

Creamy Chicken Noodle Soup

A can of chicken soup and seasoned pepper give this slow-cooked noodle soup an earthy depth.

PREP
15 MINUTES

COOK
6 TO 8 HOURS (LOW) OR
3 TO 4 HOURS (HIGH) PLUS
20 TO 30 MINUTES (HIGH)

MAKES
6 TO 8 SERVINGS

5	cups water
2	10.75-ounce cans condensed cream of chicken soup
2	cups chopped cooked chicken (about 10 ounces)
1	9- to 10-ounce package frozen mixed vegetables (cut green beans, corn, diced carrots, and peas)
1	teaspoon seasoned pepper or garlic-pepper seasoning
1½	cups dried egg noodles

OFF THE SHELF TIP Look for precooked meat in the refrigerated meat section of your supermarket—usually somewhere between the uncooked products and the sandwich meat. You'll find precooked meat in whole pieces or strips, seasoned or unseasoned.

STEP 1   In a 3½- or 4-quart slow cooker gradually stir the water into the soup. Stir or whisk until smooth. Stir in cooked chicken, frozen vegetables, and pepper.

STEP 2   Cover and cook on low-heat setting for 6 to 8 hours or on high-heat setting for 3 to 4 hours.

STEP 3   If using low-heat setting, turn slow cooker to high-heat setting. Stir in uncooked noodles. Cover and cook for 20 to 30 minutes more or just until noodles are tender.

PER 1¾ CUPS: 262 cal., 12 g total fat (3 g sat. fat), 63 mg chol., 908 mg sodium, 21 g carbo., 3 g fiber, 19 g pro.
EXCHANGES: 1 Vegetable, 1 Starch, 2 Lean Meat, 1 Fat

Chicken-Vegetable Soup

LOW FAT

START TO FINISH
25 MINUTES
MAKES
4 SERVINGS

1   16-ounce package frozen Italian vegetables (zucchini, carrots, cauliflower, lima beans, and Italian beans)
1   14.5-ounce can Italian-style stewed tomatoes, undrained
1   12-ounce can vegetable juice
1   cup chicken broth
1½   cups chopped cooked chicken (about 8 ounces)

OFF THE SHELF TIP   Italian-style stewed tomatoes are a fabulous way to add flavor to recipes without making any extra effort. Located in the canned vegetable aisle of your supermarket, these tomatoes come in an abundance of flavor combinations.

STEP 1   In a large saucepan combine frozen vegetables, undrained tomatoes, vegetable juice, and broth.

STEP 2   Bring to boiling; reduce heat. Cover and simmer about 10 minutes or until vegetables are tender. Stir in chicken. Heat through.

PER 1¾ CUPS: 206 cal., 5 g total fat (1 g sat. fat), 47 mg chol., 784 mg sodium, 18 g carbo., 4 g fiber, 18 g pro.
EXCHANGES: 2 Vegetable, 1 Starch, 2 Very Lean Meat

Chicken Tortilla Soup

Take advantage of your deli's roasted chicken to bring moist, flavorful meat to this filling but light Mexican soup.

PREP
20 MINUTES

COOK
15 MINUTES

MAKES
6 SERVINGS

1	**2- to 2.25-pound deli-roasted chicken**
2	**14-ounce cans chicken broth with roasted garlic**
1	**15-ounce can chopped tomatoes and green chile peppers, undrained**
1	**11-ounce can whole kernel corn with sweet peppers, drained**
1	**small fresh jalapeño chile pepper, seeded and finely chopped***
1	**teaspoon ground cumin**
2	**tablespoons snipped fresh cilantro**
1	**tablespoon lime juice**
	Tortilla chips with lime or regular tortilla chips, broken

STEP 1 Remove chicken meat from the frame of the deli-roasted chicken. Using 2 forks, shred enough of the chicken meat to measure 2 cups; set aside. Reserve any remaining chicken meat for another use.

STEP 2 In a large saucepan combine broth, undrained tomatoes, drained corn, jalapeño pepper, and cumin. Bring to boiling; reduce heat. Cover and simmer for 10 minutes. Stir in shredded chicken, cilantro, and lime juice. Heat through. Top each serving with tortilla chips.

***NOTE:** Because chile peppers contain volatile oils that can burn your skin and eyes, avoid direct contact with them as much as possible. When working with chile peppers, wear plastic or rubber gloves. If your bare hands do touch chile peppers, wash them well with soap and water.

PER 1½ CUPS: 183 cal., 5 g total fat (1 g sat. fat), 43 mg chol., 1,080 mg sodium, 18 g carbo., 2 g fiber, 16 g pro.
EXCHANGES: 1 Vegetable, 1 Starch, 2 Very Lean Meat

OFF THE SHELF TIP Let your supermarket work for you. When you need cooked chicken and want fresh-from-the-oven flavor, pick up a roasted chicken from the deli counter.

Creamy Chicken & Vegetable Stew

SLOW COOKER

PREP
30 MINUTES

COOK
8 TO 9 HOURS (LOW) OR
4 TO 4½ HOURS (HIGH)

MAKES
6 SERVINGS

1½ pounds skinless, boneless chicken thighs, cut into 1-inch pieces
1 tablespoon cooking oil
1 pound potatoes (3 medium), peeled and cut into 1-inch pieces
2 cups packaged peeled baby carrots
2 cups frozen cut green beans
½ cup chopped onion (1 medium)
1 teaspoon dried thyme, crushed
½ teaspoon salt
½ teaspoon poultry seasoning
2 cups water
2 0.87- to 1-ounce envelopes chicken gravy mix
1 8-ounce carton dairy sour cream

STEP 1 In a large skillet brown chicken, half at a time, in hot oil over medium-high heat. Drain off fat.

STEP 2 Transfer chicken to a 3½- or 4-quart slow cooker. Stir in potato, carrots, green beans, onion, thyme, salt, and poultry seasoning. In a small bowl stir together the water and dry gravy mix; stir into chicken mixture in slow cooker.

STEP 3 Cover and cook on low-heat setting for 8 to 9 hours or on high-heat setting for 4 to 4½ hours.

STEP 4 In a medium bowl gradually stir about 1 cup of the hot chicken mixture into the sour cream. Add sour cream mixture to cooker, stirring gently until combined.

PER 1½ CUPS: 344 cal., 14 g total fat (6 g sat. fat), 107 mg chol., 769 mg sodium, 26 g carbo., 4 g fiber, 26 g pro.
EXCHANGES: 1 Vegetable, 1½ Starch, 3 Lean Meat, 1 Fat

OFF THE SHELF TIP Packaged gravy mix is usually found in the spice aisle of the supermarket. It comes in a variety of flavors and is a simple way to add depth and flavor to dishes.

Chunky Chicken Chili

Chicken produces a light but kicky chili and goes together in a snap. Refrigerated corn bread sticks heat nearly as quickly as does a corn bread mix for a crumbly sweet accompaniment.

START TO FINISH
20 MINUTES
MAKES
4 SERVINGS

Nonstick cooking spray

12 ounces skinless, boneless chicken thighs, cut into 1-inch pieces

2 15-ounce cans chili beans with spicy chili gravy, undrained

1½ cups frozen stir-fry vegetables (yellow, green, and red peppers and onion)

¾ cup bottled salsa

STEP 1 Coat an unheated large saucepan with nonstick cooking spray. Preheat over medium-high heat. Add chicken; cook and stir until brown. Stir in undrained chili beans, frozen vegetables, and salsa.

STEP 2 Bring to boiling; reduce heat. Simmer, uncovered, about 7 minutes or until chicken is no longer pink.

PER 1¼ CUPS: 320 cal., 5 g total fat (1 g sat. fat), 70 mg chol., 930 mg sodium, 39 g carbo., 12 g fiber, 29 g pro.
EXCHANGES: ½ Vegetable, 2½ Starch, 2½ Very Lean Meat

OFF THE SHELF TIP Canned chili beans with spicy chili gravy allow you to make chili in 20 minutes that tastes like it simmered all day. Look for the beans in the canned vegetable aisle of your supermarket.

Turkey-Bean Soup

All the goods for this hearty soup keep well in the refrigerator and pantry. Have them ready for a satisfying meal when the weather cools or the snow flies and burrowing in with a steaming bowl of soup sounds divine.

LOW FAT

START TO FINISH
30 MINUTES
MAKES
4 SERVINGS

2   15-ounce cans Great Northern or white kidney (cannellini) beans, rinsed and drained
1   10.75-ounce can condensed cream of celery soup
8   ounces cooked smoked turkey sausage, halved lengthwise and sliced
1½   cups milk
1   teaspoon dried minced onion
½   teaspoon dried thyme, crushed
⅛   to ¼ teaspoon ground black pepper
1   teaspoon bottled minced garlic (2 cloves) or ¼ teaspoon garlic powder

OFF THE SHELF TIP Grab a can from the soup section. Just make sure your choice is condensed, not ready-to-serve.

STEP 1   In a large saucepan combine drained beans, soup, and sausage. Stir in milk, onion, thyme, pepper, and garlic.

STEP 2   Bring to boiling over medium-high heat, stirring occasionally; reduce heat. Cover and simmer for 10 minutes, stirring occasionally.

PER 1½ CUPS: 434 cal., 11 g total fat (3 g sat. fat), 54 mg chol., 1,129 mg sodium, 57 g carbo., 11 g fiber, 29 g pro.
EXCHANGES: ½ Milk, 2½ Starch, ½ Other Carbo., 2½ Lean Meat, ½ Fat

Seafood Chowder

START TO FINISH
25 MINUTES

MAKES
4 SERVINGS

12   ounces fresh or frozen fish fillets (such as salmon, orange roughy, or cod)

3   cups loose-pack frozen diced hash brown potatoes with onions and peppers

1   cup water

1   12-ounce can (1½ cups) evaporated milk

1   10.75-ounce can condensed cream of shrimp or cream of potato soup

⅓   cup canned cooked bacon pieces

2   teaspoons snipped fresh dill or ¾ teaspoon dried dill

¼   teaspoon ground black pepper

1   2-ounce jar diced pimiento, drained

STEP 1   Thaw fish, if frozen. Rinse fish; pat dry with paper towels. Cut fish into 1-inch pieces. Set aside.

STEP 2   Meanwhile, in a large saucepan combine frozen potatoes and the water. Bring to boiling; reduce heat. Cover and simmer about 5 minutes or until tender.

STEP 3   Stir in evaporated milk, soup, bacon, dill, and pepper. Return to boiling. Add fish and drained pimiento; reduce heat. Cover and simmer for 3 to 5 minutes more or until fish flakes easily when tested with a fork.

PER 1½ CUPS: 366 cal., 15 g total fat (7 g sat. fat), 86 mg chol., 1,045 mg sodium, 27 g carbo., 2 g fiber, 30 g pro.
EXCHANGES: 1 Milk, 1 Starch, 2½ Lean Meat, 1½ Fat

OFF THE SHELF TIP   Pull a bag of diced hash browns with onions and peppers out of the grocer's freezer case. You'll find a number of varieties alongside the diced style.

Crab-Tomato Bisque

This soup is rich and elegant and simple to prepare. Serve it at a dinner party or anytime you want to treat yourself to luxury.

START TO FINISH
15 MINUTES
MAKES
4 SERVINGS

1   19-ounce can ready-to-eat tomato basil soup
1   10.75-ounce can condensed cream of shrimp soup
1   cup vegetable broth
1   cup half-and-half, light cream, or milk
1   tablespoon dried minced onion
1   teaspoon dried parsley flakes
1   6.5-ounce can crabmeat, drained, flaked, and cartilage removed

STEP 1   In a large saucepan combine tomato basil soup, cream of shrimp soup, vegetable broth, half-and-half, onion, and parsley flakes.

STEP 2   Cook over medium heat until bubbly, stirring occasionally. Stir in crabmeat, heat through.

PER 1½ CUPS: 242 cal., 12 g total fat (6 g sat. fat), 73 mg chol., 1,447 mg sodium, 20 g carbo., 1 g fiber, 15 g pro.
EXCHANGES: 1 Starch, 2 Very Lean Meat, 2 Fat

OFF THE SHELF TIP The sweet, succulent meat from crabs is found near the canned tuna and salmon.

Clam Chowder

Want seafood on Friday? Get the pantry and freezer ingredients home earlier in the week and when week's end rolls around, this chowder meal will be ready to soothe in minutes.

PREP
15 MINUTES

COOK
15 MINUTES

MAKES
4 TO 6 SERVINGS

2   10.75-ounce cans condensed cream of celery soup

2   cups loose-pack frozen diced hash brown potatoes with onions and peppers

1   8-ounce bottle clam juice

1   6.5-ounce can minced or chopped clams, undrained

2   teaspoons Worcestershire sauce

1   teaspoon dried thyme, crushed

1   cup half-and-half or light cream
     Ground black pepper (optional)

3   slices packaged ready-to-serve cooked bacon, chopped

OFF THE SHELF TIP Packaged precooked bacon is usually found in or near your supermarket's meat counter. It heats up in the microwave (or oven) in no time.

STEP 1   In a large saucepan combine soup, frozen potatoes, clam juice, undrained clams, Worcestershire sauce, and thyme. Bring to boiling over high heat; reduce heat. Cover and simmer about 15 minutes or until potatoes are tender, stirring frequently.

STEP 2   Stir in half-and-half; heat through. If desired, season to taste with pepper. Sprinkle each serving with bacon.

PER 1½ CUPS: 383 cal., 20 g total fat (9 g sat. fat), 62 mg chol., 1,410 mg sodium, 29 g carbo., 3 g fiber, 19 g pro.
EXCHANGES: 2 Starch, 2 Lean Meat, 2½ Fat

Spicy Shrimp & Noodle Soup

LOW FAT

START TO FINISH
45 MINUTES

MAKES
6 SERVINGS

RECIPE PICTURED ON PAGE 132.

1	pound fresh or frozen uncooked medium shrimp in shells
1	tablespoon lemon juice
½	teaspoon chili powder
½	teaspoon ground cumin
½	teaspoon salt
⅛	teaspoon ground black pepper
5	cups water
2	3-ounce packages shrimp- or Oriental-flavor ramen noodles
1	16-ounce jar salsa (about 1¾ cups)
1	15-ounce can black beans, rinsed and drained
1	8.75-ounce can whole kernel corn, drained
¼	cup snipped fresh cilantro
2	tablespoons thinly sliced green onion (1)

STEP 1 Thaw shrimp, if frozen. Peel and devein shrimp. Rinse shrimp; pat dry with paper towels. In a medium bowl combine lemon juice, chili powder, cumin, salt, and pepper; add shrimp. Toss to coat. Cover and refrigerate for 30 minutes.

STEP 2 Meanwhile, in a 4-quart Dutch oven bring water to boiling over high heat. Stir in one of the noodle flavor packets (discard remaining flavor packet or reserve for another use). Break ramen noodles into pieces; add to saucepan. Return to boiling; cook for 1 minute. Add the shrimp; cook for 1 to 2 minutes more or until shrimp turn opaque. Stir in salsa, drained beans, corn, cilantro, and green onion. Heat through.

PER ABOUT 1¾ CUPS: 254 cal., 6 g total fat (0 g sat. fat), 88 mg chol., 1,090 mg sodium, 37 g carbo., 6 g fiber, 21 g pro.
EXCHANGES: 2½ Starch, 2 Very Lean Meat, ½ Fat

OFF THE SHELF TIP Look for packages of ramen noodles in the soup aisle of your supermarket. They come in a variety of flavors, both meat and vegetarian.

Broccoli Chowder

½ cup water

1 10-ounce package frozen chopped broccoli

1 tablespoon dried minced onion

1 10.75-ounce can condensed cream of chicken soup

1 cup milk

1 cup shredded cheddar cheese (4 ounces)

⅛ teaspoon cayenne pepper

Croutons (optional)

OFF THE SHELF TIP Grab a can from the soup section. Just make sure your choice is condensed, not ready-to-serve.

START TO FINISH
20 MINUTES
MAKES
4 SERVINGS

STEP 1 In a medium saucepan bring the water to boiling. Add broccoli and onion. Cover and simmer about 5 minutes or until broccoli is crisp-tender. Do not drain.

STEP 2 Stir in soup, milk, cheese, and cayenne pepper. Cook and stir about 4 minutes or until heated through. If desired, sprinkle each serving with croutons.

PER 1 CUP: 242 cal., 16 g total fat (8 g sat. fat), 40 mg chol., 824 mg sodium, 13 g carbo., 2 g fiber, 13 g pro.
EXCHANGES: ½ Vegetable, ½ Starch, 1½ Medium-Fat Meat, 2 Fat

Broccoli-Swiss Soup

Ham, cream, Swiss cheese, and broccoli mingle in broth for a satisfying soup. Roasted minced garlic adds a nice flavor depth.

2	14-ounce cans chicken broth
1	16-ounce package fresh broccoli florets
½	cup chopped onion (1 medium)
2	teaspoons bottled minced roasted garlic
1	cup shredded Swiss cheese (4 ounces)
1	cup half-and-half or light cream
½	cup cubed cooked ham
	Salt
	Ground black pepper

OFF THE SHELF TIP Save tons of time by using bottled minced roasted garlic instead of roasting and mincing your own. Look for jars with the spices or in the produce section of your supermarket. Be sure to refrigerate after opening.

START TO FINISH
25 MINUTES

MAKES
4 SERVINGS

STEP 1 In a large saucepan combine broth, broccoli, onion, and garlic. Bring to boiling; reduce heat. Cover and simmer about 10 minutes or until broccoli is very tender. In a blender or food processor blend or process the broccoli mixture, in 2 or 3 batches, until smooth.

STEP 2 Return all of the broccoli mixture to the saucepan. Return to a simmer. Add cheese; cook, stirring constantly, until melted. Stir in half-and-half and ham. Season to taste with salt and pepper.

PER 1½ CUPS: 283 cal., 18 g total fat (10 g sat. fat), 58 mg chol., 1,213 mg sodium, 14 g carbo., 4 g fiber, 18 g pro.
EXCHANGES: ½ Vegetable, 1 Starch, 2 Medium-Fat Meat, 1 Fat

Tofu-Mushroom Noodle Soup

This soup features udon noodles that are made with wheat or corn flour. If you can't locate udon noodles, substitute them with angel hair pasta, which cooks in the same amount of time.

START TO FINISH
25 MINUTES

MAKES
4 TO 6 SERVINGS

1   16-ounce package extra-firm tofu (fresh bean curd), drained and cut into ½-inch cubes

1   tablespoon soy sauce

1   tablespoon toasted sesame oil

8   ounces fresh button mushrooms, sliced (3 cups)

½   teaspoon bottled minced garlic (1 clove)

1   tablespoon cooking oil

2   14-ounce cans vegetable broth

1   10.5-ounce can condensed vegetarian vegetable soup

1   10-ounce package frozen chopped broccoli

2   ounces dried udon noodles or angel hair pasta, broken

1   to 2 tablespoons snipped fresh cilantro

PER 2 CUPS: 295 cal., 15 g total fat (2 g sat. fat), 0 mg chol., 1,545 mg sodium, 29 g carbo., 5 g fiber, 18 g pro.
EXCHANGES: 2 Vegetable, 1 Starch, 1½ Medium-Fat Meat, 1 Fat

OFF THE SHELF TIP Minced, packed in oil, and found in the produce aisle, garlic couldn't get much easier to use.

STEP 1   In a medium bowl gently stir together tofu cubes, soy sauce, and sesame oil; set aside.

STEP 2   In a large saucepan cook mushrooms and garlic over medium-high heat in hot oil for 4 minutes. Add broth, soup, broccoli, and noodles. Bring to boiling; reduce heat. Simmer, covered, for 4 to 6 minutes or until vegetables and noodles are tender, stirring occasionally.

STEP 3   Gently stir in tofu mixture; heat through. Stir in cilantro.

Tomato-Barley Soup with Garden Vegetables

Chunks of fresh chopped veggies join a prepared tomato-basil soup and barley for an aromatic treat. Serve with wheat rolls and sliced cheese for a light, satisfying soup supper.

L O W
F A T

START TO FINISH
30 MINUTES

MAKES
4 SERVINGS

2	14-ounce cans vegetable broth
¾	cup quick-cooking barley
¾	cup thinly sliced carrot
1	teaspoon dried thyme, crushed
⅛	teaspoon ground black pepper
1	19-ounce can ready-to-serve tomato-basil soup
2	cups coarsely chopped zucchini and/or yellow summer squash (2 medium)
1	cup frozen cut green beans

STEP 1 In a large saucepan combine broth, barley, carrot, thyme, and pepper. Bring to boiling; reduce heat. Cover and simmer for 10 minutes.

STEP 2 Stir in tomato-basil soup, zucchini, and frozen green beans. Return to boiling; reduce heat. Cover and simmer for 8 to 10 minutes more or until vegetables and barley are tender.

PER 1¾ CUPS: 197 cal., 3 g total fat (0 g sat. fat), 0 mg chol., 1,265 mg sodium, 40 g carbo., 6 g fiber, 7 g pro.
EXCHANGES: 2 Vegetable, 2 Starch

OFF THE SHELF TIP Simple flavor enhancers for a variety of foods, spices and dried herbs should be stored in airtight containers in cool, dark locations.

Three-Bean Chili

When you're thinking chili, putting this meat-free version on the stove alongside the standard fare is easy to do—and your vegetarian friends will appreciate the gesture. But don't be surprised to see meat lovers dipping into this sassy-flavored version too.

LOW FAT

PREP
25 MINUTES
COOK
40 MINUTES
MAKES
8 SERVINGS

2   15-ounce cans pinto beans, rinsed and drained
1   28-ounce can crushed tomatoes, undrained
1   18.8-ounce can ready-to-serve lentil soup
1   15-ounce can garbanzo beans (chickpeas), rinsed and drained
1   15-ounce can black beans, rinsed and drained
1   4-ounce can diced green chile peppers, undrained
1   cup chopped onion (1 large)
1   cup water
1   tablespoon chili powder
2   medium zucchini, halved lengthwise and sliced (about 2½ cups)
1   cup shredded Monterey Jack cheese with jalapeño peppers (4 ounces)
     Dairy sour cream (optional)
     Snipped fresh cilantro (optional)

STEP 1   In a 4- or 5-quart Dutch oven combine drained pinto beans, undrained tomatoes, lentil soup, drained garbanzo beans, drained black beans, undrained chile peppers, onion, water, and chili powder. Bring to boiling; reduce heat. Simmer, covered, for 30 minutes, stirring occasionally.

STEP 2   Stir in zucchini. Cover and cook for 10 minutes more. Remove from heat. Sprinkle each serving with cheese. If desired, serve with sour cream and garnish with cilantro.

PER 1½ CUPS: 319 cal., 7 g total fat (3 g sat. fat), 15 mg chol., 1,173 mg sodium, 48 g carbo., 15 g fiber, 18 g pro.
EXCHANGES: 1 Vegetable, 3 Starch, 1 Lean Meat

OFF THE SHELF TIP Look for canned green chiles in the Mexican section of your supermarket. They come whole and diced as well as mild and hot.

Meats

Peppery Steak with Bordelaise Sauce

Mushrooms, gravy, and red wine simmer down to a lush sauce for skillet-cooked steak. The meal's substantial, sophisticated, and on the table in 25 minutes.

START TO FINISH
25 MINUTES

MAKES
4 SERVINGS

1¼	cups water
1	cup sliced fresh mushrooms
½	cup finely chopped onion (1 medium)
1	0.87- to 1.2-ounce package brown gravy mix
¼	cup dry red wine
2	teaspoons garlic-pepper seasoning
4	beef ribeye, top sirloin, or tenderloin steaks, cut ¾ inch thick (about 1½ pounds)
2	tablespoons olive oil

OFF THE SHELF TIP Packaged gravy mix is usually found in the spice aisle of the supermarket. It comes in a variety of flavors and is a simple way to add depth and flavor to dishes.

STEP 1 For sauce, in a medium saucepan bring the water to boiling. Add the mushrooms and onion. Reduce heat. Cover and cook for 3 minutes. Stir in dry gravy mix; stir in red wine. Cook about 3 minutes or until thickened, stirring occasionally. Cover; keep warm.

STEP 2 Sprinkle garlic-pepper seasoning evenly over steaks; rub into meat. In a large heavy skillet heat oil over medium-high heat. Add steaks. Reduce heat to medium. Cook for 7 to 12 minutes for medium-rare (145°F) to medium doneness (160°F), turning once. Serve steaks with the sauce.

PER SERVING: 366 cal., 18 g total fat (5 g sat. fat), 81 mg chol., 954 mg sodium, 7 g carbo., 1 g fiber, 39 g pro.
EXCHANGES: ½ Other Carbo., 5½ Lean Meat, 1 Fat

Stroganoff-Style Beef with Broccoli

START TO FINISH
30 MINUTES

MAKES
4 SERVINGS

3   cups dried wide egg noodles
3   cups fresh small broccoli spears (12 ounces)
½   cup light dairy sour cream
1½   teaspoons prepared horseradish
½   teaspoon snipped fresh dill
1   pound beef ribeye steak, trimmed and cut into thin bite-size strips
1   small onion, cut into ½-inch slices
½   teaspoon bottled minced garlic (1 clove)
1   tablespoon cooking oil
4   teaspoons all-purpose flour
½   teaspoon ground black pepper
1   14-ounce can beef broth
3   tablespoons tomato paste
1   teaspoon Worcestershire sauce

STEP 1   Cook noodles according to package directions, adding broccoli for the last 5 minutes of cooking; drain well. Return noodle mixture to pan; cover and keep warm.

STEP 2   Meanwhile, in a small serving bowl stir together sour cream, horseradish, and dill; cover and chill until serving time.

STEP 3   In a large skillet cook half of the beef, the onion, and garlic in hot oil over medium-high heat until beef is desired doneness and onion is tender. Remove from skillet. Add remaining beef to skillet; cook and stir until beef is desired doneness. Return all of the meat mixture to the skillet; sprinkle flour and pepper over meat. Stir to coat.

STEP 4   Stir in broth, tomato paste, and Worcestershire sauce. Cook and stir until thickened and bubbly. Cook and stir for 1 minute more. Serve beef mixture on top of noodle mixture. Pass sour cream mixture.

PER SERVING: 368 cal., 15 g total fat (5 g sat. fat), 81 mg chol., 454 mg sodium, 32 g carbo., 4 g fiber, 29 g pro.
EXCHANGES: 1½ Vegetable, 1½ Starch, 3 Lean Meat, 1 Fat

OFF THE SHELF TIP   Save tons of time by using bottled minced garlic instead of mincing your own. Look for jars near the spices or in the produce section of your supermarket. Be sure to refrigerate after opening.

Beef & Broccoli with Plum Sauce

START TO FINISH
30 MINUTES

MAKES
4 SERVINGS

RECIPE PICTURED ON PAGE 136.

³/₄	cup water
¹/₂	cup bottled plum sauce
2	tablespoons reduced-sodium soy sauce
1	tablespoon cornstarch
1	teaspoon grated fresh ginger
1	tablespoon cooking oil
1	cup broccoli florets
1	small onion, cut into 1-inch pieces
1	teaspoon bottled minced garlic (2 cloves)
12	ounces beef top round steak, trimmed and cut into thin bite-size strips
3	cups coarsely chopped bok choy
2	medium plums, pitted and cut into thin wedges
	Hot cooked Chinese egg noodles, fine egg noodles, or rice

STEP 1 For sauce, in a small bowl stir together water, plum sauce, soy sauce, cornstarch, and ginger. Set aside.

STEP 2 In a nonstick wok or large skillet heat oil over medium-high heat. (Add more oil as necessary during cooking.) Add broccoli, onion, and garlic; stir-fry for 3 minutes. Remove broccoli mixture from wok. Add beef to hot wok. Cook and stir for 2 to 3 minutes or until brown. Push beef from center of wok. Stir sauce. Add sauce to center of wok. Cook and stir until thickened and bubbly.

STEP 3 Return broccoli mixture to wok. Add bok choy and plums. Stir to coat all ingredients with sauce. Cover and cook about 2 minutes more or until heated through. Serve over hot cooked noodles.

PER SERVING: 413 cal., 10 g total fat (3 g sat. fat), 74 mg chol., 533 mg sodium, 54 g carbo., 4 g fiber, 26 g pro.
EXCHANGES: 1 Vegetable, ½ Fruit, 3 Other Carbo., 3 Lean Meat

OFF THE SHELF TIP Look for plum sauce in the Asian foods section of your supermarket. This sweet and sour sauce is also called "duck sauce."

Steaks with Horseradish Cream Sauce

PREP
15 MINUTES

BAKE
10 MINUTES

OVEN
400°F

MAKES
2 TO 4 SERVINGS

1   tablespoon olive oil
2   beef tenderloin steaks, cut
        1½ inches thick (8 to 10 ounces each)
        Salt
        Ground black pepper
½   cup whipping cream
3   tablespoons horseradish mustard
        Cracked black pepper (optional)

STEP 1   Preheat oven to 400°F. In a large skillet heat oil over medium heat. Sprinkle both sides of steaks with salt and pepper; add to hot oil. Cook about 4 minutes or until brown, turning once. Transfer to a 2-quart square baking dish. Bake the steaks, uncovered, in the preheated oven for 10 to 13 minutes or until medium-rare doneness (145°F).

STEP 2   Meanwhile, in a medium bowl beat the whipping cream with an electric mixer on medium speed until soft peaks form. Fold in horseradish mustard.

STEP 3   To serve, place steaks on dinner plates and spoon the cream sauce over steaks. If desired, sprinkle with cracked black pepper.

PER SERVING: 641 cal., 47 g total fat (21 g sat. fat), 221 mg chol., 620 mg sodium, 4 g carbo., 0 g fiber, 50 g pro.
EXCHANGES: 7 Lean Meat, 5½ Fat

OFF THE SHELF TIP Mustards come in a wide variety of flavors, from mild to wow—and everywhere in between. Some are flavored with herbs and spices, others with wine, peppers, or even honey.

Dijon-Pepper Steak

Cracked black pepper adds a sharp flavor to the rich meat, and a mustard sauce is ready in just minutes.

START TO FINISH
30 MINUTES

MAKES
4 SERVINGS

4   beef sirloin steaks, cut ³/₄ inch thick (1¹/₄ pounds)
1   teaspoon cracked black pepper
2   tablespoons butter or margarine
1   10.5-ounce can condensed French onion soup
¹/₄ cup water
2   tablespoons Dijon-style mustard
1   tablespoon all-purpose flour
1   4-ounce can (drained weight) sliced mushrooms, drained
     Hot cooked noodles

OFF THE SHELF TIP Grab a can from the soup section. Just make sure your choice is condensed, not ready-to-serve.

STEP 1   Trim fat from steaks. Press pepper into both sides of each steak. In a large skillet cook steaks in hot butter over medium heat for 8 to 10 minutes for medium-rare (145°F) to medium doneness (160°F), turning once.

STEP 2   Transfer steaks to a serving platter, reserving drippings in skillet. Cover steaks; keep warm. Remove skillet from heat and allow to stand for 1 minute.

STEP 3   For sauce, in a medium bowl combine soup, water, mustard, and flour; stir into skillet. Add drained mushrooms. Cook and stir until slightly thickened and bubbly. Cook and stir for 1 minute more. Serve sauce with steaks and noodles.

PER SERVING: 451 cal., 14 g total fat (6 g sat. fat), 144 mg chol., 1,041 mg sodium, 39 g carbo., 3 g fiber, 38 g pro.
EXCHANGES: 2¹/₂ Starch, 4 Lean Meat, 1 Fat

Pot Roast with Chipotle-Fruit Sauce

Garlic-pepper seasoning, dried fruit, and chipotle peppers give this slow-cooked roast a complex, delicious kick. Serve it with hot cooked couscous or rice to soak up the sauce.

PREP
15 MINUTES

COOK
10 TO 11 HOURS (LOW)
OR 5 TO 5½ HOURS (HIGH)
PLUS 5 MINUTES

MAKES
6 TO 8 SERVINGS

1	3-pound boneless beef chuck pot roast
2	teaspoons garlic-pepper seasoning
1	7-ounce package dried mixed fruit
½	cup water
1	tablespoon finely chopped chipotle peppers in adobo sauce
1	tablespoon water
2	teaspoons cornstarch

STEP 1 Sprinkle both sides of meat with garlic-pepper seasoning. If necessary, cut meat to fit into a 3½- or 4-quart slow cooker; place meat in cooker. Add dried fruit, the ½ cup water, and the chipotle peppers.

STEP 2 Cover and cook on low-heat setting for 10 to 11 hours or on high-heat setting for 5 to 5½ hours. Transfer meat and fruit to a serving platter. Cover and keep warm.

STEP 3 Transfer cooking liquid to a bowl or glass measuring cup; skim off fat. In a medium saucepan combine the 1 tablespoon water and the cornstarch; add cooking liquid. Cook and stir until thickened and bubbly; cook and stir for 2 minutes more. Thinly slice meat. To serve, spoon sauce over sliced meat and fruit.

PER SERVING: 366 cal., 9 g total fat (3 g sat. fat), 134 mg chol., 278 mg sodium, 23 g carbo., 1 g fiber, 49 g pro.
EXCHANGES: 1½ Fruit, 7 Very Lean Meat, 1 Fat

OFF THE SHELF TIP Fetch jars of chipotle peppers in adobo sauce—dried and smoked jalapeño peppers in a tangy sauce of vinegar, pepper, and chiles—from the ethnic section of your supermarket. Take care when chopping them because they contain volatile oils that can burn your skin and eyes.

Flank Steak Sandwiches

Marinated, grilled steak slips between a toasted bun with a mushroom–roasted pepper relish to make a very dressy sandwich. Try it at a backyard picnic.

PREP
20 MINUTES

MARINATE
2 TO 24 HOURS

GRILL
17 MINUTES

MAKES
4 TO 6 SERVINGS

1	1- to 1¼-pound beef flank steak
½	cup bottled balsamic vinaigrette salad dressing
1½	cups sliced fresh portobello mushrooms
2	tablespoons butter or margarine
½	cup bottled roasted red sweet peppers, cut into strips
1	teaspoon soy sauce
4	to 6 hoagie rolls, halved lengthwise and toasted
	Balsamic vinaigrette salad dressing (optional)

STEP 1 Score both sides of steak in a diamond pattern by making shallow diagonal cuts at 1-inch intervals. Place steak in a resealable large plastic bag set in a shallow baking dish. Add the ½ cup balsamic dressing. Seal bag; turn to coat steak. Marinate in the refrigerator for at least 2 hours or up to 24 hours, turning bag occasionally.

STEP 2 Preheat grill. Drain steak, discarding marinade. Place steak on the rack of an uncovered grill directly over medium heat. Grill for 17 to 21 minutes or until medium doneness (160°F), turning once halfway through grilling.

STEP 3 Meanwhile, in a large skillet cook mushrooms in hot butter over medium-high heat just until tender. Stir in roasted red peppers and soy sauce; remove from heat. Slice steak thinly across the grain.

STEP 4 Serve steak slices in rolls. Top with mushroom mixture. If desired, drizzle with additional balsamic dressing.

PER SERVING: 503 cal., 26 g total fat (9 g sat. fat), 62 mg chol., 861 mg sodium, 35 g carbo., 2 g fiber, 32 g pro.
EXCHANGES: ½ Vegetable, 2 Starch, 3½ Lean Meat, 3 Fat

OFF THE SHELF TIP Roasted red sweet peppers are found in the condiment aisle of your supermarket. They are easy to make at home, but why take the time when jars are so easy to snap up?

Saucy Steak

PREP
30 MINUTES
COOK
45 MINUTES
MAKES
6 SERVINGS

1½	**pounds tenderized beef round steak**
2	**tablespoons cooking oil**
1	**10.75-ounce can condensed golden mushroom soup**
1	**4-ounce can (drained weight) sliced mushrooms, drained**
½	**cup water**
1	**tablespoon snipped fresh basil or 1 teaspoon dried basil, crushed**
1	**8-ounce carton dairy sour cream**
2	**tablespoons all-purpose flour**
	Hot cooked noodles or rice
1	**tablespoon snipped fresh parsley**

STEP 1   Cut meat into 6 serving-size pieces. In a large skillet cook meat, half at a t me, in hot oil over medium-high heat until brown on both sides. Drain off fat. Return all of the meat to skillet.

STEP 2   Meanwhile, in a medium bowl stir together soup, drained mushrooms, water, and, if using, dried basil. Pour over meat in skillet. Bring to boiling; reduce heat. Cover and simmer for 45 to 60 minutes or until meat is tender. Transfer meat to a serving platter, reserving mushroom mixture in skillet. Cover meat to keep warm.

STEP 3   For sauce, in a small bowl stir together sour cream and flour. Stir sour cream mixture into mushroom mixture. Cook and stir until thickened and bubbly. Cook and stir for 1 minute more. If using, stir in fresh basil.

STEP 4   Serve sauce and meat over hot cooked noodles. Sprinkle with parsley.

PER SERVING: 419 cal., 19 g total fat (8 g sat. fat), 111 mg chol., 567 mg sodium, 29 g carbo., 2 g fiber, 31 g pro.
EXCHANGES: 2 Starch, 3½ Very Lean Meat, 3 Fat

OFF THE SHELF TIP Grab a can from the soup section. Just make sure your choice is condensed, not ready-to-serve.

Steak with Mushrooms

LOW FAT SLOW COOKER

PREP
10 MINUTES

COOK
8 TO 10 HOURS (LOW)
OR 4 TO 5 HOURS (HIGH)

MAKES
4 SERVINGS

1 pound boneless beef round steak, cut 1 inch thick
2 medium onions, sliced
2 4½-ounce jars (drained weight) whole mushrooms, drained
1 12-ounce jar beef gravy
¼ cup dry red wine or apple juice

STEP 1 Trim fat from meat. Cut meat into 4 serving-size pieces. Place onion slices in a 3½- or 4-quart slow cooker. Arrange mushrooms over onions; add meat. Stir together gravy and wine. Pour over meat.

STEP 2 Cover and cook on low-heat setting for 8 to 10 hours or on high-heat setting for 4 to 5 hours.

FOR A 5- TO 6-QUART COOKER: Recipe may be doubled.

PER SERVING: 220 cal., 4 g total fat (2 g sat. fat), 51 mg chol., 814 mg sodium, 11 g carbo., 3 g fiber, 31 g pro.
EXCHANGES: 1 Vegetable, ½ Other Carbo., 4 Very Lean Meat, ½ Fat

OFF THE SHELF TIP Look for cans or jars of mushrooms in the canned vegetable aisle of your supermarket. You can buy them whole or sliced.
MAKE IT HEALTHY Grab an apple or pear, slice it, and set it out with chopped veggies to nibble while you and your family put dinner together. You'll help everyone reach the 5-cup daily fruit-veggie requirements. The high water content of fruits and vegetables also helps folks feel full sooner, so they're less likely to overconsume meat (protein) and bread (grains).

Spiced Beef Brisket

This savory slow-cooked meal will welcome you home with a delicious aroma and will produce plenty of leftovers to freeze for an easy meal on another busy day.

PREP
15 MINUTES

COOK
10 TO 11 HOURS (LOW)
OR 5 TO 5½ HOURS (HIGH)
PLUS 5 MINUTES

MAKES
10 TO 12 SERVINGS

1   3½- to 4-pound fresh beef brisket
2   cups water
¼   cup ketchup
1   envelope (½ of a 2.2-ounce package) onion soup mix
2   tablespoons Worcestershire sauce
½   teaspoon ground cinnamon
½   teaspoon bottled minced garlic (1 clove)
¼   teaspoon ground black pepper
¼   cup water
3   tablespoons all-purpose flour

STEP 1   If necessary, cut meat to fit into a 3½- or 4-quart slow cooker. Place meat in cooker.

STEP 2   In a medium bowl combine the 2 cups water, the ketchup, soup mix, Worcestershire sauce, cinnamon, garlic, and pepper. Pour over meat.

STEP 3   Cover and cook on low-heat setting for 10 to 11 hours or on high-heat setting for 5 to 5½ hours. Remove meat from cooker; keep warm.

STEP 4   For gravy, pour cooking juices into a glass measuring cup. Skim off fat. Measure 1½ cups of the cooking juices; set aside (discard the remaining juices). In a small saucepan stir the ¼ cup water into the flour. Stir in the 1½ cups cooking juices. Cook and stir until thickened and bubbly. Cook and stir 1 minute more.

STEP 5   Slice beef thinly across the grain. Serve with the hot gravy.

PER SERVING: 247 cal., 9 g total fat (3 g sat. fat), 76 mg chol., 338 mg sodium, 5 g carbo., 0 g fiber, 33 g pro.
EXCHANGES: 4½ Lean Meat

OFF THE SHELF TIP   Onion soup mix is sold in a box or a bag. You'll spot it on shelves near soups.

Asian-Style Meatballs

Mixing in sweet ginger-sesame grilling sauce or bottled stir-fry sauce and water chestnuts is the key to infusing meatballs with Asian flavor and texture.

PREP
25 MINUTES

COOK
12 MINUTES

MAKES
4 SERVINGS

1   egg, slightly beaten
¼   cup purchased shredded carrot
½   cup soft bread crumbs
1   teaspoon ground ginger
¼   teaspoon salt
¼   teaspoon garlic powder
12   ounces lean ground beef
½   of a 14-ounce jar sweet ginger-sesame grill sauce (about ¾ cup) or ¾ cup bottled stir-fry sauce
½   cup water
1   small onion, cut into thin wedges
1   8-ounce can sliced water chestnuts, drained
1   medium red or green sweet pepper, cut into 1-inch pieces
½   cup purchased shredded carrot
     Hot cooked rice

STEP 1 In a medium bowl combine egg, the ¼ cup of the carrot, the bread crumbs, ginger, salt, and garlic powder. Add meat and mix well. Shape meat mixture into 8 meatballs.

STEP 2 In a large skillet cook meatballs over medium heat until brown, turning to brown evenly (meatballs will not be done). Remove meatballs from skillet. Wipe out skillet with paper towels.

STEP 3 Add grill sauce and water to skillet; stir to combine. Add onion, drained water chestnuts, sweet pepper, and the ½ cup carrot to skillet; bring to boiling. Return meatballs to skillet. Reduce heat. Cover and simmer for 12 to 15 minutes or until meatballs are done (160°F).* Serve meatballs and sauce with hot cooked rice.

*NOTE: To check the doneness of a meatball, insert an instant-read thermometer into the center of a meatball.

PER SERVING: 537 cal., 10 g total fat (4 g sat. fat), 107 mg chol., 1,367 mg sodium, 83 g carbo., 3 g fiber, 23 g pro.
EXCHANGES: 1 Vegetable, 2 Starch, 3 Other Carbo., 2½ Medium-Fat Meat

OFF THE SHELF TIP You'll find dozens of flavors of grill sauces available. Look for them near the barbecue sauce in the condiment aisle. They can be sweet or savory, mild or sassy.

Stroganoff-Style Meatballs

White wine imparts a zippy flavor to this dress up of purchased meatballs.

PREP
15 MINUTES

COOK
20 MINUTES

MAKES
6 SERVINGS

1   10.75-ounce can condensed golden mushroom soup

½   cup dairy sour cream

½   cup milk

¼   cup dry white wine

2   tablespoons all-purpose flour

32   to 36 frozen cooked meatballs (½ ounce each)

1   4-ounce can (drained weight) sliced mushrooms, drained

    Hot cooked noodles

OFF THE SHELF TIP Straight from your grocer's freezer, frozen meatballs can be a timesaver for the busy cook. For variety look for Italian and turkey versions.

STEP 1 In a large saucepan combine soup, sour cream, milk, wine, and flour. Add meatballs and mushrooms. Bring to boiling; reduce heat. Cover and simmer about 20 minutes or until meatballs are heated through, stirring occasionally. Serve with hot cooked noodles.

PER SERVING: 436 cal., 26 g total fat (11 g sat. fat), 64 mg chol., 1,094 mg sodium, 34 g carbo., 4 g fiber, 16 g pro.
EXCHANGES: 2 Starch, 1½ Medium-Fat Meat, 3½ Fat

Tamale Pie

PREP
20 MINUTES
BAKE
22 MINUTES
OVEN
375°F
MAKES
6 SERVINGS

1   **8.5-ounce package corn muffin mix**
1   **cup shredded cheddar cheese
     (4 ounces)**
1   **4-ounce can diced green chile
     peppers, drained**
1   **pound lean ground beef or bulk
     pork sausage**
1   **15-ounce can red kidney beans,
     rinsed and drained**
1   **10-ounce can enchilada sauce
     Dairy sour cream (optional)**

STEP 1   Preheat oven to 375°F. Grease a 2-quart rectangular baking dish; set aside.

STEP 2   Prepare muffin mix according to package directions. Stir in ½ cup of the cheese and the drained chile peppers. Spread corn muffin batter into the prepared baking dish.

STEP 3   Bake in the preheated oven for 12 to 15 minutes or until a wooden toothpick inserted near the center comes out clean.

STEP 4   Meanwhile, in a large skillet cook meat over medium heat until brown. Drain off fat. Stir drained kidney beans and enchilada sauce into browned meat. Spread meat mixture over baked corn muffin mixture.

STEP 5   Bake for 7 minutes more. Sprinkle with remaining ½ cup cheese.

Bake about 3 minutes more or until cheese melts and mixture is heated through. To serve, cut into squares. If desired, serve with sour cream.

PER SERVING: 464 cal., 21 g total fat (8 g sat. fat), 67 mg chol., 778 mg sodium, 44 g carbo., 4 g fiber, 27 g pro.
EXCHANGES: 2½ Starch, ½ Other Carbo., 3 Medium-Fat Meat

OFF THE SHELF TIP Find packaged corn muffin mix in the baking aisle of your supermarket. Unopened boxes will last up to a year.

Taco Pizza

PREP
15 MINUTES

BAKE
20 MINUTES

OVEN
400°F

MAKES
6 SERVINGS

8 ounces lean ground beef and/or bulk pork sausage

¾ cup chopped red or green sweet pepper (1 medium)

1 11.5-ounce package (8) refrigerated corn bread twists

½ cup bottled salsa

3 cups shredded taco cheese (12 ounces)

STEP 1 Preheat oven to 400°F. Grease a 12-inch pizza pan; set aside. In a medium skillet cook and stir beef and sweet pepper over medium heat until meat is brown. Drain off fat. Set aside.

STEP 2 Unroll corn bread dough (do not separate into strips). Press dough into the bottom and up the edge of the prepared pan. Spread salsa on top of dough. Sprinkle with meat mixture and top with cheese.

STEP 3 Bake in the preheated oven about 20 minutes or until bottom of crust is golden when lifted slightly with a spatula. Cut into wedges.

PER SERVING: 465 cal., 30 g total fat (15 g sat. fat), 73 mg chol., 870 mg sodium, 27 g carbo., 1 g fiber, 22 g pro.
EXCHANGES: 2 Starch, 2½ High-Fat Meat, 1 Fat

OFF THE SHELF TIP Corn bread twists are a great accompaniment to dinner but also make a versatile ingredient. Look for them in the refrigerated section of your supermarket. Be sure not to freeze unbaked dough; baked dough may be frozen for up to a month.

Beef Bunburgers

These could be called Beef "Fun Burgers" because they're a great choice for informal get-togethers. Serve alongside an array of chips, dips, deli salads, and bar cookies and you'll have an instant party.

PREP
15 MINUTES
COOK
15 MINUTES
MAKES
8 SERVINGS

1½   pounds lean ground beef
½   cup chopped onion (1 medium)
⅓   cup chopped green sweet pepper
1   10.75-ounce can condensed tomato soup
1   tablespoon vinegar
1   teaspoon dry mustard
1   teaspoon poultry seasoning
½   teaspoon dried thyme, crushed
¼   teaspoon salt
8   hamburger buns, split and toasted

OFF THE SHELF TIP Grab a can from the soup section. Just make sure your choice is condensed, not ready-to-serve.

STEP 1   In a large skillet over medium heat cook ground beef, onion, and sweet pepper until beef is brown and onion is tender. Drain off fat. Stir in soup, vinegar, dry mustard, poultry seasoning, thyme, and salt.

STEP 2   Bring to boiling; reduce heat. Simmer, uncovered, about 15 minutes or until desired consistency. Serve on toasted hamburger buns.

PER SERVING: 364 cal., 19 g total fat (7 g sat. fat), 62 mg chol., 584 mg sodium, 28 g carbo., 2 g fiber, 20 g pro.
EXCHANGES: 1 Starch, 1 Other Carbo., 3 Medium-Fat Meat

Chili-Sauced Burgers & Spaghetti

This lively burger version is a twist on Cincinnati chili—a spicy chili served over spaghetti and topped with cheese. Give it a go!

PREP
20 MINUTES
COOK
15 MINUTES
MAKES
6 SERVINGS

$1/4$ cup milk

$3/4$ cup soft bread crumbs (1 slice)

$1/2$ teaspoon salt

     Dash ground black pepper

1   pound lean ground beef

$1/4$ cup chopped onion

$1/2$ teaspoon bottled minced garlic (1 clove)

1   11.25-ounce can condensed chili beef soup

$2/3$ cup water

12   ounces dried spaghetti, cooked according to package directions

$1/3$ cup shredded cheddar cheese

OFF THE SHELF TIP Save tons of time by using bottled minced garlic instead of mincing your own. Look for jars near the spices or in the produce section of your supermarket. Be sure to refrigerate after opening.

STEP 1 In a medium bowl combine milk, bread crumbs, salt, and pepper. Add ground beef; mix well. Shape into six $3/4$-inch-thick oblong patties. In a large skillet cook patties over medium heat until brown. Remove from skillet.

STEP 2 Cook onion and garlic in drippings in skillet until tender. Stir in soup and water. Return patties to skillet. Bring mixture to boiling; reduce heat. Cover and simmer for 15 minutes.

STEP 3 To serve, place patties on top of hot cooked spaghetti. Pour soup mixture over all. Sprinkle with cheddar cheese.

PER SERVING: 461 cal., 13 g total fat (6 g sat. fat), 63 mg chol., 707 mg sodium, 57 g carbo., 3 g fiber, 27 g pro.
EXCHANGES: 3 Starch, 1 Other Carbo., 3 Lean Meat

Hamburger Stroganoff

When it's cold, you want comfort in the form of browned meat, rich sauce, and soft hot noodles. Follow this recipe and you'll get what you're after in less than half an hour.

12	ounces lean ground beef
1/2	teaspoon bottled minced garlic (1 clove) or 1/8 teaspoon garlic powder
1 1/2	cups water
1 1/2	cups half-and-half, light cream, or milk
1	4-ounce can (drained weight) sliced mushrooms, drained
1	1.5-ounce envelope (beef) stroganoff sauce mix
4	ounces dried medium egg noodles (2 cups)

OFF THE SHELF TIP Stroganoff sauce mix, found in the spice aisle of your supermarket, makes dishes that are quick to prepare seem like they took hours.

START TO FINISH
25 MINUTES

MAKES
3 OR 4 SERVINGS

STEP 1 In a large saucepan cook ground beef and garlic over medium heat until meat is brown. Drain off fat.

STEP 2 Stir water, half-and-half, drained mushrooms, and dry stroganoff sauce mix into meat mixture in skillet. Bring to boiling. Stir in noodles. Reduce heat. Cover and simmer for 6 to 8 minutes or until noodles are tender, stirring occasionally.

PER SERVING: 528 cal., 34 g total fat (16 g sat. fat), 132 mg chol., 949 mg sodium, 31 g carbo., 1 g fiber, 23 g pro.
EXCHANGES: 2 Starch, 2 1/2 Medium-Fat Meat, 4 Fat

Stroganoff-Sauced Beef Roast

When you dress up a package of ready-to-go beef pot roast with a quick mushroom-studded sour cream dip and toss it all with hot noodles, you'll have a soul-stirring comfort meal on the table fast.

START TO FINISH

30 MINUTES

MAKES

3 OR 4 SERVINGS

RECIPE PICTURED

ON PAGE 138.

1   16-ounce package refrigerated
     cooked beef pot roast with gravy
2   cups fresh shiitake, cremini, or
     button mushrooms
1/2 cup dairy sour cream French
     onion-flavor dip
2   cups hot cooked noodles

STEP 1 Transfer beef with gravy to a large skillet (leave meat whole). Remove stems from shiitake mushrooms; halve or quarter mushrooms. Add mushrooms to skillet. Cover and cook over medium-low heat about 15 minutes or until heated through, stirring mushrooms once and turning roast over halfway through cooking time.

STEP 3 Use a wooden spoon to break meat into bite-size pieces. Stir onion dip into meat mixture; heat through (do not boil). Stir in hot cooked noodles.

PER SERVING: 488 cal., 17 g total fat (9 g sat. fat), 115 mg chol., 771 mg sodium, 48 g carbo., 3 g fiber, 38 g pro.
EXCHANGES: 1 Vegetable, 2 1/2 Starch, 4 Lean Meat, 1 Fat

OFF THE SHELF TIP Fully cooked meats—roasts, briskets, loins—make putting dinner on the table a snap. Add a few extra touches and you have "it cooked all day" flavor. Look for these products in your grocer's meat section.

Roast Beef & Mashed Potato Stacks

This comfort food recalls chrome-shiny diners and a sassy waitstaff. It's a layered concoction of white bread, mashed potatoes, and cooked beef tips with gravy.

FAST

START TO FINISH
15 MINUTES

MAKES
4 SERVINGS

1   17-ounce package refrigerated cooked beef tips with gravy
$1/2$ cup onion-flavored beef broth
1   20-ounce package refrigerated mashed potatoes
2   tablespoons butter or margarine
$1/8$ teaspoon ground black pepper
4   slices thick-sliced white bread

STEP 1   In a large skillet combine beef tips with gravy and broth. Cook and stir over medium heat until heated through.

STEP 2   Meanwhile, prepare mashed potatoes according to package directions, adding the butter and pepper.

STEP 3   To serve, place bread slices on 4 dinner plates. Divide mashed potatoes among bread slices. Ladle beef mixture over potatoes and bread. Serve immediately.

PER SERVING: 372 cal., 15 g total fat (6 g sat. fat), 64 mg chol., 1,174 mg sodium, 36 g carbo., 2 g fiber, 23 g pro.
EXCHANGES: 2$1/2$ Starch, 2 Medium-Fat Meat, $1/2$ Fat

OFF THE SHELF TIP   Refrigerated mashed potatoes can be found in the produce section, or sometimes the dairy section, of your supermarket. A few minutes in the microwave or on the stovetop and you're set!

Beef Burgundy

LOW FAT

PREP
20 MINUTES

COOK
20 MINUTES

MAKES
5 OR 6 SERVINGS

1   17-ounce package refrigerated cooked beef tips with gravy
1/2   teaspoon dried basil, crushed
1/4   teaspoon ground black pepper
1   10.75-ounce can condensed golden mushroom soup
1/2   cup Burgundy wine
1 1/2 cups sliced fresh mushrooms
1   cup packaged peeled baby carrots, halved lengthwise
1   cup frozen small whole onions
12   ounces dried wide egg noodles (6 cups)

OFF THE SHELF TIP Fully cooked meats—roasts, briskets, loins—make putting dinner on the table a snap. Add a few extra touches and you have "it cooked all day" flavor. Look for these products in your grocer's meat section.

STEP 1 In a large saucepan combine beef tips with gravy, basil, and pepper. Stir in soup and wine. Bring to boiling. Add mushrooms, carrot, and onions. Return to boiling; reduce heat. Cover and simmer for 20 to 25 minutes or until vegetables are tender, stirring frequently.

STEP 2 Meanwhile, cook the noodles according to package directions; drain. Serve meat mixture over noodles.

PER SERVING: 458 cal., 10 g total fat (3 g sat. fat), 106 mg chol., 1,017 mg sodium, 63 g carbo., 5 g fiber, 26 g pro.
EXCHANGES: 1/2 Vegetable, 3 Starch, 3 Other Carbo., 2 Medium-Fat Meat

Chipotle Brisket Sandwich

Sassy coleslaw slides over a serving of beef brisket as an alternative to lettuce and tomato for a tangy, filling kaiser roll sandwich.

FAST

START TO FINISH
15 MINUTES
MAKES
6 SERVINGS

1   17-ounce package refrigerated cooked, seasoned, and sliced beef brisket with barbecue sauce
1   to 2 canned chipotle peppers in adobo sauce, chopped
$1/2$ of a 16-ounce package shredded cabbage with carrot (coleslaw mix) (about 4 cups)
$1/3$ cup bottled coleslaw dressing
6   kaiser rolls, split and toasted

STEP 1   In a large saucepan combine the beef brisket with barbecue sauce and the chipotle peppers. Cook and stir over medium heat about 5 minutes or until heated through.

STEP 2   Meanwhile, in a large bowl combine shredded cabbage mixture and coleslaw dressing; toss to coat.

STEP 3   To serve, spoon beef mixture onto roll bottoms. Top with coleslaw mixture. Add roll tops.

PER SERVING: 414 cal., 18 g total fat (5 g sat. fat), 39 mg chol., 1,085 mg sodium, 47 g carbo., 2 g fiber, 16 g pro.
EXCHANGES: $1/2$ Vegetable, 2 Starch, 1 Other Carbo., $1 1/2$ Medium-Fat Meat, 2 Fat

OFF THE SHELF TIP Fetch cans of chipotle peppers in adobo sauce—dried and smoked jalapeño peppers in a tangy sauce of vinegar, pepper, and chiles—from the ethnic section of your supermarket. Take care when chopping them because they contain volatile oils that can burn your skin and eyes.

Barbecue Beef Calzones

A smart combination of refrigerated pizza dough, shredded beef in barbecue sauce, veggies, and shredded cheese produces a savory hot baked meal.

PREP
20 MINUTES

BAKE
30 MINUTES

OVEN
400°F

MAKES
4 CALZONES

1   13.8-ounce package refrigerated pizza dough
½   of an 18- to 20-ounce package refrigerated cooked shredded beef with barbecue sauce
½   of a 16-ounce package (2 cups) frozen stir-fry vegetables (yellow, green, and red peppers and onion), thawed
1   cup shredded Monterey Jack cheese with jalapeño peppers or cheddar cheese (4 ounces)
2   tablespoons cornmeal
1   tablespoon milk
¼   teaspoon garlic salt

STEP 1   Preheat oven to 400°F. Grease a 15×10×1-inch baking pan; set aside. On a lightly floured surface, unroll pizza dough. Roll to a 12-inch square. Cut into four 6-inch squares.

STEP 2   Divide shredded beef, thawed vegetables, and cheese among dough squares, placing ingredients on half of each square. Fold remaining half of each dough square over filling to form a rectangle. Press edges with the tines of a fork to seal.

STEP 3   Sprinkle 1 tablespoon of the cornmeal on prepared baking pan. Place calzones on pan; brush tops lightly with milk. In a small bowl combine remaining 1 tablespoon cornmeal and the garlic salt; sprinkle over calzones.

STEP 4   Bake in the preheated oven about 30 minutes or until golden. Serve warm.

PER CALZONE: 434 cal., 17 g total fat (8 g sat. fat), 69 mg chol., 832 mg sodium, 42 g carbo., 2 g fiber, 28 g pro.
EXCHANGES: ½ Vegetable, 1½ Starch, 1 Other Carbo., 3½ Medium-Fat Meat

OFF THE SHELF TIP Cornmeal comes from your grocer's baking aisle. It is often packaged in a tall cylinder similar to oatmeal. Use as an ingredient or to "lift" pizza or flatbread off its baking pan.

Mexican-Style Hash

LOW FAT

PREP
20 MINUTES

COOK
15 MINUTES

MAKES
4 SERVINGS

1   17-ounce package refrigerated cooked beef roast au jus

1½   cups finely chopped potato (2 medium)

1   11-ounce can whole kernel corn, drained

1   10.75-ounce can condensed tomato soup

⅓   cup chopped onion (1 small)

1½   teaspoons chili powder

¼   teaspoon ground black pepper

OFF THE SHELF TIP Grab a can from the soup section. Just make sure your choice is condensed, not ready-to-serve.

STEP 1 Drain meat, reserving juices. Chop meat.

STEP 2 In a 10-inch skillet combine chopped meat and reserved meat juices; add potato, corn, tomato soup, onion, chili powder, and pepper. Bring to boiling; reduce heat. Cover and simmer for 15 to 20 minutes or until potato is tender, stirring occasionally to prevent sticking.

PER SERVING: 334 cal., 10 g total fat (4 g sat. fat), 64 mg chol., 1,069 mg sodium, 40 g carbo., 4 g fiber, 27 g pro.
EXCHANGES: ½ Vegetable, 1½ Starch, 1 Other Carbo., 3 Lean Meat

Beef Roast with Vegetables

LOW FAT

PREP
15 MINUTES
COOK
20 MINUTES
MAKES
4 SERVINGS

1	**17-ounce package refrigerated cooked beef roast au jus**
1½	**cups packaged peeled baby carrots**
8	**ounces tiny new potatoes, quartered**
2	**stalks celery, cut into 1-inch pieces**
¼	**cup water**
½	**teaspoon dried thyme, crushed**
½	**teaspoon garlic-pepper seasoning**

STEP 1 Transfer liquid from beef roast package to a large skillet. Cut any large carrots in half lengthwise. Add carrots, potatoes, celery, and the water to skillet. Place beef roast on top of vegetables. Sprinkle thyme and garlic-pepper seasoning over all. Bring to boiling; reduce heat. Cover and simmer about 20 minutes or until vegetables are tender and meat is heated through.

STEP 2 Serve meat with vegetables and juices.

PER SERVING: 239 cal., 9 g total fat (4 g sat. fat), 64 mg chol., 591 mg sodium, 18 g carbo., 3 g fiber, 25 g pro.
EXCHANGES: ½ Vegetable, 1 Starch, 3 Lean Meat

OFF THE SHELF TIP Fully cooked meats—roasts, briskets, loins—make putting dinner on the table a snap. A few extra touches and you have "it cooked all day" flavor. Look for in your grocer's meat section.

Beef Ragout

START TO FINISH
25 MINUTES
MAKES
6 SERVINGS

10	ounces dried wide egg noodles
1	17-ounce package refrigerated cooked beef tips with gravy
1	10.75-ounce can condensed cheddar cheese soup
1	9-ounce package frozen Italian-style green beans
1	4.5-ounce jar (drained weight) whole mushrooms, drained
$^1/_2$	cup water
3	tablespoons tomato paste
2	tablespoons dried minced onion
$^1/_2$	cup dairy sour cream

OFF THE SHELF TIP Look for cans and jars of mushrooms in the canned vegetable aisle of your supermarket. You can buy them whole or sliced.

STEP 1 Prepare noodles according to package directions. Drain and keep warm.

STEP 2 Meanwhile, in a 4-quart Dutch oven combine beef tips with gravy, soup, green beans, drained mushrooms, water, tomato paste, and onion. Bring to boiling; reduce heat. Cover and simmer for 10 to 15 minutes or until green beans are crisp-tender, stirring occasionally. Stir in sour cream; cook for 2 to 3 minutes more or until heated through. Serve over hot cooked noodles.

PER SERVING: 378 cal., 13 g total fat (5 g sat. fat), 90 mg chol., 954 mg sodium, 49 g carbo., 4 g fiber, 22 g pro.
EXCHANGES: $^1/_2$ Vegetable, 3 Starch, 2 lean Meat, 1 Fat

Roasted Vegetable & Pastrami Panini

Bring home a jar or pint of roasted grilled or deli-marinated veggies and layer them with pastrami and provolone for scrumptious sandwich flavor that you wouldn't expect from your kitchen.

START TO FINISH
30 MINUTES

MAKES
4 SERVINGS

4 thin slices provolone cheese (2 ounces)
8 ½-inch slices sourdough or Vienna bread
1 cup roasted or grilled vegetables from the deli or deli-marinated vegetables, coarsely chopped
4 thin slices pastrami (3 ounces)
1 tablespoon olive oil or basil-flavored olive oil

OFF THE SHELF TIP Flavored olive oils add extra dimension to all kinds of dishes. Use them for sauteeing vegetables and meats, in salad dressings, and for dipping chunks of crusty bread.

STEP 1 Place a cheese slice on each of 4 of the bread slices. Spread vegetables evenly over cheese. Top with pastrami and remaining 4 bread slices. Brush the outsides of the sandwiches with oil.

STEP 2 If desired, wrap a brick completely in foil. Heat a nonstick griddlepan or large skillet over medium heat. Place a sandwich on heated pan; place brick on top to flatten slightly.* Cook for 4 to 6 minutes or until sandwich is golden and cheese is melted, turning once. Repeat for remaining sandwiches.

*NOTE: Or place sandwich on a covered indoor grill or panini grill. Close lid; grill for 4 to 5 minutes or until golden and cheese is melted.

PER SERVING: 314 cal., 16 g total fat (6 g sat. fat), 29 mg chol., 689 mg sodium, 30 g carbo., 2 g fiber, 12 g pro.
EXCHANGES: ½ Vegetable, 2 Starch, 1 High-Fat Meat, 1 Fat

Reuben Loaf

Hot roll mix combines with traditional Reuben fixings to make this sandwich in a sliceable loaf form. It's a measured way to enjoy this decadent treat.

PREP
30 MINUTES

RISE
30 MINUTES

BAKE
25 MINUTES

OVEN
375°F

MAKES
10 SERVINGS

1   **16-ounce package hot roll mix**
1   **cup bottled Thousand Island salad dressing**
1   **pound sliced cooked corned beef**
8   **ounces Swiss cheese, thinly sliced or shredded**
1   **14- to 16-ounce jar or can sauerkraut, rinsed and drained**

STEP 1   Prepare the hot roll mix according to package directions. Let dough rest for 5 minutes. Meanwhile, line an extra-large baking sheet with foil; grease foil. Set aside.

STEP 2   On a lightly floured surface, divide dough in half. Roll each half into a 12×8-inch rectangle. On each dough rectangle, layer $\frac{1}{4}$ cup of the salad dressing, half of the corned beef, half of the cheese, and half of the drained sauerkraut, spreading to within 1 inch of the edges. Starting from a long side, roll up each rectangle to form a loaf. Brush edges with water and press to seal.

STEP 3   Place loaves, seam sides down, on the prepared baking sheet. Lightly cover; let rise in a warm place for 30 minutes. After 20 minutes preheat oven to 375°F.

STEP 4   Make 4 diagonal slits, $\frac{1}{4}$ inch deep, in the top of each loaf. Bake in the preheated oven for 25 to 30 minutes or until golden. Serve with remaining $\frac{1}{2}$ cup salad dressing.

PER SERVING: 492 cal., 27 g total fat (8 g sat. fat), 91 mg chol., 1,305 mg sodium, 41 g carbo., 1 g fiber, 22 g pro.
EXCHANGES: 2½ Starch, 2 High-Fat Meat, 2 Fat

OFF THE SHELF TIP   Hot roll mix can be found in the baking aisle of your supermarket. It contains all of the ingredients to make it rise.

Shredded Pork Sandwiches

PREP
15 MINUTES

COOK
8 TO 10 HOURS (LOW) OR
4 TO 5 HOURS (HIGH)

MAKES
8 TO 10 SERVINGS

RECIPE PICTURED
ON PAGE 142.

1	2¹/₂- to 3-pound pork sirloin roast
¹/₂	teaspoon garlic powder
¹/₂	teaspoon ground ginger
¹/₂	teaspoon dried thyme, crushed
1	cup chicken broth
¹/₂	cup vinegar
¹/₂	teaspoon cayenne pepper
8	to 10 hoagie rolls, split

STEP 1 Remove string from meat, if present. Trim fat from pork roast. If necessary, cut roast to fit into a 3¹/₂- or 4-quart slow cooker. In a small bowl combine garlic powder, ginger, and thyme. Sprinkle mixture over meat and rub in with fingers. Transfer meat to the cooker. Pour broth over meat.

STEP 2 Cover and cook on low-heat setting for 8 to 10 hours or on high-heat setting for 4 to 5 hours.

STEP 3 Remove meat from cooker, reserving cooking liquid. Using 2 forks, shred meat and place in a large bowl. Add 1 cup of the cooking liquid, the vinegar, and cayenne pepper to meat in bowl; toss to combine. Serve on hoagie rolls.

PER SERVING: 292 cal., 7 g total fat (2 g sat. fat), 79 mg chol., 402 mg sodium, 23 g carbo., 1 g fiber, 31 g pro.
EXCHANGES: 1¹/₂ Starch, 4 Very Lean Meat, ¹/₂ Fat

OFF THE SHELF TIP Simple flavor enhancers for a variety of foods, spices and dried herbs should be stored in airtight containers in cool, dark locations.

Pork & Slaw Barbecue Rolls

Pork shoulder slow-cooks with cider vinegar and brown sugar to join a deli coleslaw topper between halves of toasted kaiser rolls for a complete sandwich meal.

PREP
10 MINUTES

COOK
10 TO 12 HOURS (LOW) OR
5 TO 6 HOURS (HIGH)

MAKES
16 SERVINGS

1	4- to 5-pound pork shoulder blade roast
³/₄	cup cider vinegar
2	tablespoons packed brown sugar
¹/₂	teaspoon salt
¹/₂	teaspoon crushed red pepper
¹/₄	teaspoon ground black pepper
16	kaiser rolls, split and toasted
	Purchased deli coleslaw

STEP 1 Cut roast to fit into a 4- to 6-quart slow cooker; place meat in slow cooker. In a small bowl combine vinegar, brown sugar, salt, red pepper, and black pepper. Pour over meat.

STEP 2 Cover and cook on low-heat setting for 10 to 12 hours or on high-heat setting for 5 to 6 hours.

STEP 3 Transfer roast to a cutting board; reserve cooking juices. When cool enough to handle, cut meat off bones and coarsely chop. In a medium bowl combine meat and as much of the juices as desired to moisten. Spoon meat onto roll bottoms. Top with coleslaw. Add roll tops.

PER SERVING: 272 cal., 6 g total fat (2 g sat. fat), 41 mg chol., 563 mg sodium, 34 g carbo., 1 g fiber, 18 g pro.
EXCHANGES: 2 Starch, 2 Lean Meat

OFF THE SHELF TIP Check with your butcher when purchasing a pork shoulder roast. These roasts may not be on display in the meat case but are usually available.

Balsamic & Garlic Pork

FAST

START TO FINISH
15 MINUTES
MAKES
4 SERVINGS

4	boneless pork loin chops, cut ½ inch thick (12 to 16 ounces)
½	teaspoon dried rosemary, crushed
¼	teaspoon salt
1	tablespoon olive oil
2	teaspoons bottled minced roasted garlic
½	cup bottled balsamic salad dressing
1	tablespoon honey mustard

STEP 1 Sprinkle chops with rosemary and salt, rubbing into the surface of the meat.

STEP 2 In a large nonstick skillet heat oil over medium heat. Add chops; cook for 8 to 12 minutes or until tender and juices run clear (160°F), turning once halfway through cooking. Remove chops, reserving drippings in skillet; keep chops warm while preparing sauce.

STEP 3 For sauce, in the same skillet cook garlic in hot drippings for 30 seconds. Stir in salad dressing and honey mustard. Bring to boiling. To serve, spoon sauce over chops.

PER SERVING: 276 cal., 18 g total fat (4 g sat. fat), 54 mg chol., 562 mg sodium, 5 g carbo., 0 g fiber, 22 g pro.
EXCHANGES: ½ Other Carbo., 3 Lean Meat, 2 Fat

OFF THE SHELF TIP Save tons of time by using bottled minced roasted garlic instead of roasting and mincing your own. Look for jars near the spices or in the produce section of your supermarket. Be sure to refrigerate after opening.

Apricot-Glazed Pork Roast

A five-spice rub imparts a symphony of flavor to roast pork, which is finished with a shiny apricot glaze. Bring this to the table for a holiday meal and you'll kindle a fresh new round of "what'll we have for dinner"!

PREP
20 MINUTES

CHILL
1 TO 2 HOURS

ROAST
1 1/4 HOURS

STAND
15 MINUTES

OVEN
325°F

MAKES
8 SERVINGS

RECIPE PICTURED ON PAGE 137.

1 1/2	teaspoons ground cumin
1/2	teaspoon garlic salt
1/2	teaspoon ground cinnamon
1/2	teaspoon ground ginger
1/4	teaspoon ground cloves
1	2 1/2- to 3-pound boneless pork top loin roast (single loin)
1	cup apricot preserves
2	to 3 tablespoons white wine vinegar

STEP 1 For rub, in a small bowl stir together cumin, garlic salt, cinnamon, ginger, and cloves. Sprinkle rub mixture evenly over roast, rub into meat. Wrap roast in plastic wrap and refrigerate for 1 to 2 hours.

STEP 2 Preheat oven to 325°F. Unwrap roast and discard plastic wrap. Place roast on a rack in a shallow roasting pan. Insert an oven-going meat thermometer into center of roast. Roast in the preheated oven for 1 to 1 1/2 hours or until meat thermometer registers 135°F.

STEP 3 Meanwhile, for glaze, in a small saucepan cook and stir apricot preserves and vinegar over medium heat until preserves are melted. Remove from heat. Brush roast generously with the glaze. Roast about 15 minutes more or until meat thermometer registers 155°F, brushing 2 or 3 times with the glaze.

STEP 4 Remove roast from oven; cover with foil. Let stand for 15 minutes. The temperature of the roast after standing should be 160°F. Reheat remaining glaze and pass with roast.

PER SERVING: 326 cal., 9 g total fat (3 g sat. fat), 77 mg chol., 125 mg sodium, 28 g carbo., 1 g fiber, 31 g pro.
EXCHANGES: 2 Other Carbo., 4 Lean Meat

OFF THE SHELF TIP Look for apricot preserves with the other jams and jellies in your supermarket. You thought these products just paired with bread and peanut butter! They are fabulous for cooking too!

Oriental Pork Sandwiches

Slow-cooking pork with soy and hoisin produces an Asian-influenced sandwich delicacy. Plate the sandwiches with a green salad topped with mandarin oranges for a well-rounded meal.

PREP
25 MINUTES

COOK
10 TO 12 HOURS (LOW) OR
5½ TO 6 HOURS (HIGH)

MAKES
6 TO 8 SERVINGS

1	2½- to 3-pound pork shoulder roast
1	cup apple juice or apple cider
2	tablespoons soy sauce
2	tablespoons hoisin sauce
1½	teaspoons purchased five-spice powder or Homemade Five-Spice Powder
6	to 8 kaiser rolls, split and toasted
1½	to 2 cups shredded Chinese cabbage (napa) or packaged shredded broccoli (broccoli slaw mix)

STEP 1   Trim fat from meat. If necessary, cut roast to fit into a 3½- or 4-quart slow cooker. Place meat in cooker. In a small bowl combine apple juice, soy sauce, hoisin sauce, and five-spice powder. Pour over roast.

STEP 2   Cover and cook on low-heat setting for 10 to 12 hours or on high-heat setting for 5½ to 6 hours.

STEP 3   Remove meat from cooker, reserving juices. Remove meat from bone; discard bone. Using 2 forks, shred meat. Place meat on roll bottoms. Top with Chinese cabbage; add roll tops. Skim fat from juices. Serve juices in individual serving bowls for dipping.

PER SERVING: 366 cal., 9 g total fat (3 g sat. fat), 73 mg chol., 818 mg sodium, 39 g carbo., 2 g fiber, 29 g pro.
EXCHANGES: 2 Starch, ½ Other Carbo., 3½ Lean Meat

HOMEMADE FIVE-SPICE POWDER: In a blender combine 3 tablespoons ground cinnamon, 6 star anise or 2 teaspoons anise seeds, 1½ teaspoons fennel seeds, 1½ teaspoons whole Szechwan peppercorns or whole black peppercorns, and ¾ teaspoon ground cloves. Cover and blend to a fine powder. Store in a tightly covered container. Makes ⅓ cup.

OFF THE SHELF TIP Prepared five-spice powder can be found in the spice aisle of most grocery stores, but you may prefer the flavor of the homemade version.

Peppery Pork Sandwiches

PREP
25 MINUTES

BAKE
2½ HOURS

OVEN
325°F

MAKES
8 OR 9 SERVINGS

1   large onion, thinly sliced
1   2- to 2½-pound boneless pork shoulder roast
1   tablespoon hot paprika
2   14.5-ounce cans diced tomatoes, undrained
1   4-ounce can diced green chile peppers, undrained
2   teaspoons dried oregano, crushed
1   teaspoon ground black pepper
¼   teaspoon salt
8   or 9 (6-inch) French-style rolls, split and toasted

OFF THE SHELF TIP Look for canned green chiles in the Mexican section of your supermarket. They come whole and diced as well as mild and hot.

STEP 1   Preheat oven to 325°F. Arrange onion slices in bottom of a 4-quart Dutch oven. Sprinkle pork roast evenly with paprika. Place roast on top of onion. In a medium bowl combine undrained tomatoes, undrained chile peppers, oregano, black pepper, and salt. Pour over roast in Dutch oven.

STEP 2   Bake, covered, in the preheated oven for 2½ to 3 hours or until roast is very tender. Remove pork to cutting board, reserving tomato mixture in Dutch oven. Using 2 forks, shred meat. Skim fat from tomato mixture. Add shredded meat to tomato mixture; stir until combined. Heat through. Spoon pork mixture onto roll bottoms. Replace tops.

PER SERVING: 383 cal., 18 g total fat (6 g sat. fat), 79 mg chol., 964 mg sodium, 29 g carbo., 3 g fiber, 25 g pro.
EXCHANGES: 1 Vegetable, 2 Starch, 2½ Lean Meat, 1½ Fat

Maple-Pecan Glazed Pork Chops

FAST

START TO FINISH
15 MINUTES
MAKES
4 SERVINGS

4	boneless pork loin chops, cut $^3/_4$ inch thick (about 1 pound)
	Salt
	Ground black pepper
4	tablespoons butter or margarine, softened
2	tablespoons pure maple syrup or maple-flavor syrup
$^1/_3$	cup chopped pecans, toasted

STEP 1 Trim fat from chops. Sprinkle chops with salt and pepper. In a 12-inch skillet melt 1 tablespoon of the butter over medium-high heat. Add chops; cook for 8 to 12 minutes or until tender and juices run clear (160°F), turning once. Transfer chops to a serving platter.

STEP 2 Meanwhile, in a small bowl combine the remaining 3 tablespoons butter and the maple syrup. Spread butter mixture evenly over cooked chops. Let stand about 1 minute or until melted. Sprinkle with pecans.

PER SERVING: 333 cal., 23 g total fat (10 g sat. fat), 98 mg chol., 310 mg sodium, 8 g carbo., 1 g fiber, 23 g pro.
EXCHANGES: ½ Other Carbo., 3½ Very Lean Meat, 4 Fat

OFF THE SHELF TIP You thought maple syrup was reserved for pancakes and waffles! Look for it in the cereal aisle of your supermarket and expand its use in your cooking repertoire.

Cheesy Chops & Corn Bread Dressing

Green chile peppers, corn bread stuffing, and nacho cheese make a filling and unusual pork loin chop bake.

PREP
20 MINUTES

BAKE
40 MINUTES

OVEN
400°F

MAKES
4 SERVINGS

3　cups packaged corn bread stuffing mix
1　4-ounce can diced green chile peppers, undrained
$\frac{1}{2}$　cup orange juice or water
$\frac{1}{4}$　cup butter or margarine, melted
4　pork loin chops, cut 1 inch thick (about 2$\frac{1}{2}$ pounds)
　Salt
　Ground black pepper
1　9-ounce can nacho cheese sauce or dip ($\frac{3}{4}$ cup)

OFF THE SHELF TIP Look for canned green chiles in the Mexican section of your supermarket. They come whole and diced as well as mild and hot.

STEP 1 Preheat oven to 400°F. In a medium bowl stir together dry stuffing mix, undrained chile peppers, orange juice, and melted butter. Spoon stuffing mixture evenly into the bottom of a 3-quart rectangular baking dish. Arrange chops over stuffing mixture in baking dish. Season chops with salt and pepper.

STEP 2 Bake, uncovered, in the preheated oven about 30 minutes or until an instant-read thermometer inserted horizontally into centers of chops registers 140°F (make sure thermometer does not touch bone). Carefully spoon cheese sauce over chops and stuffing mixture. Bake about 10 minutes more or until thermometer registers 160°F.

PER SERVING: 624 cal., 30 g total fat (13 g sat. fat), 131 mg chol., 1,346 mg sodium, 42 g carbo., 2 g fiber, 44 g pro.
EXCHANGES: 3 Starch, 5 Lean Meat, 2$\frac{1}{2}$ Fat

Pork Chops with Raspberries

Pull out a skillet and follow this recipe for seasoned chops and a quick-cooking fruited sauce and you'll have a luscious dinner on the table in just 20 minutes.

LOW FAT

START TO FINISH
25 MINUTES

MAKES
4 SERVINGS

RECIPE PICTURED ON PAGE 136.

³/₄ cup chicken broth
1 tablespoon packed brown sugar
1 tablespoon white balsamic vinegar
1¹/₂ teaspoons cornstarch
Dash ground allspice
4 pork rib chops, cut ³/₄ inch thick (about 1¹/₂ pounds)
¹/₂ teaspoon salt
¹/₄ teaspoon ground black pepper
¹/₄ teaspoon dried basil, crushed
1 tablespoon cooking oil
1 cup fresh raspberries

STEP 1 In a small bowl stir together broth, brown sugar, balsamic vinegar, cornstarch, and allspice; set aside.

STEP 2 Trim fat from chops. Sprinkle both sides of chops with salt, pepper, and basil. In a 12-inch skillet heat oil over medium heat. Add chops; cook chops for 8 to 12 minutes or until tender and juices run clear (160°F), turning once. Transfer chops to a serving platter. Cover and keep warm. Drain fat from skillet.

STEP 3 Stir vinegar mixture. Add to skillet. Cook and stir over medium heat until slightly thickened and bubbly. Cook and stir for 2 minutes more. Gently stir in raspberries; heat through. To serve, spoon raspberry mixture over chops.

PER SERVING: 206 cal., 9 g total fat (2 g sat. fat), 53 mg chol., 516 mg sodium, 8 g carbo., 2 g fiber, 22 g pro.
EXCHANGES: ¹/₂ Other Carbo., 3 Very Lean Meat, 1¹/₂ Fat

OFF THE SHELF TIP Chicken and beef broth come in cans and cartons and are handy to keep on your shelf. If you prefer, for each cup of broth dissolve 1 teaspoon of instant beef or chicken bouillon granules in 1 cup boiling water.

Pork Chops with Orange-Dijon Sauce

Boneless pork sirloin chops slow-cook along with thyme, mustard, and tart orange for a satisfying meal that's ready when you arrive home.

SLOW COOKER

PREP
15 MINUTES

COOK
6 TO 7 HOURS (LOW) OR
3 TO 3½ HOURS (HIGH)

MAKES
6 SERVINGS

6	boneless pork sirloin chops, cut 1 inch thick
	Salt
	Ground black pepper
½	teaspoon dried thyme, crushed
1	cup orange marmalade
⅓	cup Dijon-style mustard
¼	cup water

STEP 1 Sprinkle both sides of chops lightly with salt and pepper. Sprinkle chops with thyme. Place chops in a 3½- or 4-quart slow cooker. In a small bowl combine orange marmalade and mustard. Remove 2 tablespoons of the mixture; cover and refrigerate. Combine remaining mixture and the water. Pour over chops.

STEP 2 Cover and cook on low-heat setting for 6 to 7 hours or on high-heat setting for 3 to 3½ hours. Transfer chops to a serving platter; discard cooking liquid. Spread reserved marmalade mixture over chops.

PER SERVING: 409 cal., 15 g total fat (5 g sat. fat), 166 mg chol., 212 mg sodium, 9 g carbo., 1 g fiber, 56 g pro.
EXCHANGES: ½ Other Carbo., 7½ Lean Meat, 2½ Fat

OFF THE SHELF TIP Orange marmalade is not just for toast anymore! Use it in recipes to add a splash of citrus flavor.

Pork Chops Dijon

START TO FINISH
30 MINUTES

MAKES
4 SERVINGS

3   tablespoons Dijon-style mustard
2   tablespoons bottled reduced-calorie
     Italian salad dressing
¼   teaspoon ground black pepper
4   pork loin chops, cut ½ inch thick
     (about 1½ pounds)
     Nonstick cooking spray
1   medium onion, halved and sliced

STEP 1 In a small bowl combine mustard, Italian dressing, and pepper; set aside.

STEP 2 Trim fat from the chops. Coat an unheated 10-inch skillet with nonstick cooking spray. Preheat the skillet over medium-high heat. Add the chops; cook until brown on both sides, turning once. Remove chops from skillet.

STEP 3 Add onion to skillet. Cook and stir over medium heat for 3 minutes. Push onion aside; return chops to skillet. Spread mustard mixture over chops. Cover and cook over medium-low heat about 15 minutes or until tender and juices run clear (160°F). Spoon onion over chops.

PER SERVING: 163 cal., 5 g total fat (2 g sat. fat), 53 mg chol., 403 mg sodium, 2 g carbo., 0 g fiber, 22 g pro.
EXCHANGES: 3 Very Lean Meat, 1 Fat

OFF THE SHELF TIP Grab a bottle of salad dressing from your supermarket and use it to marinate meats and vegetables or drizzle over finished dishes for an extra pop of flavor.

Barbecue Pork Ribs

Enjoy delicious ribs any time of year without standing over a hot grill. Shred any leftovers to serve on sandwich buns.

SLOW COOKER

PREP
25 MINUTES

COOK
10 TO 12 HOURS (LOW) OR
5 TO 6 HOURS (HIGH)
PLUS 5 MINUTES

MAKES
4 TO 6 SERVINGS

3	to 3½ pounds pork country-style ribs
1	cup ketchup
½	cup finely chopped onion (1 medium)
¼	cup packed brown sugar
1	tablespoon Worcestershire sauce
½	teaspoon chili powder
½	teaspoon liquid smoke
¼	teaspoon garlic powder
¼	teaspoon bottled hot pepper sauce

OFF THE SHELF TIP Liquid smoke adds a lovely smokiness to recipes. Look for it in the condiment aisle of your supermarket.

STEP 1   Place ribs in a 3½- or 4-quart slow cooker.

STEP 2   For sauce, in a small bowl combine ketchup, onion, brown sugar, Worcestershire sauce, chili powder, liquid smoke, garlic powder, and hot pepper sauce. Pour sauce over ribs, turning to coat.

STEP 3   Cover and cook on low-heat setting for 10 to 12 hours or on high-heat setting for 5 to 6 hours.

STEP 4   Transfer ribs to a serving platter; cover to keep warm. Skim fat from surface of sauce; pour sauce into a medium saucepan. Bring sauce to boiling; reduce heat slightly. Boil gently, uncovered, for 5 to 7 minutes or until thickened to desired consistency (should have about 1 cup). Pass sauce with ribs.

PER SERVING: 419 cal., 15 g total fat (5 g sat. fat), 121 mg chol., 891 mg sodium, 33 g carbo., 2 g fiber, 38 g pro.
EXCHANGES: 2 Other Carbo., 5 Medium-Fat Meat

Barbecued Ribs & Kraut

PREP
15 MINUTES

COOK
25 MINUTES

MAKES
3 SERVINGS

1   14.5-ounce can sauerkraut,
     rinsed and drained
2   cups loose-pack frozen diced hash
     brown potatoes with onions and
     peppers
1   30.4-ounce package refrigerated
     cooked pork ribs in barbecue sauce
1/4 cup chicken broth

STEP 1 In a large nonstick skillet combine drained sauerkraut and frozen potatoes. Cut ribs into 2-rib portions; arrange on top of sauerkraut mixture.

STEP 2 In a small bowl combine any barbecue sauce from ribs package and the chicken broth; drizzle over the potato mixture in the skillet. Cover and cook over medium heat about 25 minutes or until heated through.

PER SERVING: 751 cal., 43 g total fat (16 g sat. fat), 111 mg chol., 2,700 mg sodium, 54 g carbo., 7 g fiber, 39 g pro.
EXCHANGES: 1 Vegetable, 3 Starch, 4 Medium-Fat Meat, 4 Fat

OFF THE SHELF TIP Pull a bag of diced hash browns with onions and peppers out of the grocer's freezer case. You'll find a number of varieties alongside the diced style.

Country-Style Stuffed Peppers

PREP
30 MINUTES
BAKE
25 MINUTES
OVEN
375°F
MAKES
8 STUFFED PEPPER HALVES

4	medium green sweet peppers
1	pound bulk pork sausage
1	cup purchased shredded carrot
1/2	cup finely chopped celery (1 stalk)
1 1/2	cups shredded smoked Gouda, smoked cheddar, or regular cheddar cheese (6 ounces)
1/2	cup packaged corn bread stuffing mix

STEP 1 Preheat oven to 375°F. Cut sweet peppers in half lengthwise. Remove seeds and membranes. In a covered large saucepan cook sweet pepper halves in enough boiling water to cover for 4 to 5 minutes or just until tender; drain well. Pat dry with paper towels.

STEP 2 Meanwhile, in a large skillet cook sausage, carrot, and celery until sausage is brown. Drain off fat. Stir 1 cup of the cheese and the dry stuffing mix into sausage mixture.

STEP 3 Spoon about 1/2 cup of the stuffing mixture into each sweet pepper half. Place pepper halves, filling sides up, in a 15×10×1-inch baking pan.

STEP 4 Bake, uncovered, in the preheated oven for 20 minutes. Sprinkle tops with remaining 1/2 cup cheese. Bake, uncovered, about 5 minutes more or until cheese is melted and stuffing is heated through.

PER STUFFED PEPPER HALF: 304 cal., 23 g total fat (10 g sat. fat), 60 mg chol., 815 mg sodium, 11 g carbo., 2 g fiber, 13 g pro.
EXCHANGES: 1/2 Vegetable, 1/2 Starch, 2 Medium-Fat Meat, 2 1/2 Fat

OFF THE SHELF TIP Purchased shredded carrot is a huge timesaver for the busy cook. Don't forget about purchased coleslaw mix too. Look for both near the bagged lettuce in the supermarket.

Sausage-Cavatelli Skillet

Bullet-shape cavatelli pasta joins sausage or beef, spaghetti sauce, and mozzarella for a fast-fixing, hearty meal. Round it out with green salad and a glass of wine— weeknight meals couldn't be better.

START TO FINISH
30 MINUTES
MAKES
4 SERVINGS

8   ounces dried cavatelli (1³/₄ cups)
1   pound bulk Italian sausage or lean ground beef
³/₄ cup chopped green sweet pepper (1 medium) (optional)
1   20-ounce jar spaghetti sauce with mushrooms
1   cup shredded mozzarella cheese (4 ounces)

STEP 1 Cook cavatelli according to package directions; drain well.

STEP 2 Meanwhile, in a large skillet cook sausage and, if desired, sweet pepper over medium heat until sausage is brown. Drain off fat. Stir in spaghetti sauce; cook about 2 minutes or until heated through. Stir in the drained cavatelli. Sprinkle with cheese. Cover and cook about 2 minutes more or until cheese melts.

PER SERVING: 677 cal., 32 g total fat (13 g sat. fat), 93 mg chol., 1,469 mg sodium, 60 g carbo., 4 g fiber, 32 g pro.
EXCHANGES: ¹/₂ Vegetable, 2 Starch, 1¹/₂ Other Carbc., 3¹/₂ High-Fat Meat, ¹/₂ Fat

OFF THE SHELF TIP Available in a multitude of flavors, spaghetti and pasta sauces can change the character of a dish. Try a variety spiked with basil or roasted peppers for extra flavor punch.

MEAL ROUND-OUTS

FRUITS & VEGETABLES
Fruit: slices or sections, fresh or canned
Veggies: fresh chopped, steamed, grilled, canned
Greens: mixed, spinach
Potatoes: whole or half baked in the microwave or heat-and-eat

GRAINS
Bread: sourdough, whole wheat, flatbread, tortillas
Cornbread
Rice: long-cooking or quick-heat
Pasta: white or whole wheat
Couscous

PROTEINS
Meat: deli slices
Fish & seafood, canned or refrigerated: tossed into salad
Eggs, hard-cooked: chopped or sliced
Cheese: cottage, slices
Beans

FATS
Fats are flavorful and filling—just a little does the trick. Shredded cheese garnish, olives chopped fine and tossed with salads or pasta, meats sauteed in olive or nut oil generally provide all the fat and flavor needed.

Peach-Mustard Glazed Ham

Sweet-salty ham has always been a match for fruit and mustard. This glazed version celebrates the peach and is quickly produced on the grill.

PREP
20 MINUTES
GRILL
8 MINUTES
MAKES
4 SERVINGS

2	teaspoons packed brown sugar
2	teaspoons spicy brown mustard
2	tablespoons peach or apricot nectar
1	1-pound cooked ham slice,
	cut ¾ to 1 inch thick
1	recipe Fruit Salsa

STEP 1	Preheat grill. For the glaze, in a small bowl combine brown sugar and mustard. Gradually whisk in peach nectar until smooth. To prevent ham from curling, make shallow cuts around the edge at 1-inch intervals. Brush one side of the ham slice with the glaze.

STEP 2	Place ham, glazed side down, on the greased rack of an uncovered grill directly over medium-high heat. Grill for 4 minutes. Brush ham with remaining glaze; turn ham. Grill 4 to 6 minutes more or until heated through, brushing occasionally with glaze. Serve with Fruit Salsa.

FRUIT SALSA: In a small bowl combine 1 cup finely chopped, drained canned peaches; ½ cup finely chopped sweet green pepper; ½ cup canned crushed pineapple, drained; ¼ cup finely chopped red onion; 1 tablespoon lime juice; 1 tablespoon honey; and 1 jalapeño pepper, seeded and finely chopped*. Makes 2 cups.

PER SERVING: 285 cal., 10 g total fat (3 g sat. fat), 65 mg chol., 1,526 mg sodium, 29 g carbo., 3 g fiber, 20 g pro.
EXCHANGES: 3 Other Carbo., 3 Medium-Fat Mea

*NOTE: Because chile peppers contain volatile oils that can burn your skin and eyes avoid direct contact with them as much as possible. When working with chile peppers, wear plastic or rubber gloves. If your bare hands do touch chile peppers, wash them well with soap and water.

OFF THE SHELF TIP Look for peach nectar in the juice aisle of your supermarket. It is thicker than typical juice and adds to the silky coating on this ham.

Lamb Chops with Cranberry Relish

Aromatic rosemary joins orange and cranberry for a quickly broiled and oh-so-elegant dinner.

PREP
15 MINUTES

BROIL
10 MINUTES

MAKES
4 SERVINGS

½   cup purchased cranberry-orange relish

¼   cup chopped pecans, toasted

2   tablespoons orange juice

2   teaspoons snipped fresh rosemary or ½ teaspoon dried rosemary, crushed

8   lamb loin chops, cut ¾ inch thick (about 2½ pounds)

     Salt

     Ground black pepper

OFF THE SHELF TIP Cranberry-orange relish is a seasonal product. In the winter, look for it in the specialty section of your supermarket. In the summertime (when cranberries aren't at their peak), look for the product in the frozen foods aisle near the other packaged fruits.

STEP 1 Preheat broiler. In a small bowl combine cranberry-orange relish, pecans, orange juice, and rosemary. Set aside.

STEP 2 Trim fat from chops. Place chops on the unheated rack of a broiler pan. Season generously with salt and pepper. Broil 3 to 4 inches from the heat for 9 to 11 minutes or until medium doneness (160°F), turning once. Spread relish mixture over chops. Broil for 1 minute more.

PER SERVING: 324 cal., 13 g total fat (3 g sat. fat), 100 mg chol., 172 mg sodium, 18 g carbo., 1 g fiber, 33 g pro.
EXCHANGES: 1 Other Carbo., 4 Lean Meat, ½ Fat

Lamb Burgers with Feta & Mint

Mint and lamb are traditional partners, and for good reason. Here they star in a burger finished with feta for a Greek isle experience.

PREP
15 MINUTES
GRILL
14 MINUTES
MAKES
4 SERVINGS

1¹/₂	pounds ground lamb or lean ground beef
4	lettuce leaves
4	kaiser rolls, split and toasted
4	tomato slices
¹/₂	cup crumbled feta cheese with peppercorns (2 ounces)
1	tablespoon snipped fresh mint

OFF THE SHELF TIP Packages of crumbled feta cheese with seasonings offer double the flavor. Look for feta with basil and tomato, garlic and herbs, or peppercorns.

STEP 1   Preheat grill. Shape ground meat into four ³/₄-inch-thick patties. Place patties on the greased rack of an uncovered grill directly over medium heat. Grill for 14 to 18 minutes or until done (160°F),* turning once.

STEP 2   Place lettuce on roll bottoms. Top with patties, tomato slices, feta cheese, mint, and roll tops.

*NOTE: The internal color of a burger is not a reliable doneness indicator. A lamb or beef patty cooked to 160°F is safe, regardless of color. To measure the doneness of a patty, insert an instant-read thermometer through the side of the patty to a depth of 2 to 3 inches.

PER SERVING: 554 cal., 30 g total fat (13 g sat. fat), 130 mg chol., 615 mg sodium, 32 g carbo., 1 g fiber, 38 g pro.
EXCHANGES: 1 Vegetable, 2 Starch, 4¹/₂ Medium-Fat Meat, 1 Fat

Saucy Lamb Meatballs

PREP
35 MINUTES

COOK
15 MINUTES

MAKES
4 OR 5 SERVINGS

1   egg, slightly beaten
3/4   cup soft bread crumbs (1 slice)
3/4   teaspoon salt
1/8   teaspoon ground cinnamon
1/8   teaspoon ground black pepper
1   pound ground lamb
1   10.75-ounce can condensed cream of mushroom soup
1   4-ounce can (drained weight) sliced mushrooms, drained
1/2   cup orange juice
1/4   cup water
    Dash ground black pepper
1/2   cup dairy sour cream
1   tablespoon all-purpose flour
    Hot cooked noodles

STEP 1   In a large bowl combine egg, the 1/4 cup orange juice, the bread crumbs, salt, cinnamon, and the 1/8 teaspoon pepper. Add lamb; mix well. Shape into 1 1/2-inch meatballs. In a large skillet cook meatballs over medium heat until brown, turning to brown evenly (meatballs will not be done). Drain off fat.

STEP 2   In a medium bowl combine soup, drained mushrooms, the 1/2 cup orange juice, the water, and the dash pepper; pour over meatballs. Bring to boiling; reduce heat. Cover and simmer for 15 to 20 minutes or until the meatballs are done (160°F).

STEP 4   In a small bowl stir together sour cream and flour; add to meatball mixture. Cook and stir until thickened and bubbly.

Cook and stir for 1 minute more. Serve over hot cooked noodles.

PER SERVING: 592 cal., 26 g total fat (9 g sat. fat), 183 mg chol., 1,221 mg sodium, 58 g carbo., 3 g fiber, 32 g pro.
EXCHANGES: 2 Starch, 2 Other Carbo., 4 Medium-Fat Meat, 1/2 Fat

OFF THE SHELF TIP   Grab a can from the soup section. Just make sure your choice is condensed, not ready-to-serve.

Greek-Style Lamb Skillet

Pasta cooks right in the juice-broth with lamb for a one-skillet meal infused with cinnamon, steering the flavor to sunny Greece.

START TO FINISH
30 MINUTES

MAKES
4 SERVINGS

RECIPE PICTURED ON PAGE 133.

12	ounces ground lamb or ground beef
1	14.5-ounce can diced tomatoes with onion and garlic, undrained
1	5.5-ounce can (²/₃ cup) tomato juice
½	cup onion-flavored beef broth
½	teaspoon ground cinnamon
1	cup dried medium shell macaroni or elbow macaroni
1	cup loose-pack frozen cut green beans
½	cup crumbled feta cheese (2 ounces)

OFF THE SHELF TIP Diced tomatoes are a fabulous way to add flavor to recipes without making any extra effort. Located in the canned vegetable aisle of your supermarket, these tomatoes come in an abundance of flavor combinations.

STEP 1 In a large skillet cook ground meat over medium heat until brown. Drain off fat. Stir undrained tomatoes, tomato juice, broth, and cinnamon into meat in skillet. Bring to boiling.

STEP 2 Stir dried macaroni and frozen green beans into meat mixture. Return to boiling; reduce heat. Cover and simmer for 15 to 20 minutes or until macaroni and green beans are tender. Sprinkle with feta cheese.

PER SERVING: 411 cal., 21 g total fat (10 g sat. fat), 75 mg chol., 1,013 mg sodium, 32 g carbo., 2 g fiber, 23 g pro.
EXCHANGES: 1 Vegetable, 2 Starch, 2 Medium-Fat Meat, 2 Fat

Poultry

Saucy Cranberry Chicken

PREP
15 MINUTES

BAKE
1 ½ HOURS

OVEN
325°F

MAKES
4 TO 6 SERVINGS

RECIPE PICTURED ON PAGE **130.**

1	16-ounce can whole cranberry sauce
1	cup bottled Russian salad dressing or French salad dressing
1	envelope (½ of a 2.2-ounce package) onion soup mix
2½	to 3 pounds meaty chicken pieces (breast halves, thighs, and/or drumsticks)
	Hot cooked rice (optional)

STEP 1 Preheat oven to 325°F. In a medium bowl stir together cranberry sauce, salad dressing, and dry soup mix. If desired, skin chicken. Arrange chicken pieces, meaty sides down, in a 3-quart rectangular baking dish. Pour cranberry mixture over chicken pieces.

STEP 2 Bake, uncovered, in the preheated oven about 1½ hours or until the chicken is tender and no longer pink (170°F for breast pieces; 180°F for thighs and drumsticks), stirring glaze and spooning over chicken once or twice. If desired, serve over hot cooked rice.

PER SERVING: 810 cal., 47 g total fat (7 g sat. fat), 141 mg chol., 901 mg sodium, 54 g carbo., 2 g fiber, 43 g pro.
EXCHANGES: 3½ Other Carbo., 6 Lean Meat, 6 Fat

OFF THE SHELF TIP Onion soup mix is sold in a packet or a bag. You'll spot it on shelves near soups. Be sure to use within six months of purchase.

Plum Wonderful Chicken

PREP
40 MINUTES

BAKE
35 MINUTES

OVEN
350°F

MAKES
6 SERVINGS

RECIPE PICTURED ON PAGE 129.

2	tablespoons olive oil or cooking oil
2½	to 3 pounds meaty chicken pieces (breast halves, thighs, and/or drumsticks), skinned
¼	cup chopped onion
1	teaspoon grated fresh ginger
½	teaspoon bottled minced garlic (1 clove)
⅓	cup bottled plum sauce
¼	cup frozen lemonade concentrate
¼	cup bottled chili sauce
2	tablespoons reduced-sodium soy sauce
1	tablespoon lemon juice
1	teaspoon dry mustard
3	cups hot cooked rice
	Thinly sliced green onion (optional)
	Sesame seeds, toasted (optional)

STEP 1 Preheat oven to 350°F. In a large skillet heat oil over medium heat. Add half the chicken; cook about 10 minutes or until brown, turning often to brown evenly on all sides. Transfer browned chicken pieces to a 3-quart rectangular baking dish. Repeat with remaining chicken. Drain fat from skillet, reserving 1 tablespoon in the skillet. Add onion, ginger, and garlic to skillet. Cook and stir about 5 minutes or until onion is tender.

STEP 2 Meanwhile, for sauce, in a small bowl stir together plum sauce, lemonade concentrate, chili sauce, soy sauce, lemon juice, and dry mustard. Carefully stir into onion mixture in skillet. Bring to boiling; reduce heat. Cover and simmer for 5 minutes; spoon sauce over chicken in dish.

STEP 3 Bake, uncovered, in the preheated oven for 35 to 40 minutes or until chicken is tender and no longer pink (170°F for breast pieces; 180°F for thighs and drumsticks), spooning sauce over chicken twice during baking. Serve chicken and sauce over rice. If desired, sprinkle with green onion and sesame seeds.

PER SERVING: 366 cal., 12 g total fat (2 g sat. fat), 77 mg chol., 405 mg sodium, 37 g carbo., 1 g fiber, 28 g pro.
EXCHANGES: 1½ Starch, 1 Other Carbo., 3½ Lean Meat

OFF THE SHELF TIP Look for plum sauce in the Oriental section of your supermarket. This sweet and sour sauce is also called "duck sauce."

Cashew Chicken

Sliced mushrooms and golden mushroom soup slow-cook with ginger, soy, carrots, and celery to give this chicken strip meal luscious depth of flavor.

LOW FAT   SLOW COOKER

PREP
15 MINUTES

COOK
6 TO 8 HOURS (LOW) OR
3 TO 4 HOURS (HIGH)

MAKES
6 SERVINGS

1   10.75-ounce can condensed golden mushroom soup
2   tablespoons soy sauce
½   teaspoon ground ginger
1½   pounds chicken breast tenderloins or skinless, boneless chicken breasts, cut lengthwise into 1-inch-wide strips
1   cup sliced fresh mushrooms or one 4-ounce can (drained weight) sliced mushrooms, drained
1   cup sliced celery (2 stalks)
1   cup purchased shredded carrot
1   8-ounce can sliced water chestnuts, drained
½   cup cashews
    Hot cooked rice

OFF THE SHELF TIP Look for water chestnuts in the Oriental section of your supermarket. They come whole and sliced; chose sliced for this dish.

STEP 1   In a 3½- or 4-quart slow cooker combine soup, soy sauce, and ginger. Stir in chicken, mushrooms, celery, carrot, and drained water chestnuts.

STEP 2   Cover and cook on low-heat setting for 6 to 8 hours or on high-heat setting for 3 to 4 hours.

STEP 3   Stir cashews into chicken mixture. Serve over hot cooked rice.

PER SERVING: 364 cal., 9 g total fat (2 g sat. fat), 68 mg chol., 789 mg sodium, 38 g carbo., 3 g fiber, 33 g pro.
EXCHANGES: 1 Vegetable, 1 Starch, 1 Other Carbo., 4 Very Lean Meat, 1 Fat

Quick Thai Chicken

FAST

START TO FINISH
20 MINUTES

MAKES
4 SERVINGS

RECIPE PICTURED
ON PAGE 131.

¾ cup unsweetened coconut milk
¼ cup peanut butter
¼ teaspoon ground ginger
¼ teaspoon ground black pepper
4 skinless, boneless chicken breast halves (about 1¼ pounds)
1 tablespoon cooking oil
4 green onions, cut into 1-inch pieces
¼ cup honey-roasted peanuts, coarsely chopped

STEP 1 In a small bowl stir together coconut milk, peanut butter, ginger, and pepper; set aside.

STEP 2 In a large skillet cook chicken in hot oil over medium heat for 8 to 10 minutes or until chicken is tender and no longer pink (170°F), turning once halfway through cooking. Remove from skillet; keep warm.

STEP 3 For sauce, add green onion to skillet. Cook and stir about 2 minutes or until tender. Stir in coconut milk mixture. Cook and stir until bubbly.

STEP 4 To serve, spoon the sauce over chicken. Sprinkle with peanuts.

PER SERVING: 398 cal., 27 g total fat (13 g sat. fat), 66 mg chol., 173 mg sodium, 9 g carbo., 3 g fiber, 33 g pro.
EXCHANGES: ½ Starch, 4½ Lean Meat, 2½ Fat

OFF THE SHELF TIP Look for cans of unsweetened coconut milk in the Oriental section of your supermarket. Don't confuse this product with cream of coconut, which is commonly used in drinks such as a piña colada.

Margarita Fajitas with Sub-Lime Salsa

Say "margarita" and you immediately think of a kicked-back, celebrate-the-evening kind of mood. So when you stir the lime juice and tequila into this grilled chicken marinade, you know a fiesta meal will be happening soon.

LOW FAT

PREP
20 MINUTES

MARINATE
1 HOUR

GRILL
12 MINUTES

MAKES
4 SERVINGS

RECIPE PICTURED ON PAGE 130.

1	15-ounce can black beans, rinsed and drained
1	8-ounce can pineapple tidbits (juice pack), drained
¼	cup finely chopped red onion
2	fresh jalapeño chile peppers, seeded and finely chopped*
2	tablespoons snipped fresh cilantro
1	canned chipotle pepper in adobo sauce, drained and finely chopped
4	teaspoons lime juice
¼	teaspoon salt
4	skinless, boneless chicken breast halves (1¼ pounds)
¼	cup tequila
¼	cup lime juice
1	tablespoon cooking oil
¼	teaspoon salt
¼	teaspoon ground black pepper
8	6- to 7-inch flour tortillas

STEP 1 For salsa, in a medium bowl stir together drained black beans, drained pineapple, onion, jalapeño peppers, cilantro, chipotle pepper, the 4 teaspoons lime juice, and ¼ teaspoon salt. Cover and refrigerate while chicken marinates.

STEP 2 Place the chicken in a large resealable plastic bag set in a large bowl. In a small bowl stir together tequila, the ¼ cup lime juice, the oil, ¼ teaspoon salt, and black pepper. Pour over chicken in bag; seal bag. Marinate in the refrigerator for 1 hour, turning bag occasionally. Meanwhile, wrap tortillas in heavy foil; set aside.

STEP 3 Preheat grill. Drain chicken, discarding marinade. Place chicken on the rack of an uncovered grill directly over medium heat. Grill 12 to 15 minutes or until chicken is no longer pink (170°F), turning once halfway through grilling. During the last 5 minutes of grilling, place foil-wrapped tortillas next to chicken on grill rack until warm, turning once.

STEP 4 Cut chicken into ½-inch slices. Divide chicken among tortillas and top with salsa. Roll up.

***NOTE:** Because chile peppers contain volatile oils that can burn your skin and eyes, avoid direct contact with them as much as possible. When working with chile peppers, wear plastic or rubber gloves. If your bare hands do touch chile peppers, wash them well with soap and water.

PER SERVING: 489 cal., 7 g total fat (2 g sat. fat), 82 mg chol., 835 mg sodium, 61 g carbo., 8 g fiber, 46 g pro.
EXCHANGES: ½ Fruit, 3½ Starch, 5 Very Lean Meat

OFF THE SHELF TIP Fetch cans of chipotle peppers in adobo sauce—dried and smoked jalapeño peppers in a tangy sauce of vinegar, pepper, and chiles—from the ethnic section of your supermarket. Take care when chopping them because they contain volatile oils that can burn your skin and eyes.

Baked Parmesan Chicken

Parmesan and chicken are a favorite pair, and there are so many ways to bake them together. If you're looking for a recipe that does not include tomato sauce, try this one, which features a crunchy baked Italian-seasoned crust.

LOW FAT EASY

PREP
10 MINUTES

BAKE
30 MINUTES

OVEN
375°F

MAKES
4 SERVINGS

½   cup crushed cornflakes
2   tablespoons grated Parmesan cheese
¼   teaspoon dried Italian seasoning, crushed
4   skinless, boneless chicken breast halves (1¼ pounds)
3   tablespoons butter or margarine, melted

STEP 1   Preheat oven to 375°F. In a shallow bowl combine cornflakes, cheese, and Italian seasoning. Dip chicken pieces in melted butter; roll in cornflake mixture. Place on a baking rack in a shallow baking pan.

STEP 2   Bake in the preheated oven about 30 minutes or until chicken is tender and no longer pink (170°F).

PER SERVING: 287 cal., 12 g total fat (7 g sat. fat), 109 mg chol., 318 mg sodium, 9 g carbo., 0 g fiber, 35 g pro.
EXCHANGES: ½ Starch, 4½ Very Lean Meat, 1½ Fat

OFF THE SHELF TIP For a quick version, snatch a package of cornflake crumbs off your grocer's shelf (you'll likely find them with the packaged bread crumbs). For more texture, toss some cornflakes in a plastic bag and crush them with a rolling pin.

Pastry-Wrapped Chicken

Make this elegant dish to cap off a splendid weekend. Honey-mustard sauce coats Swiss cheese–topped chicken breasts that bake in crescent roll pastry.

PREP
30 MINUTES

BAKE
12 MINUTES

OVEN
400°F

MAKES
4 SERVINGS

2   tablespoons butter or margarine
½   teaspoon dried tarragon, crushed
4   skinless, boneless chicken breast halves (about 1¼ pounds)
1   8-ounce package (8) refrigerated crescent rolls
1   cup shredded Swiss cheese (4 ounces)
1   recipe Honey Mustard Sauce

STEP 1 Preheat oven to 400°F. In a large skillet melt butter over medium heat; stir in tarragon. Add chicken; cook for 8 to 10 minutes or until tender and no longer pink (170°F), turning once. Remove from skillet.

STEP 2 Meanwhile, separate crescent rolls into 4 rectangles. Pinch perforations to seal. On a lightly floured surface, roll each dough rectangle into a 6½×4½-inch rectangle. Divide cheese among rectangles, sprinkling in center of each rectangle. Place chicken breast halves on cheese. Fold dough over chicken and cheese. Crimp edges to seal.

STEP 3 Place bundles, seam sides down, on an ungreased baking sheet. Bake in the preheated oven about 12 minutes or until pastry is golden. Serve with Honey Mustard Sauce.

HONEY MUSTARD SAUCE: In a small bowl stir together ¼ cup mayonnaise or salad dressing and 2 tablespoons honey mustard. Makes about ⅓ cup.

PER SERVING: 621 cal., 38 g total fat (13 g sat. fat), 132 mg chol., 808 mg sodium, 25 g carbo., 0 g fiber, 45 g pro.
EXCHANGES: 1½ Starch, 4½ Very Lean Meat, 1 High-Fat Meat, 5½ Fat

OFF THE SHELF TIP Refrigerated crescent rolls can be found in the refrigerated breads section of your supermarket. Opening the package starts the leavening process. You must bake the dough within two hours of opening.

Orange Chicken & Fried Rice

Orange juice concentrate is just one of the secrets of this quick-cooking skillet meal. Infused with ginger and garlic and served with flavored fried rice and chopped cashews, the dish has plenty of texture too.

1	6-ounce package Oriental-flavor fried rice mix
2	tablespoons butter or margarine
1	pound packaged skinless, boneless chicken breast strips (stir-fry strips)
8	green onions, bias-sliced into 1-inch pieces
1	teaspoon bottled minced garlic (2 cloves) or ¼ teaspoon garlic powder
1	teaspoon ground ginger
1	tablespoon frozen orange juice concentrate, thawed
¼	cup chopped cashews

OFF THE SHELF TIP Look for stir-fry steak and chicken strips in the meat section of your supermarket.

START TO FINISH
25 MINUTES

MAKES
4 SERVINGS

STEP 1 Cook rice according to package directions.

STEP 2 Meanwhile, in a large skillet melt butter over medium-high heat. Add chicken strips, green onion, garlic, and ginger; cook and stir for 3 to 5 minutes or until chicken is no longer pink.

STEP 3 Stir orange juice concentrate into cooked rice. Stir rice mixture into chicken mixture in skillet. Cook and stir until heated through. Sprinkle each serving with cashews.

PER SERVING: 396 cal., 13 g total fat (5 g sat. fat), 82 mg chol., 985 mg sodium, 38 g carbo., 2 g fiber, 32 g pro.
EXCHANGES: 2½ Starch, 3½ Very Lean Meat, 2 Fat

Lemon Chicken with Asparagus

Lemon and chicken make a lovely pairing that appeals any time of the year but make an especially delightful combo with in-season asparagus.

LOW FAT

START TO FINISH
25 MINUTES

MAKES
4 SERVINGS

Nonstick cooking spray
4   skinless, boneless chicken breast halves (about 1¼ pounds)
1   pound fresh asparagus
1   cup water
1   10.75-ounce can condensed cream of chicken or cream of asparagus soup
¾   cup chicken broth
1   tablespoon lemon juice
    Hot cooked couscous

OFF THE SHELF TIP Grab a can from the soup section. Just make sure your choice is condensed, not ready-to-serve.

STEP 1 Lightly coat a large skillet with nonstick cooking spray. Preheat skillet over medium heat. Add chicken; cook for 8 to 10 minutes or until tender and no longer pink (170°F), turning once. Meanwhile, snap off and discard woody bases from asparagus. If desired, scrape off scales.

STEP 2 Remove chicken from skillet; cover and keep warm. In the same skillet combine asparagus and the water. Bring to boiling; reduce heat. Cover and simmer for 3 to 5 minutes or until asparagus is crisp-tender. Drain.

STEP 3 Meanwhile, in a small saucepan combine soup, broth, and lemon juice. Cook and stir until heated through. Serve sauce with chicken, asparagus, and hot cooked couscous.

PER SERVING: 354 cal., 8 g total fat (3 g sat. fat), 88 mg chol., 844 mg sodium, 27 g carbo., 3 g fiber, 40 g pro.
EXCHANGES: 1 Vegetable, 1½ Starch, 5 Very Lean Meat, ½ Fat

Dijon Chicken & Mushrooms

START TO FINISH
30 MINUTES

MAKES
4 SERVINGS

3 tablespoons butter or margarine

2 cups sliced fresh mushrooms

4 skinless, boneless chicken breast halves (about 1¼ pounds)

1 10.75-ounce can condensed cream of chicken soup

¼ cup dry white wine

¼ cup water

2 tablespoons Dijon-style mustard

½ teaspoon dried thyme or tarragon, crushed

Hot cooked pasta

OFF THE SHELF TIP Mustards come in a wide variety of flavors from mild to wow—and everywhere in between. Some are flavored with herbs and spices, wine, peppers, or even honey.

STEP 1 In a large skillet melt 1 tablespoon of the butter over medium-high heat. Add mushrooms; cook for 3 to 4 minutes or until tender. Remove mushrooms from skillet. In same skillet cook chicken in the remaining 2 tablespoons butter for 8 to 10 minutes or until tender and no longer pink (170°F), turning to brown evenly.

STEP 2 Meanwhile, in a small bowl stir together soup, wine, water, mustard, and thyme.

STEP 3 Return mushrooms to skillet; add soup mixture. Bring to boiling; reduce heat. Simmer, uncovered, for 2 minutes. Serve chicken and soup mixture over hot cooked pasta.

PER SERVING: 498 cal., 18 g total fat (8 g sat. fat), 112 mg chol., 947 mg sodium, 37 g carbo., 2 g fiber, 41 g pro.
EXCHANGES: ½ Vegetable, 1½ Starch, 1 Other Carbo., 5 Very Lean Meat, 3 Fat

Cranberry Chicken

Sweet stuff such as apples, honey, and lemonade concentrate joins cranberry sauce and onions to slow-cook chicken to tangy perfection with sauce to spare.

PREP
15 MINUTES

COOK
6 TO 7 HOURS (LOW) OR
3 TO 3½ HOURS (HIGH)

MAKES
6 SERVINGS

2	medium apples, cored and cut into wedges
1	medium onion, thinly sliced
6	skinless, boneless chicken breast halves (about 2 pounds)
1	16-ounce can whole cranberry sauce
¼	cup frozen lemonade concentrate, thawed
2	tablespoons quick-cooking tapioca
2	tablespoons honey
¼	teaspoon salt
2	6- to 6.25-ounce packages long grain and wild rice mix

STEP 1 In a 3½- or 4-quart slow cooker combine apples and onion. Place chicken on top of apple mixture. In a medium bowl combine cranberry sauce, lemonade concentrate, tapioca, honey, and salt. Pour over mixture in slow cooker.

STEP 2 Cover and cook on low-heat setting for 6 to 7 hours or on high-heat setting for 3 to 3½ hours.

STEP 3 In a large saucepan prepare long grain and wild rice with seasoning packets according to package directions. Serve chicken and apple mixture over rice.

PER SERVING: 565 cal., 2 g total fat (1 g sat. fat), 88 mg chol., 993 mg sodium, 96 g carbo., 4 g fiber, 40 g pro.
EXCHANGES: 1 Fruit, 4 Starch, 1 Other Carbo., 4 Very Lean Meat

OFF THE SHELF TIP Quick-cooking tapioca is used in many slow cooker recipes to thicken the mixture. It is used in place of flour or cornstarch, which tend to break down when cooked for the long periods of time slow cooking calls for. Look for the tapioca in the baking aisle of the supermarket.

Chicken with Buttermilk Gravy

The aroma of broiled chicken and savory, herbed gravy will stir your senses as it cooks; its flavor and texture will satisfy your palate with each bite.

LOW FAT   EASY

PREP
15 MINUTES

BROIL
12 MINUTES

MAKES
6 SERVINGS

⅓   cup seasoned fine dry bread crumbs
2   tablespoons grated Parmesan cheese
½   teaspoon paprika
6   skinless, boneless chicken breast halves (about 2 pounds)
3   tablespoons butter or margarine, melted
     Salt (optional)
     Ground black pepper (optional)
1   1-ounce envelope chicken gravy mix
1   cup buttermilk
¼   teaspoon dried sage, crushed

STEP 1   Preheat broiler. In a shallow dish combine bread crumbs, Parmesan cheese, and paprika; set aside. Brush chicken with some of the melted butter. If desired, sprinkle with salt and pepper. Dip chicken into crumb mixture, turning to coat evenly.

STEP 2   Arrange chicken on the unheated rack of a broiler pan. Drizzle with any remaining melted butter. Broil 4 to 5 inches from the heat for 12 to 15 minutes or until chicken is tender and no longer pink (170°F), turning once halfway through broiling.

STEP 3   Meanwhile, for gravy, in a small saucepan prepare chicken gravy mix according to package directions, except use the 1 cup buttermilk in place of the water called for in the package directions. Stir sage into gravy. Serve with chicken.

PER SERVING: 288 cal., 9 g total fat (5 g sat. fat), 107 mg chol., 644 mg sodium, 10 g carbo., 0 g fiber, 38 g pro.
EXCHANGES: ½ Starch, 5 Very Lean Meat, 1 Fat

OFF THE SHELF TIP Don't look for seasoned bread crumbs in the bread section of your supermarket. Instead, try packaged goods, near stuffing mixes and mac 'n' cheese.

Chicken Breasts in Herbed Tomato Sauce

Stirring sour cream into a skillet of browned chicken breasts and tomato sauce adds a rich, full flavor.

START TO FINISH
40 MINUTES

MAKES
4 SERVINGS

4 skinless, boneless chicken breast halves (about 1¼ pounds)
2 tablespoons olive oil or cooking oil
1 10.75-ounce can condensed tomato soup
¼ cup water
1 teaspoon dried minced onion
1 teaspoon dried basil, crushed
½ teaspoon dried oregano, crushed
   Dash ground black pepper
½ cup dairy sour cream
   Hot cooked noodles

STEP 1 In a 10-inch skillet cook chicken in hot oil over medium-high heat about 5 minutes or until brown, turning once. In a medium bowl stir together soup, water, dried minced onion, basil, oregano, and pepper; pour over chicken. Bring to boiling; reduce heat. Cover and simmer about 15 minutes or until chicken is tender and no longer pink (170°F). Remove chicken to platter; keep warm.

STEP 2 For sauce, spoon sour cream into a small bowl; gradually whisk about ½ cup of the pan juices into sour cream. Return sour cream mixture to skillet. Cook and stir until heated through (do not boil).

STEP 3 Arrange chicken on hot cooked noodles. Spoon some of the sauce over chicken; pass remaining sauce.

PER SERVING: 431 cal., 15 g total fat (5 g sat. fat), 119 mg chol., 560 mg sodium, 33 g carbo., 2 g fiber, 39 g pro.
EXCHANGES: 1 Starch, 1 Other Carbo., 5 Very Lean Meat, 2 Fat

OFF THE SHELF TIP Grab a can from the soup section. Just make sure your choice is condensed, not ready-to-serve.

Chicken & Vegetables Alfredo with Rice

FAST

START TO FINISH
25 MINUTES
MAKES
4 SERVINGS

4   skinless, boneless chicken breast halves (about 1 pounds) or 8 skinless, boneless chicken thighs
1   tablespoon butter
2½   cups frozen stir-fry vegetables (such as broccoli, carrots, onions, and red sweet peppers)
1⅓   cups uncooked instant white rice
1   10-ounce container refrigerated light Alfredo pasta sauce
1   cup milk
2   tablespoons grated or finely shredded Parmesan cheese (optional)

STEP 1   In a large skillet cook chicken in hot butter over medium heat for 6 to 8 minutes or until chicken is brown, turning once. Remove chicken from skillet.

STEP 2   Add frozen vegetables, rice, Alfredo sauce, and milk to skillet. Bring to boiling, stirring occasionally; reduce heat. Top with chicken.

STEP 3   Cover and cook over medium-low heat for 6 to 8 minutes or until chicken is tender and no longer pink (170°F for breasts; 180°F for thighs), stirring once or twice. If desired, sprinkle with Parmesan cheese.

PER SERVING: 433 cal., 13 g total fat (8 g sat. fat), 105 mg chol., 638 mg sodium, 39 g carbo., 2 g fiber, 38 g pro.
EXCHANGES: 1 Vegetable, 5 Starch, 2½ Very Lean Meat, 2 Fat

OFF THE SHELF TIP Refrigerated pasta sauces come in a wide variety of flavors including Alfredo and tomato-based sauces. They are fabulous convenience products, but note that their shelf life is shorter than their jarred counterparts.

Hawaiian-Style Barbecue Pizza

PREP
20 MINUTES

BAKE
20 MINUTES

OVEN
425°F

MAKES
4 SERVINGS

1	14-ounce Italian bread shell
½	cup bottled barbecue sauce
1½	cups shredded pizza cheese (6 ounces)
1	15.25-ounce can tropical fruit salad, drained
1	to 1½ cups purchased roasted chicken cut into strips or chunks (about ½ of a chicken)
¼	of a small red or yellow onion, thinly sliced and separated into rings
¼	cup thinly sliced green onion (2)

OFF THE SHELF TIP Prebaked Italian bread shells are a huge timesaver for the busy cook. Pizza during the week no longer has to be from a delivery joint; you can top the shell with your favorite ingredients, bake, and dinner is ready.

STEP 1 Preheat oven to 425°F. Place bread shell on a baking sheet. Spread barbecue sauce over bread shell. Sprinkle with ½ cup of the cheese. Arrange drained fruit salad, chicken, and onion rings on top.

STEP 2 Bake in the preheated oven for 10 minutes. Sprinkle with remaining 1 cup cheese and the green onion. Bake about 10 minutes more or until heated through and cheese is melted.

PER SERVING: 606 cal., 21 g total fat (8 g sat. fat), 64 mg chol., 1,114 mg sodium, 74 g carbo., 4 g fiber, 32 g pro.
EXCHANGES: ½ Fruit, 4½ Starch, 2½ Medium-Fat Meat, ½ Fat

Chicken with Noodles

FAST

START TO FINISH
20 MINUTES
MAKES
4 SERVINGS

8	ounces dried egg noodles (4 cups)
1	10.75-ounce can condensed cream of chicken soup
½	cup milk
1	2.25-ounce can sliced, pitted ripe olives, drained
2	tablespoons chopped bottled roasted red sweet pepper
¼	teaspoon dried marjoram, crushed
⅛	teaspoon ground black pepper
2	cups chopped cooked chicken (10 ounces)
1	cup frozen peas
¼	cup dry white wine or chicken broth

STEP 1 Cook noodles according to package directions. Drain and keep warm.

STEP 2 Meanwhile, in a large saucepan combine soup and milk. Stir in olives, red pepper, marjoram, and black pepper; bring to boiling, stirring occasionally. Stir in chicken, peas, and wine; heat through. Stir in cooked noodles.

PER SERVING: 506 cal., 15 g total fat (4 g sat. fat), 125 mg chol., 827 mg sodium, 55 g carbo., 5 g fiber, 33 g pro.
EXCHANGES: 4 Starch, 2½ Very Lean Meat, 2 Fat

OFF THE SHELF TIP Roasted red sweet peppers are found in the condiment aisle of your supermarket. They are easy to make at home, but why take the time when jars are so easy to snap up?

Chipotle Chicken Enchiladas

Simple, sassy, and satisfying, this enchilada dish comes together quickly and bakes in less than an hour. Take the bake time to unwind, walk the dog, or play a game of catch.

PREP
25 MINUTES
BAKE
40 MINUTES
OVEN
350°F
MAKES
4 SERVINGS

2½   cups chopped cooked chicken (12 ounces)
1   to 2 teaspoons ground dried chipotle chile pepper
1   10.75-ounce can condensed cream of chicken soup
1   8-ounce carton dairy sour cream
1   4-ounce can diced green chile peppers, undrained
8   7- to 8-inch flour tortillas
2   cups shredded cheddar cheese (8 ounces)
¼   cup sliced green onion (2)

PER SERVING: 786 cal., 47 g total fat (24 g sat. fat), 169 mg chol., 1,376 mg sodium, 42 g carbo., 2 g fiber, 47 g pro.
EXCHANGES: 3 Starch, 5½ Lean Meat, 5½ Fat

OFF THE SHELF TIP Look for canned green chiles in the Mexican section of your supermarket. They come whole and diced as well as mild and hot.

STEP 1   Preheat oven to 350°F. Grease a 3-quart rectangular baking dish; set aside. In a medium bowl combine chicken and chipotle chile pepper; set aside.

STEP 2   For sauce, in a large bowl combine soup, sour cream, and undrained green chile peppers. Stir ½ cup of the sauce into the chicken mixture.

STEP 3   Divide chicken mixture among tortillas. Sprinkle 1½ cups of the cheese and the green onion over chicken mixture on tortillas. Roll up tortillas; place, seam sides down, in prepared baking dish. Pour remaining sauce over all. Cover with foil.

STEP 4   Bake in the preheated oven about 35 minutes or until edges are bubbly. Uncover; sprinkle with the remaining ½ cup cheese. Bake, uncovered, about 5 minutes more or until cheese is melted.

Chicken & Pasta Salad with Tomatoes

START TO FINISH

25 MINUTES

MAKES

4 SERVINGS

1   16-ounce package frozen pasta and vegetables in a seasoned sauce (such as pasta, broccoli, peas, and carrots in onion-and-herb-seasoned sauce)

1   5-ounce can chunk-style chicken, drained and flaked, or 1 cup chopped cooked chicken or turkey (5 ounces)

½   cup dairy sour cream chive-flavor dip

1   cup coarsely chopped tomatoes (2 medium)

½   cup shredded cheddar cheese (2 ounces)

STEP 1 In a 2-quart saucepan cook frozen pasta and vegetables according to package directions.

STEP 2 Meanwhile, in a large bowl stir together chicken and sour cream dip. Gently fold the undrained cooked pasta mixture and the tomato into the chicken mixture. Cover and quick-chill in the freezer for 10 minutes.

STEP 3 To serve, sprinkle with cheddar cheese.

PER SERVING: 329 cal., 18 g total fat (10 g sat. fat), 58 mg chol., 935 mg sodium, 24 g carbo., 5 g fiber, 18 g pro.
EXCHANGES: 1 Vegetable, 1 Starch, 2 Lean Meat, 2 Fat

OFF THE SHELF TIP Cans of chicken are perfect for last-minute cooking because they need no thawing. Just add to the recipe and heat through. You can find them near the cans of tuna at the supermarket.

Easy Chicken Turnovers

1   15-ounce package rolled refrigerated unbaked piecrusts (2 crusts)
1   10-ounce can chunk-style chicken, drained and broken up, or 1½ cups chopped cooked chicken (about 8 ounces)
1   cup frozen mixed vegetables or peas and carrots
1   cup shredded cheddar cheese (4 ounces)
⅓   cup bottled or refrigerated pasta sauce or bottled barbecue sauce
    Milk

PREP
25 MINUTES

BAKE
25 MINUTES

STAND
10 MINUTES

OVEN
400°F

MAKES
4 SERVINGS

STEP 1   Let piecrusts stand at room temperature according to package directions.

STEP 2   Preheat oven to 400°F. For filling, in a large bowl stir together chicken, frozen vegetables, cheese, and pasta sauce.

STEP 3   Unroll piecrusts; cut each crust in half. Spoon one-fourth of the filling (about ¾ cup) onto one half of each piecrust piece. Moisten edges of piecrust pieces with water. Fold each piecrust piece in half over filling to make a turnover. Seal edges of turnovers with the tines of a fork; prick tops. Place on an ungreased baking sheet.

STEP 4   Brush turnovers with milk. Bake in the preheated oven about 25 minutes or until crusts are light brown. Let stand for 10 minutes before serving.

MAKE-AHEAD DIRECTIONS: Prepare filling as directed in Step 2. Cover and refrigerate for up to 24 hours. Let piecrusts stand at room temperature according to package directions. Continue as directed in Step 3.

PER SERVING: 714 cal., 41 g total fat (19 g sat. fat), 85 mg chol., 859 mg sodium, 60 g carbo., 2 g fiber, 27 g pro.
EXCHANGES: 3 Starch, 1 Other Carbo., 3 Medium-Fat Meat, 5 Fat

OFF THE SHELF TIP   You'll find the refrigerated piecrusts—a lifesaver for a busy cook—in the refrigerated baked goods section of your supermarket. If you do get cracks in your crust as you work with it, simply wet your fingers with cold water and press cracks together.

Maple-Mustard-Sauced Turkey Thighs

PREP
20 MINUTES

COOK
6 TO 7 HOURS (LOW) OR
3 TO 3½ HOURS (HIGH)

MAKES
4 SERVINGS

1	pound new potatoes, quartered
2	to 2½ pounds turkey thighs (about 2 thighs), skinned
⅓	cup coarse-grain brown mustard
¼	cup maple syrup or maple-flavor syrup
1	tablespoon quick-cooking tapioca

STEP 1 Place potatoes in a 3½- or 4-quart slow cooker. Place turkey thighs on potatoes. In a small bowl stir together mustard, syrup, and tapioca. Pour over turkey.

STEP 2 Cover and cook on low-heat setting for 6 to 7 hours or on high-heat setting for to 3 to 3½ hours.

PER SERVING: 377 cal., 10 g total fat (3 g sat. fat), 93 mg chol., 369 mg sodium, 36 g carbo., 2 g fiber, 36 g pro.
EXCHANGES: 1½ Starch, 1 Other Carbo., 4 Very Lean Meat, ½ Fat

OFF THE SHELF TIP Mustards come in a wide variety of flavors, from mild to wow—and everywhere in between. Some are flavored with herbs and spices, others with wine, and yet others with peppers or even honey.

TREAT YOURSELF TO LUXURY
After a day away from home, arriving home to a table that's set and ready for you is a luxurious treat. It feels good, even if you were the one who set the table before heading out. You can rotate the honor among your family, too.

Apricot Turkey Steaks

START TO FINISH
25 MINUTES

MAKES
4 SERVINGS

1	6-ounce package chicken-flavor rice and vermicelli mix
2	turkey breast tenderloins (about 1¼ pounds)
1	5.5-ounce can (⅔ cup) apricot nectar
½	teaspoon salt
⅛	teaspoon ground cinnamon
	Dash ground black pepper
3	tablespoons apricot preserves
1½	teaspoons cornstarch

PER SERVING: 374 cal., 2 g total fat (1 g sat. fat), 88 mg chol., 1,054 mg sodium, 48 g carbo., 1 g fiber, 39 g pro.
EXCHANGES: 2 Starch, 1 Other Carbo., 4 Very Lean Meat

STEP 1   Prepare rice mix according to package directions; keep warm.

STEP 2   Meanwhile, split each turkey breast tenderloin in half horizontally to make 4 turkey steaks. In a large skillet combine apricot nectar, salt, cinnamon, and pepper. Add turkey steaks. Bring to boiling; reduce heat. Cover and simmer about 10 minutes or until turkey is no longer pink (170°F).

STEP 3   Transfer turkey steaks to a serving platter, reserving cooking liquid in the skillet. Keep turkey warm.

STEP 4   For sauce, in a small bowl combine apricot preserves and cornstarch; stir into cooking liquid in the skillet. Cook and stir until thickened and bubbly. Cook and stir for 2 minutes more. Spoon rice mixture onto the serving platter. Pour some of the sauce over turkey; pass remaining sauce.

OFF THE SHELF TIP   Look for apricot preserves with the other jams and jellies in your supermarket. And you thought these products just paired with bread and peanut butter! They are fabulous for cooking too. Apricot nectar can be found in the juice aisle.

Five-Spice Turkey Stir-Fry

LOW FAT

START TO FINISH
25 MINUTES

MAKES
4 SERVINGS

1	4.4-ounce package beef lo mein noodle mix
12	ounces turkey breast tenderloin, cut into bite-size strips
¼	teaspoon five-spice powder or Homemade Five-Spice Powder (page 89)
¼	teaspoon salt
¼	teaspoon ground black pepper
2	tablespoons cooking oil
½	of a 16-ounce package (2 cups) frozen stir-fry vegetables (yellow, green, and red peppers and onion)
2	tablespoons chopped honey-roasted peanuts or peanuts

PER SERVING: 314 cal., 11 g total fat (2 g sat. fat), 76 mg chol., 670 mg sodium, 26 g carbo., 3 g fiber, 27 g pro.
EXCHANGES: 1 Vegetable, 1½ Starch, 3 Very Lean Meat, 1½ Fat

OFF THE SHELF TIP Frozen mixed vegetable combinations give crunch and color to meals and make a convenient ingredient in fast-to-cook one-dish meals. Some come with sauces and/or seasonings, so check the package to be sure you're buying what the recipe specifies.

STEP 1 Prepare noodle mix according to package directions. Set aside. In a small bowl toss together turkey strips, five-spice powder, salt, and pepper; set aside.

STEP 2 Pour 1 tablespoon of the oil into a wok or large skillet. Heat over medium-high heat. Carefully add frozen vegetables to hot oil; cook and stir for 3 minutes. Remove vegetables from wok. Add remaining 1 tablespoon oil to hot wok. Add turkey mixture to wok; cook and stir for 2 to 3 minutes or until turkey is no longer pink. Return cooked vegetables to wok. Cook and stir about 1 minute more or until heated through.

STEP 3 To serve, divide noodle mixture among 4 dinner plates. Top with turkey mixture. Sprinkle with peanuts.

Mexican Turkey Pie

PREP
25 MINUTES

BAKE
24 MINUTES

OVEN
400°F

MAKES
6 SERVINGS

1	8.5-ounce package corn muffin mix
1	cup all-purpose flour
1	9-ounce can plain bean dip
½	cup bottled chunky salsa
2	cups chopped cooked turkey breast (10 ounces)
1	4-ounce can diced green chile peppers, drained
1	2.25-ounce can sliced, pitted ripe olives, drained
1	cup shredded sharp American cheese (4 ounces)
	Bottled chunky salsa (optional)

STEP 1   Preheat oven to 400°F. Grease a 12-inch pizza pan; set aside. For crust, prepare corn muffin mix according to package directions, except stir in ¾ cup of the flour with the dry corn muffin mix. Using a wooden spoon, stir in as much of the remaining flour as you can. Turn out dough onto a lightly floured surface. Knead in the remaining flour to make a moderately soft dough. Shape dough into a ball. Roll dough into a 13-inch circle. Carefully transfer the dough to prepared pizza pan, building up edge slightly.

STEP 2   Bake crust about 12 minutes or until golden.

STEP 3   Meanwhile, in a small bowl combine bean dip and the ½ cup salsa. Spread over hot crust. Top with turkey breast, chile peppers, and drained olives. Sprinkle with cheese. Bake in the 400° oven for 12 to 15 minutes more or until hot. If desired, serve with additional salsa.

PER SERVING: 435 cal., 14 g total fat (4 g sat. fat), 71 mg chol., 1,505 mg sodium, 54 g carbo., 3 g fiber, 22 g pro.
EXCHANGES: 3½ Starch, 1 Very Lean Meat, 1 High-Fat Meat, ½ Fat

OFF THE SHELF TIP Find packaged corn muffin mix in the baking aisle of your supermarket. Unopened boxes will last up to a year.

Plum Wonderful Chicken, page 107.

ABOVE: **Margarita Fajitas with Sub-Lime Salsa**, page 110. BELOW: **Saucy Cranberry Chicken**, page 106. OPPOSITE PAGE: **Quick Thai Chicken**, page 109.

ABOVE: **Spicy Shrimp & Noodle Soup**, page 51. BELOW: **Black Bean & Sausage Posole**, page 38. OPPOSITE PAGE: **Greek-Style Lamb Skillet**, page 104.

ABOVE: **Glazed Brussels Sprouts**, page 210. BELOW: **Savory Couscous**, page 222. OPPOSITE PAGE: **Tuna Spinach Braid**, page 171.

ABOVE: **Beef & Broccoli with Plum Sauce**, page 60. BELOW: **Pork Chops with Raspberries**, page 93. OPPOSITE PAGE: **Apricot-Glazed Pork Roast**, page 88.

Stroganoff-Sauced Beef Roast, page 75.

Fettuccine Vegetable Toss, page 196.

ABOVE: **Shrimply Divine Pasta**, page 178. BELOW: **Ravioli Skillet Lasagna**, page 193. OPPOSITE PAGE: **Turkey Manicotti with Chive Cream Sauce**, page 149.

ABOVE: **Shredded Pork Sandwiches**, page 85. BELOW: **Hot Artichoke & Roasted Red Pepper Dip**, page 8. OPPOSITE PAGE: **Mediterranean Alfredo Pizza**, page 198.

Chocolate-Covered Strawberry Cakes, page 246.

Nutty Turkey Tenderloins

Mustard-coated turkey tenderloins bake to perfection in less than 20 minutes along with corn bread stuffing and a topping of chopped nuts.

PREP
15 MINUTES
BAKE
18 MINUTES
OVEN
375°F
MAKES
4 SERVINGS

2   turkey breast tenderloins (about 1 pound)
¼   cup creamy Dijon-style mustard blend
1   cup packaged corn bread stuffing mix
½   cup finely chopped pecans
2   tablespoons butter, melted

STEP 1   Preheat oven to 375°F. Split each turkey breast tenderloin in half horizontally to make 4 turkey steaks. Brush turkey generously with the mustard blend. In a shallow dish combine dry stuffing mix and pecans; dip turkey in stuffing mixture, turning to coat both sides. Place in a shallow baking pan. Drizzle with melted butter.

STEP 2   Bake, uncovered, in the preheated oven for 18 to 20 minutes or until turkey is tender and no longer pink (170°F).

PER SERVING: 395 cal., 21 g total fat (5 g sat. fat), 84 mg chol., 566 mg sodium, 21 g carbo., 1 g fiber, 30 g pro.
EXCHANGES: 1 Starch, 4 Very Lean Meat, 4 Fat

OFF THE SHELF TIP Made with crumbled savory corn bread, white bread cubes, and herbs, this stuffing is a tasty break from the traditional.

Turkey Tenderloin with Bean & Corn Salsa

START TO FINISH
25 MINUTES

MAKES
4 SERVINGS

1	pound turkey breast tenderloin
	Salt
	Ground black pepper
¼	cup red jalapeño chile pepper jelly
1¼	cups bottled black bean and corn salsa
2	tablespoons snipped fresh cilantro

STEP 1 Preheat broiler. Split turkey breast tenderloin in half horizontally to make 4 turkey steaks. Place turkey on the unheated rack of a broiler pan. Season with salt and pepper. Broil 4 to 5 inches from the heat for 5 minutes.

STEP 2 Meanwhile, in a small saucepan melt jelly. Turn turkey and brush with 2 tablespoons of the jelly. Broil for 4 to 6 minutes more or until tender and no longer pink (170°F). Transfer turkey to a serving plate. Spoon remaining jelly over turkey; cover and keep warm.

STEP 3 In a small saucepan heat the salsa. Spoon salsa over the turkey. Sprinkle with cilantro.

PER SERVING: 196 cal., 2 g total fat (1 g sat. fat), 66 mg chol., 377 mg sodium, 16 g carbo., 1 g fiber, 27 g pro.
EXCHANGES: ½ Starch, 1 Other Carbo., 3½ Very Lean Meat

OFF THE SHELF TIP Look for jalapeño jelly in the jam and jelly aisle of the supermarket. Other uses? Take a block of cream cheese and cover it with the jelly. Serve with crackers for an instant appetizer. It also adds a surprise spicy-sweetness to a fried egg sandwich.

Turkey Steaks with Cranberry-Orange Sauce

Purchased relish, plus a splash of orange liqueur or juice, joins wild rice mix as a fitting pairing with sauteed turkey tenderloin.

LOW FAT

START TO FINISH
30 MINUTES
MAKES
4 SERVINGS

1   6-ounce package long grain and wild rice mix
1   pound turkey breast tenderloin
    Salt
    Ground black pepper
2   tablespoons butter or margarine
1   10-ounce package frozen cranberry-orange relish, thawed
2   tablespoons orange liqueur or orange juice

STEP 1   Cook rice mix according to package directions.

STEP 2   Meanwhile, split turkey breast tenderloin in half horizontally. Cut each piece in half, making 4 portions. Sprinkle turkey with salt and pepper. In a large skillet melt butter over medium heat. Add turkey; cook for 10 to 12 minutes or until tender and no longer pink (170°F), turning once.

STEP 3   Transfer turkey to a serving platter. Keep warm. Remove skillet from heat; let cool for 2 minutes. Carefully add cranberry-orange relish to drippings in skillet; stir in liqueur. Return to heat; cook and stir over low heat until heated through. Spoon sauce over turkey. Serve with rice.

PER SERVING: 481 cal., 8 g total fat (4 g sat. fat), 84 mg chol., 941 mg sodium, 68 g carbo., 0 g fiber, 31 g pro.
EXCHANGES: 2½ Starch, 2 Other Carbo., 3½ Very Lean Meat

OFF THE SHELF TIP   Cranberry-orange relish is a seasonal product. In the winter, look for it in the specialty section of your supermarket. In the summertime (when cranberries aren't at their peak), look for the product in the frozen foods aisle near the other packaged fruits.

Dijon-Turkey Potpie

PREP
25 MINUTES

BAKE
15 MINUTES

OVEN
375°F

MAKES
4 SERVINGS

1½   cups frozen broccoli, cauliflower, and carrot mix

1   11.5-ounce package (8) refrigerated corn bread twists

1   1.8-ounce envelope white sauce mix

10   ounces cooked turkey breast portion, chopped (about 2 cups)

2   tablespoons Dijon-style mustard

1   teaspoon instant chicken bouillon granules

STEP 1   Preheat oven to 375°F. Place frozen vegetables in a colander. Run hot water over vegetables just until thawed. Drain well. Cut up any large pieces.

STEP 2   Meanwhile, unroll dough. Separate into 16 pieces. Set aside.

STEP 3   In a medium saucepan prepare white sauce mix according to package directions, except after mixture starts to boil, stir in vegetables, chopped turkey, mustard, and bouillon granules. Return to boiling; reduce heat. Cook and stir for 1 minute more.

STEP 4   Transfer turkey mixture to a 2-quart rectangular baking dish. Arrange corn bread dough pieces in a single layer on top of the turkey mixture.

STEP 5   Bake, uncovered, in the preheated oven for 15 to 20 minutes or until corn bread topping is golden.

PER SERVING: 496 cal., 18 g total fat (6 g sat. fat), 50 mg chol., 1,875 mg sodium, 51 g carbo., 1 g fiber, 29 g pro.
EXCHANGES: ½ Vegetable, 3½ Starch, 3 Very Lean Meat, 2 Fat

OFF THE SHELF TIP   Corn bread twists are a great accompaniment to dinner but also make a versatile ingredient. Look for them in the refrigerated section of your supermarket. Be sure not to freeze unbaked dough; baked dough may be frozen for up to a month.

Turkey Manicotti with Chive Cream Sauce

A simple cream cheese sauce makes this dish—large pasta shells stuffed with a blend of chopped cooked turkey and broccoli—elegant enough to serve to visitors.

PREP
30 MINUTES

BAKE
25 MINUTES

OVEN
350°F

MAKES
6 SERVINGS

RECIPE PICTURED ON PAGE **141.**

12	dried manicotti shells
1	8-ounce tub cream cheese spread with chive and onion
⅔	cup milk
¼	cup grated Romano or Parmesan cheese
2	cups chopped cooked turkey (10 ounces)
1	10-ounce package frozen chopped broccoli, thawed and drained
1	4-ounce jar diced pimientos, drained
¼	teaspoon ground black pepper
	Grated Romano or Parmesan cheese (optional)

STEP 1 Cook manicotti shells according to package directions; drain. Rinse with cold water; drain again. Meanwhile, for sauce, in a heavy small saucepan heat cream cheese over medium-low heat until melted, stirring constantly. Slowly stir in milk until smooth. Stir in the ¼ cup Romano cheese.

STEP 2 Preheat oven to 350°F. For filling, in a medium bowl combine ¾ cup of the sauce, the turkey, drained broccoli, drained pimientos, and pepper. Using a small spoon, carefully fill each manicotti shell with about ⅓ cup filling. Arrange filled shells in a 3-quart rectangular baking dish. Pour remaining sauce over shells. Cover with foil.

STEP 3 Bake in the preheated oven for 25 to 30 minutes or until heated through. If desired, sprinkle each serving with additional grated cheese.

MAKE-AHEAD DIRECTIONS: Prepare as directed through Step 2, except cover with plastic wrap and refrigerate assembled manicotti for up to 24 hours. Bake, covered, in a preheated 350°F oven for 35 to 40 minutes or until heated through.

PER SERVING: 381 cal., 17 g total fat (10 g sat. fat), 78 mg chol., 256 mg sodium, 32 g carbo., 3 g fiber, 22 g pro.
EXCHANGES: ½ Vegetable, 2 Starch, 2 Lean Meat, 2 Fat

OFF THE SHELF TIP Packaged cream cheese is used in so many ways in convenience cooking. It comes in a variety of sizes and flavors. Whipped cream cheese (called spreadable cream cheese) is often combined with other flavors such as herbs, vegetables, or fruits. Use cream cheese within a week of opening.

Turkey Strudel

PREP
20 MINUTES
BAKE
20 MINUTES
OVEN
350°F
MAKES
6 SERVINGS

2   8-ounce packages (16) refrigerated crescent rolls
6   ounces Havarti cheese with dill, thinly sliced*
2   cups chopped cooked turkey or chicken (10 ounces)
1   4-ounce can (drained weight) sliced mushrooms, drained

STEP 1   Preheat oven to 350°F. Unroll crescent roll dough. On a large baking sheet, press dough from one of the packages into a 12×8-inch rectangle; set aside. On a sheet of waxed paper, press dough from remaining package into another 12×8-inch rectangle; set aside.

STEP 2   Arrange cheese slices on top of the dough rectangle on the baking sheet, leaving a ½-inch space around the edges. Top with turkey and drained mushrooms. Invert remaining dough rectangle over filling; peel off waxed paper. Pinch edges to seal. Cut 3 slits in top.

STEP 3   Bake in the preheated oven for 20 to 25 minutes or until golden.

***NOTE:** If you can't find Havarti cheese with dill, substitute 6 ounces regular Havarti cheese and sprinkle with 1 teaspoon dried dill after placing cheese on dough.

PER SERVING: 472 cal., 29 g total fat (3 g sat. fat), 71 mg chol., 868 mg sodium, 30 g carbo., 1 g fiber, 26 g pro.
EXCHANGES: 3 Starch, 2 Lean Meat, 1 High-Fat Meat, 2½ Fat

OFF THE SHELF TIP Look for precooked meat in the refrigerated meat section of your supermarket—usually somewhere between the uncooked products and the sandwich meat. You'll find precooked meat in whole pieces and strips, seasoned and unseasoned.

Turkey-Potato Bake

PREP
15 MINUTES
BAKE
30 MINUTES
STAND
10 MINUTES
OVEN
400°F
MAKES
4 SERVINGS

2¼	cups water
1	4.5- to 5-ounce package dry julienne potato mix
2	cups chopped cooked turkey or chicken breast (10 ounces)
1	cup shredded cheddar cheese (4 ounces)
1	teaspoon dried parsley flakes
⅔	cup milk

STEP 1 Preheat oven to 400°F. Bring the water to boiling. Meanwhile, in a 2-quart square baking dish combine dry potatoes and sauce mix from potato mix. Stir in turkey, ½ cup of the cheddar cheese, and the parsley. Stir in the boiling water and milk.

STEP 2 Bake, uncovered, in the preheated oven for 30 to 35 minutes or until potatoes are tender. Sprinkle with the remaining ½ cup cheese. Let stand for 10 minutes before serving (mixture will thicken on standing).

PER SERVING: 373 cal., 15 g total fat (8 g sat. fat), 87 mg chol., 994 mg sodium, 27 g carbo., 1 g fiber, 32 g pro.
EXCHANGES: 2 Starch, 2½ Very Lean Meat, 1 High-Fat Meat, ½ Fat

OFF THE SHELF TIP Packaged mixes made with dehydrated potatoes make handy side dishes or recipe ingredients. You'll frequently find them near the canned vegetables or with the stuffing mixes.

Mock Monte Cristo Sandwiches

Maybe you remember Monte Cristos from those diners with a mini jukebox at every table. The sandwich features savory deli turkey, ham, and Swiss grilled between pieces of French toast. Make this quick version for a fun Friday night meal.

PREP
10 MINUTES

BAKE
15 MINUTES

OVEN
400°F

MAKES
6 HALF SANDWICHES

6	slices frozen French toast
2	tablespoons honey mustard
3	ounces sliced cooked turkey breast
3	ounces sliced cooked ham
3	ounces thinly sliced Swiss cheese

STEP 1 Preheat oven to 400°F. Lightly grease a baking sheet; set aside. To assemble sandwiches, spread 1 side of each of the frozen French toast slices with honey mustard. Layer 3 of the toast slices, mustard sides up, with the turkey, ham, and cheese. Cover with remaining toast slices, mustard sides down. Place sandwiches on prepared baking sheet.

STEP 2 Bake in the preheated oven for 15 to 20 minutes or until sandwiches are heated through, turning sandwiches over once halfway through baking. Cut each sandwich in half diagonally.

PER HALF SANDWICH: 221 cal., 9 g total fat (4 g sat. fat), 75 mg chol., 704 mg sodium, 21 g carbo., 1 g fiber, 14 g pro.
EXCHANGES: 1½ Starch, 1½ Medium-Fat Meat

OFF THE SHELF TIP Check the freezer case for a selection of frozen breakfast dishes. Frozen French toast will be located with the frozen waffles and breakfast pastries.

Turkey-Vegetable Goulash

PREP
20 MINUTES

COOK
6 TO 8 HOURS (LOW) OR
3 TO 4 HOURS (HIGH)
PLUS 20 TO 30
MINUTES (HIGH)

MAKES
6 SERVINGS

1	pound uncooked ground turkey
1	14.5-ounce can diced tomatoes with basil, oregano, and garlic, undrained
1½	cups water
1	10-ounce package frozen mixed vegetables
1	8-ounce can tomato sauce
1	cup chopped celery (2 stalks)
⅓	cup chopped onion (1 small)
1	0.87- to 1-ounce envelope turkey gravy mix
1	cup dried fine egg noodles
⅓	cup shredded sharp cheddar, Monterey Jack, or Parmesan cheese

STEP 1 In a large skillet cook ground turkey over medium heat until brown. Drain off fat. Transfer turkey to a 3½- or 4-quart slow cooker. Stir in undrained tomatoes, water, frozen vegetables, tomato sauce, celery, onion, and dry gravy mix.

STEP 2 Cover and cook on low-heat setting for 6 to 8 hours or on high-heat setting for 3 to 4 hours.

STEP 3 If using low-heat setting, turn slow cooker to high-heat setting. Stir in uncooked noodles. Cover and cook for 20 to 30 minutes more or until noodles are tender. Sprinkle each serving with shredded cheese.

PER SERVING: 251 cal., 9 g total fat (3 g sat. fat), 73 mg chol., 918 mg sodium, 22 g carbo., 3 g fiber, 19 g pro.
EXCHANGES: 1½ Vegetable, 1 Starch, 2 Medium-Fat Meat

OFF THE SHELF TIP Packaged gravy mix is usually found in the spice aisle of the supermarket. It comes in a variety of flavors and provides a simple way to add depth and flavor to dishes.

Mexican Stromboli

Wrap cooked turkey and beans, salsa, and peppery cheese in pizza dough, bake, and enjoy the oohs and aahs when serving this lively dish to a tough-to-please crowd.

LOW FAT

PREP
30 MINUTES

BAKE
25 MINUTES

COOL
10 MINUTES

OVEN
375°F

MAKES
8 SERVINGS

12	ounces uncooked ground turkey or chicken breast
1	15-ounce can black beans or pinto beans, rinsed and drained
1	cup bottled salsa
	Nonstick cooking spray
2	10 or 13.8-ounce packages refrigerated pizza dough
¾	cup shredded Monterey Jack cheese with jalapeño peppers or Monterey Jack cheese (3 ounces)
	Water
1	tablespoon cornmeal
	Bottled salsa

STEP 1 Preheat oven to 375°F. For filling, in a large skillet cook turkey over medium-high heat until no longer pink; drain off fat. Stir in half of the drained beans (about ¾ cup) and the 1 cup salsa. Place the remaining beans in a small bowl and mash with a potato masher or fork; add mashed beans to the turkey mixture. Heat through. Set aside.

STEP 2 Lightly coat a 15×10×1-inch baking pan with nonstick cooking spray; set aside. On a lightly floured surface, unroll 1 package of the pizza dough. Roll into a 10-inch square.

STEP 3 Spoon half of the cheese down the center of the dough square to within 1 inch of edges. Spoon half of the turkey mixture (about 1¾ cups) over the cheese, spreading to a 4-inch-wide strip. Moisten the dough edges with water. Bring the side edges of dough together over the filling, stretching as necessary; pinch to seal well. Fold the ends up; pinch to seal well. Place, seam side down, on the prepared baking pan. Repeat with the remaining dough, cheese, and turkey mixture. Prick the tops of each stromboli with a fork. Brush the tops with water. Sprinkle the tops of the stromboli with cornmeal.

STEP 4 Bake in the preheated oven for 25 to 30 minutes or until golden. Cool for 10 minutes before serving. Serve with additional salsa.

PER SERVING: 331 cal., 10 g total fat (4 g sat. fat), 45 mg chol., 762 mg sodium, 43 g carbo., 4 g fiber, 20 g pro.
EXCHANGES: 3 Starch, 1½ Medium-Fat Meat

OFF THE SHELF TIP Refrigerated pizza dough is found with the refrigerated biscuits in the supermarket. If using it for traditional pizza, prebake for a few minutes for a crisp crust. Never freeze unbaked dough; baked dough may be frozen for up to a month.

Fish & Seafood

Fish Fillets with Yogurt Dressing

Choose a favorite fish fillet, then bake it in a poppy seed dressing that you'll also combine with yogurt for a cooling drizzler sauce.

LOW FAT

PREP
15 MINUTES

MARINATE
20 MINUTES

BAKE
4 TO 6 MINUTES PER ½-INCH THICKNESS

OVEN
450°F

MAKES
4 SERVINGS

1   pound fresh or frozen skinless cod, orange roughy, or other fish fillets, ½ to 1 inch thick
⅔   cup bottled poppy seed salad dressing
3   tablespoons thinly sliced green onion
1   teaspoon snipped fresh thyme or ¼ teaspoon dried thyme, crushed
½   cup plain yogurt

STEP 1   Thaw fish, if frozen.* Rinse fish; pat dry with paper towels. Cut into 4 serving-size pieces. For marinade, in a large bowl combine ½ cup of the salad dressing, 2 tablespoons of the green onion, and ½ teaspoon of the fresh thyme (or ⅛ teaspoon dried thyme). Add fish fillets. Turn to coat. Cover and marinate in the refrigerator for 20 to 30 minutes.

STEP 2   Preheat oven to 450°F. Drain fillets; discard the marinade. Measure the thickness of the fish. Place fish in a greased 2-quart rectangular baking dish, tucking under any thin edges.

STEP 3   Bake fish, uncovered, in the preheated oven until fish flakes easily when tested with a fork (allow 4 to 6 minutes per ½-inch thickness of fish). Transfer fish to a serving platter.

STEP 4   Meanwhile, for sauce, in a small serving bowl stir together yogurt, remaining salad dressing, remaining 1 tablespoon green onion, and remaining ½ teaspoon thyme. Serve sauce with fish.

*NOTE: To quickly thaw fish, place 1 pound unwrapped frozen fish in a microwave-safe 2-quart square baking dish. Cover and cook on 30% power (medium-low) for 5 to 6 minutes, turning and, if necessary, separating fillets or steaks after 3 minutes. When thawed the fish should be pliable and cold on the outside but still slightly icy in the center of thick areas.

PER SERVING: 182 cal., 9 g total fat (2 g sat. fat), 55 mg chol., 201 mg sodium, 3 g carbo., 0 g fiber, 22 g pro.
EXCHANGES: 3 Very Lean Meat, 1½ Fat

OFF THE SHELF TIP   Bottled dressings aren't just good for topping your salads. Grab a bottle from your supermarket and use to marinate meats or vegetables or drizzle over finished dishes for an extra pop of flavor.

Beer-Battered Cod

If you have a can of beer on hand, a little flour, salt, pepper, and oil, you're just some cod fillets and a few minutes away from a hot and satisfying comfort dish.

START TO FINISH
35 MINUTES

MAKES
4 SERVINGS

6	4- to 6-ounce fresh or frozen cod fillets
	Cooking oil for deep-fat frying
2	cups self-rising flour
½	teaspoon salt
½	teaspoon ground black pepper
1	12-ounce can beer

STEP 1 Thaw fish, if frozen. Rinse fish; pat dry with paper towels. In a heavy 3-quart saucepan or deep-fat fryer heat 2 inches of oil to 365°F.

STEP 2 Meanwhile, in a large bowl stir together flour, salt, and pepper. Sprinkle both sides of fish with 2 tablespoons of the flour mixture. Add beer to remaining flour mixture and stir until combined. Dip fish pieces, 1 at a time, in the batter, coating well. (Batter will be thick.)

STEP 3 Fry fish, 1 or 2 pieces at a time, for 4 to 6 minutes or until golden and fish flakes easily when tested with a fork. Drain on paper towels; keep warm in a 300°F oven while frying remaining fish.

PER SERVING: 635 cal., 29 g total fat (4 g sat. fat), 72 mg chol., 1,181 mg sodium, 50 g carbo., 2 g fiber, 37 g pro.
EXCHANGES: 2½ Starch, 1 Other Carbo., 4 Very Lean Meat, 5 Fat

OFF THE SHELF TIP If you're buying frozen fish fillets, look for a package of individually wrapped fillets. You can remove just the number you need and save the remaining for another meal.

Fish with Black Bean Sauce

Use your blender to smooth black beans and teriyaki for a thick sauce topper to complement fish.

LOW FAT

START TO FINISH
25 MINUTES

MAKES
6 SERVINGS

1½ pounds fresh or frozen skinless sea bass or orange roughy fillets, cut into 6 portions
1   15-ounce can black beans, rinsed and drained
3   tablespoons teriyaki sauce
2   tablespoons hoisin sauce
    Nonstick cooking spray
2   cups hot cooked rice

OFF THE SHELF TIP Look for hoisin sauce in the Oriental section of your supermarket. This sweet and sour sauce is also called "Peking sauce."

STEP 1 Thaw fish, if frozen. Rinse fish; pat dry with paper towels. In a blender or food processor combine the drained beans, teriyaki sauce, and hoisin sauce. Cover and blend or process until nearly smooth.

STEP 2 Lightly coat a 12-inch skillet with nonstick cooking spray. Preheat over medium-high heat. Carefully place fish portions in skillet; cook about 4 minutes or until brown, turning once. Add bean mixture to fish. Bring to boiling; reduce heat to medium. Cover and simmer about 8 minutes or until fish flakes easily when tested with a fork.

STEP 3 To serve, spoon some of the sauce onto a plate; place fish portion on the sauce. Serve remaining sauce with hot cooked rice.

PER SERVING: 276 cal., 3 g total fat (1 g sat. fat), 46 mg chol., 617 mg sodium, 35 g carbo., 4 g fiber, 28 g pro.
EXCHANGES: 1 Starch, 1 Other Carbo., 3½ Very Lean Meat

Salmon with Feta & Pasta

Tangy crumbled feta cheese adds a piquant complement to sweet salmon and tender pasta. Toss in salty kalamata olives to rev the Greek-style flavor quotient up a notch.

START TO FINISH
25 MINUTES

MAKES
5 SERVINGS

12	ounces fresh or frozen skinless salmon fillet
8	ounces dried rotini pasta
	Nonstick cooking spray
1	teaspoon bottled minced garlic (2 cloves)
	Salt
2	cups chopped roma tomato (5 medium)
1	cup sliced green onion (8)
⅓	cup sliced pitted ripe olives
3	tablespoons snipped fresh basil
½	teaspoon coarsely ground black pepper
2	teaspoons olive oil
1	4-ounce package crumbled feta cheese

STEP 1 Thaw fish, if frozen. Rinse fish; pat dry with paper towels. Cut into 1-inch pieces. Cook rotini according to package directions. Drain well. Return to pan. Cover and keep warm.

STEP 2 Meanwhile, lightly coat an unheated large nonstick skillet with nonstick cooking spray. Preheat skillet over medium-high heat. Add garlic. Cook and stir for 15 seconds. Lightly sprinkle fish pieces with salt. Add fish to skillet. Cook fish for 4 to 6 minutes or until fish flakes easily when tested with a fork, turning occasionally. Stir in tomato, green onion, olives, basil, and pepper. Heat through.

STEP 3 In a large bowl toss together hot pasta and olive oil. Add salmon mixture and feta cheese; gently toss to combine.

PER SERVING: 373 cal., 13 g total fat (5 g sat. fat), 56 mg chol., 443 mg sodium, 41 g carbo., 3 g fiber, 24 g pro.
EXCHANGES: ½ Vegetable, 2½ Starch, 2½ Lean Meat, ½ Fat

OFF THE SHELF TIP Save tons of time by using bottled minced garlic instead of mincing your own. Look for jars near the spices or in the produce section of your supermarket. Be sure to refrigerate after opening.

Parmesan Baked Fish

PREP
15 MINUTES

BAKE
12 MINUTES

OVEN
450°F

MAKES
4 SERVINGS

4	4-ounce fresh or frozen skinless salmon fillets or other firm fish fillets, ¾ to 1 inch thick
	Nonstick cooking spray
¼	cup light mayonnaise or salad dressing
2	tablespoons grated Parmesan cheese
1	tablespoon snipped fresh chives or sliced green onion
1	teaspoon Worcestershire sauce for chicken

OFF THE SHELF TIP Fresh herbs are available year-round in most supermarkets. Look for them in packages in the specialty section of the produce aisle. Snip them with kitchen scissors.

STEP 1   Thaw fish, if frozen (see note, page 156). Rinse fish; pat dry with paper towels. Preheat oven to 450°F. Coat a 2-quart square or rectangular baking dish with nonstick cooking spray.

STEP 2   Arrange fillets in dish. In a small bowl stir together mayonnaise, Parmesan cheese, chives, and Worcestershire sauce. Spread mayonnaise mixture over fillets.

STEP 3   Bake, uncovered, in the preheated oven for 12 to 15 minutes or until fish flakes easily when tested with a fork.

PER SERVING: 252 cal., 16 g total fat (3 g sat. fat), 77 mg chol., 200 mg sodium, 2 g carbo., 0 g fiber, 25 g pro.
EXCHANGES: 3½ Lean Meat, 1½ Fat

Browned Butter Salmon

PREP
20 MINUTES

BROIL
8 MINUTES

MAKES
4 SERVINGS

4   fresh or frozen salmon or halibut steaks, cut 1 inch thick (about 1½ pounds)
     Salt
     Ground black pepper
2   tablespoons butter or margarine
2   tablespoons pure maple syrup
1   teaspoon finely shredded orange peel

STEP 1   Thaw fish, if frozen (see note page 156). Rinse fish; pat dry with paper towels. Sprinkle both sides of fish steaks with salt and pepper; set aside. In a small saucepan cook the butter over medium heat about 3 minutes or until golden brown, stirring occasionally. Remove from heat. Cool for 10 minutes. Stir in maple syrup and orange peel (mixture may thicken).

STEP 2   Meanwhile, preheat broiler. Line an unheated broiler pan with foil; grease the rack. Place the fish on the prepared rack of the broiler pan. Spread both sides of each fish steak with the browned butter mixture. Broil 4 inches from the heat for 5 minutes. Using a wide spatula, carefully turn fish over. Broil for 3 to 7 minutes more or until fish flakes easily when tested with a fork.

PER SERVING: 277 cal., 12 g total fat (5 g sat. fat), 105 mg chol., 322 mg sodium, 7 g carbo., 0 g fiber, 34 g pro.
EXCHANGES: ½ Other Carbo., 5 Very Lean Meat, 1½ Fat

OFF THE SHELF TIP Pure maple syrup boasts a sweet, mellow flavor that blends superbly with fish, poultry, and pork. Maple-flavor syrup is artificially flavored and possesses a more intense flavor. For most recipes you can substitute the flavored syrup for the real thing.

Fish Stew

L O W
F A T

START TO FINISH
30 MINUTES

MAKES
6 SERVINGS
(ABOUT 9½ CUPS)

1	pound fresh or frozen skinless, boneless sea bass, red snapper, and/or catfish fillets
1	medium onion, cut into wedges
1	tablespoon cooking oil
2	10.75-ounce cans condensed tomato soup
2	cups refrigerated diced red-skinned potatoes
1	14.5-ounce can stewed tomatoes, undrained and cut up
1½	cups water
1	10-ounce package frozen mixed vegetables
½	teaspoon dried thyme, crushed
⅛	teaspoon ground black pepper

OFF THE SHELF TIP Check out the refrigerator case at your supermarket for packages of refrigerated potatoes. They come sliced, diced, and mashed, as well as shredded into hash browns.

STEP 1   Thaw fish, if frozen (see note, page 156). Cut fish into 1-inch cubes; set aside. In a 4-quart Dutch oven cook onion in hot oil over medium-high heat until tender.

STEP 2   Stir in soup, potatoes, undrained tomatoes, water, frozen mixed vegetables, thyme, and pepper. Bring to boiling. Stir in fish cubes; reduce heat. Cover and simmer about 10 minutes or until fish flakes easily when tested with a fork and vegetables are tender.

PER SERVING: 252 cal., 6 g total fat (1 g sat. fat), 31 mg chol., 847 mg sodium, 32 g carbo., 5 g fiber, 19 g pro.
EXCHANGES: 1 Vegetable, 2 Starch, 2 Very Lean Meat, ½ Fat

Herb-Crusted Salmon with Roasted Pepper Cream

There are so many simple ways to enjoy salmon. This one dresses up a bread crumb crust with mustard, then tantalizes the tongue with a light cream-based sweet red pepper sauce.

PREP
10 MINUTES

BAKE
20 MINUTES

COOK
15 MINUTES

OVEN
400°F

MAKES
4 SERVINGS

4   6-ounce fresh or frozen skinless, boneless salmon fillets
2   tablespoons honey-Dijon mustard
3   tablespoons seasoned fine dry bread crumbs
1   cup whipping cream
½   cup chopped bottled roasted red sweet peppers, drained
1   tablespoon honey-Dijon mustard

STEP 1 Thaw fish, if frozen. Rinse fish; pat dry with paper towels. Preheat oven to 400°F. Brush 1 side of each fillet with the 2 tablespoons honey-Dijon mustard. Sprinkle with bread crumbs. Place fish, crumb sides up, in a 3-quart rectangular baking dish.

STEP 2 Bake, uncovered, in the preheated oven for 20 to 25 minutes or until crumbs are golden and fish flakes easily when tested with a fork.

STEP 3 Meanwhile, in a medium saucepan combine whipping cream, roasted peppers, and the 1 tablespoon honey-Dijon mustard. Bring to boiling; reduce heat. Boil gently, uncovered, about 15 minutes or until reduced to 1 cup. Serve sauce over fish.

PER SERVING: 576 cal., 32 g total fat (15 g sat. fat), 227 mg chol., 359 mg sodium, 11 g carbo., 0 g fiber, 57 g pro.
EXCHANGES: 1 Starch, 7 Lean Meat, 2 Fat

OFF THE SHELF TIP Don't look for seasoned bread crumbs in the bread section of your supermarket. Instead, try the packaged goods section, near stuffing mixes and mac 'n' cheese.

Lime-Poached Mahi Mahi

START TO FINISH
20 MINUTES

MAKES
4 SERVINGS

4	6-ounce fresh or frozen mahi mahi or catfish fillets, ½ to ¾ inch thick
2	teaspoons seasoned pepper
1	tablespoon olive oil
⅓	cup frozen margarita mix concentrate, thawed
2	cups hot cooked basmati or long grain rice

STEP 1 Thaw fish, if frozen. If necessary, skin fish. Rinse fish; pat dry with paper towels. Rub both sides of fish with seasoned pepper.

STEP 2 In a large nonstick skillet cook the fish fillets in hot oil over medium-high heat for 1 to 2 minutes on each side or until light brown. Reduce heat to medium-low. Carefully add margarita mix to skillet. Cook, covered, for 6 to 8 minutes or until fish flakes easily when tested with a fork. Serve fish and sauce with rice.

PER SERVING: 336 cal., 5 g total fat (1 g sat. fat), 124 mg chol., 150 mg sodium, 41 g carbo., 0 g fiber, 34 g pro.
EXCHANGES: 1½ Starch, 1 Other Carbo., 4 Very Lean Meat, ½ Fat

OFF THE SHELF TIP Look for frozen margarita mix near the frozen juices in the supermarket. If you have any left over, store in a freezer-safe resealable plastic bag. Next time you cook Mexcian, you'll be ready for margaritas!

Orange-Sauced Fish with Broccoli

Your microwave brings this dish together quickly. The sauce is a smart pairing of orange marmalade and lemon juice.

PREP
15 MINUTES

MICROWAVE
12 MINUTES

MAKES
4 SERVINGS

1	pound fresh or frozen fish fillets, ½ to ¾ inch thick
1	10-ounce package frozen chopped broccoli
1	tablespoon water
1	cup water
½	cup orange marmalade
¼	teaspoon salt
1	cup uncooked quick-cooking couscous
	Salt
	Ground black pepper
1	tablespoon butter or margarine
2	teaspoons lemon juice

STEP 1 Thaw fish, if frozen (see note, page 156). Rinse fish; pat dry with paper towels. Cut fish into 4 serving-size portions; set aside.

STEP 2 Place broccoli and the 1 tablespoon water in a microwave-safe 2-quart square baking dish. Cover with vented plastic wrap. Microwave on 100% power (high) for 4 to 6 minutes or until crisp-tender, giving the dish a half turn and stirring broccoli halfway through cooking.

STEP 3 Stir the 1 cup water, 2 tablespoons of the orange marmalade, and the ¼ teaspoon salt into the broccoli. Stir in couscous. Spread couscous mixture evenly in dish. Arrange fish on top of the couscous mixture, folding under any thin edges; sprinkle fish with additional salt and pepper.

STEP 4 Cover with vented plastic wrap. Microwave on high for 7 to 9 minutes or until fish flakes easily when tested with a fork, giving the dish a half-turn halfway through cooking.

STEP 5 For sauce, in a small microwave-safe bowl combine remaining 6 tablespoons marmalade, the butter, and lemon juice. Microwave on high about 1 minute or until butter melts and sauce is bubbly. Stir sauce; drizzle over fish.

PER SERVING: 420 cal., 5 g total fat (2 g sat. fat), 62 mg chol., 312 mg sodium, 66 g carbo., 5 g fiber, 29 g pro.
EXCHANGES: 1 Vegetable, 2 Starch, 2 Other Carbo., 3 Very Lean Meat, ½ Fat

OFF THE SHELF TIP Orange marmalade is not just for toast anymore! Use it in recipes to add a splash of citrus flavor.

Sesame-Coated Tilapia Salad

FAST

START TO FINISH
20 MINUTES

MAKES
4 SERVINGS

1	pound fresh or frozen tilapia fillets
¼	cup all-purpose flour
¼	cup sesame seeds
½	teaspoon ground black pepper
⅔	cup bottled honey-Dijon salad dressing
2	tablespoons cooking oil
1	5-ounce package baby spinach and red leaf lettuce or baby spinach with radicchio

STEP 1 Thaw fish, if frozen (see note, page 156). Rinse fish; pat dry with paper towels. Cut fish into 4 serving-size pieces.

STEP 2 In a shallow bowl combine flour, sesame seeds, and pepper. Transfer 2 tablespoons of the salad dressing to a small bowl. Brush all sides of the fish pieces with the 2 tablespoons salad dressing. Firmly press both sides of each fish piece into sesame mixture.

STEP 3 In a 12-inch skillet heat oil over medium heat. Cook coated fish in hot oil about 6 minutes or until fish flakes easily when tested with a fork, turning once.

STEP 4 Divide spinach mixture among 4 dinner plates; top each with a fish piece. Drizzle with the remaining salad dressing.

PER SERVING: 423 cal., 30 g total fat (4 g sat. fat), 56 mg chol., 252 mg sodium, 15 g carbo., 4 g fiber, 26 g pro.
EXCHANGES: 1½ Vegetable, ½ Other Carbo., 2½ Very Lean Meat, 6 Fat

OFF THE SHELF TIP Bottled dressings aren't just good for topping your salads. Grab a bottle from your supermarket and use to marinate meats and vegetables or drizzle over finished dishes for an extra pop of flavor.

Snapper Veracruz

EASY

PREP
15 MINUTES
BAKE
30 MINUTES
OVEN
300°F
MAKES
4 SERVINGS

1¼ to 1½ pounds fresh or frozen red snapper fillets or firm-textured whitefish fillets such as catfish, ½ to ¾ inch thick, skinned

1 14.5-ounce can Mexican-style stewed tomatoes, undrained

1 cup pitted ripe olives

2 tablespoons olive oil

1 10-ounce package seasoned yellow rice

OFF THE SHELF TIP Mexican-style stewed tomatoes add flavor to recipes without making any extra effort. Located in the canned vegetable aisle of your supermarket, canned tomatoes come in an abundance of flavor combinations.

STEP 1 Thaw fish, if frozen. Rinse fish; pat dry with paper towels. Cut fish into 4 serving-size pieces. Preheat oven to 300°F.

STEP 2 In a large ovenproof skillet combine undrained tomatoes and olives. Top with fish fillets; drizzle with olive oil. Bake, uncovered, in the preheated oven for 15 minutes. Spoon some of the tomato mixture over the fish and bake about 15 minutes more or until fish flakes easily when tested with a fork.

STEP 3 Meanwhile, prepare rice according to package directions. Serve fish and sauce with rice.

PER SERVING: 566 cal., 19 g total fat (3 g sat. fat), 52 mg chol., 1,466 mg sodium, 63 g carbo., 3 g fiber, 36 g pro.
EXCHANGES: 1 Vegetable, 4 Starch, 3 Very Lean Meat, 2½ Fat

South-of-the-Border Snapper

It's easy to meet your fish and seafood quotient with this dish. Just bake snapper with your favorite chunky salsa and a topping of shredded cheese.

PREP
10 MINUTES
BAKE
15 MINUTES
OVEN
425°F
MAKES
4 SERVINGS

4   4-ounce fresh or frozen red snapper, sole, or cod fillets, about ½ inch thick
½   cup bottled chunky salsa
¾   cup shredded reduced-fat Monterey Jack and/or cheddar cheese

STEP 1   Thaw fish, if frozen (see note, page 156). Rinse fish; pat dry with paper towels. Preheat oven to 425°F.

STEP 2   Place fish in a 2-quart rectangular baking dish, tucking under any thin edges. Spoon salsa over fish and sprinkle with cheese.

STEP 3   Bake in the preheated oven about 15 minutes or until fish flakes easily when tested with a fork.

PER SERVING: 177 cal., 5 g total fat (3 g sat. fat), 56 mg chol., 277 mg sodium, 1 g carbo., 0 g fiber, 29 g pro.
EXCHANGES: 4 Very Lean Meat, 1 Fat

OFF THE SHELF TIP   Salsa is one of the most versatile condiments around. Located in the Mexcian section of your supermarket, it comes in an array of flavors and heat levels.

Sweet Mustard Halibut

Hearty halibut tastes great with a honey-mustard-salsa condiment. This healthful seafood dish takes just minutes to prepare.

PREP
10 MINUTES
BAKE
8 MINUTES
OVEN
450°F
MAKES
4 SERVINGS

1	to 1¼ pounds fresh or frozen halibut steaks, ¾ inch thick
½	cup bottled chunky salsa
2	tablespoons honey
2	tablespoons Dijon-style mustard

STEP 1 Thaw fish, if frozen (see note, page 156). Rinse fish; pat dry with paper towels. Preheat oven to 450°F.

STEP 2 Arrange fish in a 2-quart square or rectangular baking dish. Bake, uncovered, in the preheated oven about 6 minutes or until fish flakes easily when tested with a fork. Drain liquid from fish.

STEP 3 Meanwhile, in a small bowl stir together the salsa and honey. Spread mustard over drained fish; spoon salsa mixture on top of mustard. Bake for 2 to 3 minutes more or until salsa mixture is hot.

PER SERVING: 176 cal., 4 g total fat (0 g sat. fat), 36 mg chol., 362 mg sodium, 11 g carbo., 0 g fiber, 24 g pro.
EXCHANGES: ½ Other Carbo., 3½ Very Lean Meat, ½ Fat

OFF THE SHELF TIP Mustards come in a wide variety of flavors from mild to wow—and everywhere in between. Some are flavored with herbs and spices, wine, peppers, or even honey.

Easy Baked Fish

Easy says it all. Frozen fish portions plus stuffing mix are brightened with lemon juice and ready in less than 30 minutes.

PREP
10 MINUTES
BAKE
18 MINUTES
OVEN
425°F
MAKES
4 SERVINGS

½ cup packaged herb-seasoned stuffing mix, finely crushed

2 tablespoons butter, melted

2 7.6-ounce packages frozen Caesar Parmesan or grill-flavored fish portions (4 portions total)

2 teaspoons lemon juice

STEP 1 Preheat oven to 425°F. In a small bowl combine dry stuffing mix and melted butter; toss until well mixed.

STEP 2 Place frozen fish portions in a greased 2-quart rectangular baking dish. Sprinkle with lemon juice. Sprinkle crumb mixture over fish.

STEP 3 Bake in the preheated oven for 18 to 20 minutes or until fish flakes easily when tested with a fork.

PER SERVING: 183 cal., 9 g total fat (4 g sat. fat), 76 mg chol., 401 mg sodium, 6 g carbo., 1 g fiber, 18 g pro.
EXCHANGES: ½ Starch, 3 Very Lean Meat, 1 Fat

OFF THE SHELF TIP Packaged stuffing comes in a variety of flavors. Look for it in the bread section of the supermarket. It comes in boxes, canisters, and bags.

Tuna Spinach Braid

PREP
25 MINUTES

BAKE
18 MINUTES

OVEN
375°F

MAKES
4 TO 6 SERVINGS

RECIPE PICTURED
ON PAGE **135.**

1   **10-ounce package frozen chopped spinach, thawed and well drained**
1   **9.25-ounce can chunk white tuna (water pack), drained and broken into chunks**
1   **cup light ricotta cheese or cream-style cottage cheese, drained**
½   **cup grated Parmesan cheese**
½   **teaspoon bottled minced garlic (1 clove)**
1   **8-ounce package (8) refrigerated crescent rolls**
3   **thick slices provolone cheese (3 ounces)**
    Chopped tomato (optional)
    Grated Parmesan cheese (optional)

STEP 1   Preheat oven to 375°F. For filling, in a medium bowl stir together drained spinach, tuna, ricotta cheese, the ½ cup Parmesan cheese, and the garlic; set aside.

STEP 2   Unroll and separate crescent roll dough into 4 rectangles. On an ungreased baking sheet or shallow baking pan, place rectangles together, overlapping edges slightly to form a 14×10-inch rectangle. Firmly press edges and perforations together to seal.

STEP 3   Spread filling in a 3½-inch-wide strip lengthwise down the center of dough. Top with provolone, cutting cheese as necessary to cover the filling.

STEP 4   Make cuts in dough at 1-inch intervals on both long sides of rectangle just to the edge of the filling. Fold dough strips diagonally over filling, overlapping strips and alternating from side to side to give a braided appearance.

STEP 5   Bake in the preheated oven for 18 to 20 minutes or until golden. Serve warm. If desired, serve with chopped tomato and additional grated Parmesan cheese.

PER SERVING: 507 cal., 28 g total fat (11 g sat. fat), 69 mg chol., 1,208 mg sodium, 29 g carbo., 2 g fiber, 38 g pro.
EXCHANGES: 1 Vegetable, 1½ Starch, 4½ Lean Meat, 2½ Fat

OFF THE SHELF TIP   Save tons of time by using bottled minced garlic instead of mincing your own. Look for jars near the spices or in the produce section of your supermarket. Be sure to refrigerate after opening.

Creamy Tuna Mac

Peas, tuna, and flavored sour cream dip rev up the appeal of already beloved mac 'n' cheese. A simple salad or apple slices is all you need to round out this meal.

START TO FINISH
25 MINUTES

MAKES
4 TO 6 SERVINGS

1   7.25-ounce package macaroni and cheese dinner mix
1   cup frozen peas
½   cup dairy sour cream ranch-, onion-, or chive-flavor dip
1   6-ounce can solid white tuna, drained and broken into chunks
    Crushed potato chips (optional)

STEP 1   Cook macaroni from dinner mix according to package directions, except add peas for the last 2 minutes of cooking. Drain. Continue according to dinner mix package directions.

STEP 2   Stir sour cream dip into macaroni mixture. Gently stir in tuna. Heat through. If desired, sprinkle each serving with crushed potato chips.

PER SERVING: 368 cal., 9 g total fat (4 g sat. fat), 47 mg chol., 888 mg sodium, 50 g carbo., 2 g fiber, 23 g pro.
EXCHANGES: 3 Starch, 2 Very Lean Meat, 1 Fat

OFF THE SHELF TIP Canned tuna is a staple in many kitchens. It can be dressed up into a casserole and dressed down into a simple, yet comforting sandwich.

Salmon-Sour Cream Turnovers

PREP
15 MINUTES

BAKE
25 MINUTES

STAND
20 MINUTES

OVEN
375°F

MAKES
4 SERVINGS

1   15-ounce package rolled refrigerated unbaked piecrusts (2 crusts)
⅓   cup dairy sour cream chive-flavor dip
1   tablespoon all-purpose flour
2   6-ounce cans skinless, boneless salmon, drained and flaked
½   cup chopped celery (1 stalk)
¼   cup finely chopped red or green sweet pepper
   Milk
1   teaspoon sesame seeds

PER SERVING: 658 cal., 36 g total fat (15 g sat. fat), 80 mg chol., 996 mg sodium, 57 g carbo., 1 g fiber, 20 g pro.
EXCHANGES: 3½ Starch, 2½ Lean Meat, 5 Fat

OFF THE SHELF TIP You'll find the refrigerated piecrusts—a lifesaver for a busy cook—in the refrigerated baked goods section of your supermarket. If you do get cracks in your crust as you work with it, simply wet your fingers with cold water and press cracks together.

STEP 1 Preheat oven to 375°F. Let piecrusts stand at room temperature for 15 minutes as directed on package.

STEP 2 Meanwhile, in a medium bowl stir together sour cream dip and flour. Fold in salmon, celery, and sweet pepper.

STEP 3 Unroll piecrusts. Spread half of the salmon mixture onto one half of each piecrust, spreading to within 1 inch of the edges. Moisten edges with water. Carefully lift and fold piecrusts in half over filling; turn edges under. Seal edges with the tines of a fork. Cut slits in tops of turnovers to allow steam to escape. Brush tops of turnovers with milk; sprinkle with sesame seeds. Transfer turnovers to a large baking sheet.

STEP 4 Bake in the preheated oven for 25 to 30 minutes or until pastry is golden. Let stand for 5 minutes before removing from baking sheet.

Broccoli-Salmon Pasta

Pasta and veggies cook in the same pot. Once they're done, the other ingredients mix in and simmer for a texture-rich salmon-pasta toss. No salmon? Use tuna instead.

START TO FINISH
20 MINUTES

MAKES
4 SERVINGS

1½   cups dried penne, cut ziti, or gemelli pasta
2   cups frozen broccoli florets
1   10.75-ounce can condensed cheddar cheese soup
½   cup milk
1   tablespoon Dijon-style mustard
½   teaspoon dried dill
⅛   teaspoon ground black pepper
2   6-ounce cans skinless, boneless salmon or tuna, drained
¼   cup sliced green onion (2)

OFF THE SHELF TIP Grab a can from the soup section. Just make sure your choice is condensed, not ready-to-serve.

STEP 1   In a large saucepan cook pasta according to package directions, adding broccoli for the last 3 minutes of cooking. Drain well; return to saucepan.

STEP 2   Stir soup, milk, mustard, dill, and pepper into the pasta mixture. Cook over low heat until heated through, stirring occasionally. Gently fold in salmon and green onion; heat through.

PER SERVING: 315 cal., 10 g total fat (3 g sat. fat), 58 mg chol., 1,049 mg sodium, 34 g carbo., 4 g fiber, 25 g pro.
EXCHANGES: ½ Vegetable, 2 Starch, 2½ Lean Meat

Shrimp-Artichoke Skillet

START TO FINISH
25 MINUTES

MAKES
4 SERVINGS

1   14-ounce can artichoke hearts, drained
⅓   cup chopped onion (1 small)
1   tablespoon butter or margarine
1   10.75-ounce can condensed golden mushroom soup
¾   cup half-and-half or light cream
¼   cup dry sherry
½   cup finely shredded Parmesan cheese (2 ounces)
12   ounces cooked, peeled, and deveined shrimp*
2   cups hot cooked rice

OFF THE SHELF TIP Canned artichoke hearts are found in the canned vegetable aisle of the supermarket. Artichoke hearts can also be found marinated in jars and frozen.

STEP 1 Quarter artichoke hearts; set aside. In a large skillet cook onion in hot butter until tender. Add soup, half-and-half, and sherry, stirring until smooth. Add Parmesan cheese; heat and stir until melted.

STEP 2 Add artichoke hearts and shrimp; heat through. Serve over hot cooked rice.

*****NOTE:** If shrimp have tails, remove them.

PER SERVING: 422 cal., 14 g total fat (8 g sat. fat), 202 mg chol., 1,349 mg sodium, 38 g carbo., 4 g fiber, 28 g pro.
EXCHANGES: 1 Vegetable, 2 Starch, 3 Very Lean Meat, 3 Fat

Shrimp Alfredo

Sliced fresh zucchini gives this Alfredo-style noodle and shrimp dish a sophisticated flavor edge. Try this recipe with shrimp on one occasion, crabmeat on another.

EASY

START TO FINISH
25 MINUTES

MAKES
2 SERVINGS

1½   cups water
½   cup milk
2   tablespoons butter or margarine
1   4.4-ounce package noodles with Alfredo-style sauce
1½   cups thinly sliced zucchini (1 medium)
6   ounces frozen peeled, deveined, cooked shrimp, thawed, or 6 ounces chunk-style imitation crabmeat

STEP 1   In a medium saucepan combine water, milk, and butter. Bring to boiling. Stir in noodle mix. Return to boiling; reduce heat. Simmer, uncovered, for 5 minutes.

STEP 2   Stir in zucchini. Return to a gentle boil; cook, uncovered, about 3 minutes more or until noodles are tender.

STEP 3   Gently stir in shrimp. Heat through. Remove from heat; let stand for 3 to 5 minutes or until slightly thickened.

PER SERVING: 486 cal., 21 g total fat (12 g sat. fat), 264 mg chol., 1,279 mg sodium, 44 g carbo., 2 g fiber, 30 g pro.
EXCHANGES: 1 Vegetable, 2½ Starch, 3 Very Lean Meat, 3½ Fat

OFF THE SHELF TIP Frozen, peeled, and deveined cooked shrimp can shave a lot of time off recipe preparation. If using the imitation crab option, look for packages of it in the meat section of your supermarket.

Shrimp over Rice

LOW FAT

START TO FINISH
25 MINUTES

MAKES
4 SERVINGS

1   cup instant rice

3   cups water

1   12-ounce package frozen peeled, deveined shrimp

1   15.5-ounce jar chunky-style meatless spaghetti sauce (about 2 cups)

¼   cup dry red wine

¼   teaspoon Worcestershire sauce
    Several dashes bottled hot pepper sauce

OFF THE SHELF TIP Bottled pasta sauce comes in a huge variety of flavors. The type you choose will determine how spicy and herby your recipe turns out.

STEP 1   Prepare rice according to package directions. Set aside.

STEP 2   Meanwhile, in a large saucepan bring the water to boiling. Add frozen shrimp. Return to boiling; reduce heat. Simmer, uncovered, for 1 to 3 minutes or until shrimp turn opaque. Drain in a colander.

STEP 3   In the same large saucepan combine spaghetti sauce, red wine, Worcestershire sauce, and hot pepper sauce. Bring to boiling. Stir in shrimp; heat through. Serve shrimp mixture over rice.

PER SERVING: 246 cal., 2 g total fat (0 g sat. fat), 129 mg chol., 657 mg sodium, 34 g carbo., 3 g fiber, 21 g pro.
EXCHANGES: 1 Vegetable, 2 Other Carbo., 3 Very Lean Meat

Shrimply Divine Pasta

START TO FINISH
25 MINUTES

MAKES
FOUR 1½-CUP SERVINGS

RECIPE PICTURED ON PAGE 140.

12   ounces fresh or frozen peeled and deveined medium shrimp
6   ounces dried mafalda (or other pasta)
1½   teaspoons bottled minced garlic (3 cloves)
1   tablespoon olive oil or cooking oil
2   tablespoons butter
2   tablespoons all-purpose flour
1   teaspoon dried basil, crushed
¼   teaspoon salt
⅛   teaspoon ground black pepper
2   cups half-and-half or light cream
4   cups packaged prewashed baby spinach or torn spinach
½   cup finely shredded Parmesan cheese (2 ounces)
    Freshly ground black pepper or crushed red pepper (optional)

STEP 1 Thaw shrimp, if frozen. Rinse shrimp; pat dry with paper towels. Cook pasta according to the package directions. Drain well; keep warm.

STEP 2 Meanwhile, for sauce, in a large skillet cook garlic in hot oil over medium-high heat for 15 seconds. Add shrimp. Cook and stir for 2 to 3 minutes or until shrimp turn opaque. Remove shrimp.

STEP 3 In the same skillet melt butter. Stir in flour, basil, salt, and the ⅛ teaspoon pepper. Stir in half-and-half. Cook and stir over medium heat until thickened and bubbly. Cook and stir for 1 minute more. Return shrimp to skillet and add spinach and cheese. Cook for 1 to 2 minutes more or until shrimp is heated through and spinach is wilted.

STEP 4 Toss shrimp mixture and pasta together. If desired, sprinkle with pepper.

PER SERVING: 550 cal., 28 g total fat (15 g sat. fat), 196 mg chol., 557 mg sodium, 43 g carbo., 2 g fiber, 32 g pro.
EXCHANGES: ½ Vegetable, 2½ Starch, 1 Lean Meat, 3 Fat

OFF THE SHELF TIP Save tons of time by using bottled minced garlic instead of mincing your own. Look for jars near the spices or in the produce section of your supermarket. Be sure to refrigerate after opening.

Saucy Shrimp over Polenta

LOW
FAT

START TO FINISH
25 MINUTES

MAKES
6 SERVINGS

18   fresh or frozen peeled and deveined cooked shrimp, tails removed (about 8 ounces)
1   16-ounce tube refrigerated cooked polenta, cut crosswise into 12 slices
1   tablespoon cooking oil
2   cups frozen whole kernel corn
1⅓ cups chopped roma tomato (4 medium)
3   tablespoons balsamic vinegar
1   teaspoon dried thyme, crushed
½   teaspoon ground cumin
¼   teaspoon salt

STEP 1   Thaw shrimp, if frozen. Rinse shrimp; pat dry with paper towels. Set aside. In a large skillet cook polenta slices in hot oil over medium heat for 5 to 8 minutes or until golden brown, turning once. Transfer to a serving platter; keep warm.

STEP 2   In the same large skillet combine frozen corn, tomato, balsamic vinegar, thyme, cumin, and salt. Cook and stir over medium heat about 5 minutes or until heated through. Stir in shrimp. Cook and stir until heated through.

STEP 3   Using a slotted spoon, spoon shrimp mixture over polenta slices.

PER SERVING: 196 cal., 3 g total fat (1 g sat. fat), 74 mg chol., 483 mg sodium, 30 g carbo., 4 g fiber, 12 g pro.
EXCHANGES: ½ Vegetable, 2 Starch, 1 Very Lean Meat

OFF THE SHELF TIP   Refrigerated tubes of polenta are typically located in the produce section of your supermarket. You can slice and fry it, crumble it, or even follow the package directions to reconstitute into cornmeal mush.

Spanish-Style Rice with Seafood

A package of Spanish-flavored rice is the base for this skillet-based quick dish of peas, chopped tomatoes, ready-to-go shrimp, and a spritz of hot sauce.

L O W
F A T

START TO FINISH
25 MINUTES

MAKES
4 SERVINGS

1	5.6- to 6.2-ounce package Spanish-style rice mix
1¾	cups water
1	tablespoon butter or margarine
	Several dashes bottled hot pepper sauce
1	12-ounce package frozen peeled, deveined shrimp
1	cup frozen peas
½	cup chopped tomato (1 medium)

STEP 1 In a large skillet stir together rice mix, water, butter, and hot pepper sauce. Bring to boiling; reduce heat. Cover and simmer for 5 minutes.

STEP 2 Stir frozen shrimp into rice mixture. Return to boiling; reduce heat. Cover and simmer for 2 to 3 minutes more or until shrimp turn opaque. Remove from heat. Stir in peas. Cover and let stand for 10 minutes. Sprinkle with chopped tomato before serving.

PER SERVING: 282 cal., 5 g total fat (2 g sat. fat), 137 mg chol., 897 mg sodium, 36 g carbo., 3 g fiber, 23 g pro.
EXCHANGES: 2½ Starch, 2½ Very Lean Meat

OFF THE SHELF TIP Bottled hot pepper sauce is found in the condiment aisle of the supermarket. You can choose from mild to over-the-top hot.

Thai Shrimp & Sesame Noodles

Pad Thai lovers will be back for seconds of this dish. Yum! If shrimp's not your thing, swap it out for strips of chicken breasts.

PREP
30 MINUTES

COOK
10 MINUTES

MAKES
4 SERVINGS

1¾ pounds fresh or frozen medium shrimp

½ cup bottled Italian vinaigrette salad dressing

2 tablespoons chunky peanut butter

1 tablespoon soy sauce

1 tablespoon honey

1 teaspoon grated fresh ginger

½ teaspoon crushed red pepper

2 teaspoons toasted sesame oil

1 8-ounce package dried capellini or angel hair pasta

1 tablespoon cooking oil

1 cup bias-sliced carrot (2 medium)

6 green onions, cut into 1-inch pieces

2 tablespoons snipped fresh cilantro

¼ cup chopped peanuts (optional)

STEP 1 Thaw shrimp, if frozen. Peel and devein shrimp. Rinse shrimp; pat dry with paper towels. Set aside. In a small bowl combine salad dressing, peanut butter, soy sauce, honey, ginger, red pepper, and sesame oil; set aside.

STEP 2 Cook pasta according to package directions; drain. Keep warm.

STEP 3 Meanwhile, pour cooking oil into a wok or large skillet. Preheat over medium-high heat. Stir-fry carrot and green onion about 3 minutes or until crisp-tender. Remove vegetables from wok. Add shrimp, half at a time, to wok. Stir-fry for 1 to 2 minutes or until shrimp turn opaque. Add the dressing mixture to the wok. Cook and stir until heated through. Return all of the shrimp and the vegetables to the wok. Cook and stir until heated through. Add cooked pasta; toss to combine.

STEP 4 Transfer mixture to a serving bowl. Sprinkle with cilantro and, if desired, peanuts.

PER SERVING: 656 cal., 29 g total fat (3 g sat. fat), 226 mg chol., 634 mg sodium, 56 g carbo., 4 g fiber, 41 g pro.
EXCHANGES: 3 Starch, 1 Other Carbo., 5 Very Lean Meat, 4 Fat

OFF THE SHELF TIP Bottled dressings aren't just good for topping your salads. Grab a bottle from your supermarket and use to marinate meats or vegetables or drizzle over finished dishes for an extra pop of flavor.

Cajun Shrimp & Rice

Plop these ingredients in the slow cooker before heading out—set the table before you go—and this sassy meal will be waiting when you return. Open your favorite beverage, then put up your feet and enjoy dinner.

PREP
20 MINUTES
COOK
5 TO 6 HOURS (LOW) OR
3 TO 3½ HOURS (HIGH)
PLUS 15 MINUTES (HIGH)
MAKES
6 SERVINGS

1	28-ounce can diced tomatoes, undrained
1	14-ounce can chicken broth
1	cup chopped onion (1 large)
1	cup chopped green sweet pepper (1 large)
1	6-ounce package long grain and wild rice mix
¼	cup water
1	teaspoon bottled minced garlic (2 cloves)
½	teaspoon Cajun seasoning
1	pound cooked peeled and deveined shrimp
	Bottled hot pepper sauce (optional)

STEP 1 In a 3½- or 4-quart slow cooker combine undrained tomatoes, broth, onion, sweet pepper, uncooked rice mix with seasoning packet, water, garlic, and Cajun seasoning.

STEP 2 Cover and cook on low-heat setting for 5 to 6 hours or on high-heat setting for 3 to 3½ hours.

STEP 3 If using low-heat setting, turn slow cooker to high-heat setting. Stir shrimp into rice mixture. Cover and cook for 15 minutes more. If desired, pass hot pepper sauce.

PER SERVING: 223 cal., 2 g total fat (0 g sat. fat), 147 mg chol., 1,063 mg sodium, 32 g carbo., 3 g fiber, 21 g pro.
EXCHANGES: 1 Vegetable, 2 Starch, 2 Very Lean Meat

OFF THE SHELF TIP Frozen peeled and deveined cooked shrimp can shave a lot of time off recipe preparation.

Crab Cakes with Red Pepper Relish

Crab cakes are traditional on the coast. This simple-to-make version features a simple red pepper relish complement—a fresh alternative to mayo-based seasoning.

PREP

35 MINUTES

BAKE

12 MINUTES

OVEN

450°F

MAKES

4 SERVINGS

1	egg, slightly beaten
1	cup soft bread crumbs (1⅓ slices)
3	tablespoons mayonnaise or salad dressing
2	tablespoons thinly sliced green onion (1)
1	tablespoon snipped fresh dill or 1 teaspoon dried dill
1	teaspoon seafood seasoning
¼	teaspoon ground black pepper
1	16-ounce can pasteurized crabmeat or two 6.5-ounce cans crabmeat, drained, flaked, and cartilage removed
3	tablespoons fine dry bread crumbs
2	teaspoons cooking oil
1	recipe Red Pepper Relish

STEP 1 Preheat oven to 450°F. For crab cakes, in a medium bowl combine egg, soft bread crumbs, mayonnaise, green onion, dill, seafood seasoning, and pepper. Stir in crabmeat. Divide mixture into 8 portions. Moisten hands and form each portion into a 2½-inch patty.

STEP 2 Place crab cakes in a greased shallow baking pan. In a small bowl combine dry bread crumbs and oil; sprinkle over crab cakes, pressing to stick.

STEP 3 Bake, uncovered, in the preheated oven for 12 to 15 minutes or until light brown. (Or in a 12-inch skillet cook crab cakes in 2 tablespoons hot oil over medium-high heat for 5 to 6 minutes or until brown, turning once halfway through cooking. Add additional oil if necessary. Drain on paper towels.) Serve crab cakes with Red Pepper Relish.

RED PEPPER RELISH: In a small bowl stir together half of a 7-ounce jar roasted red sweet peppers, drained and chopped; 1 tablespoon drained, chopped oil-packed dried tomatoes; and ¼ teaspoon seafood seasoning.

MAKE-AHEAD DIRECTIONS: Prepare crab cakes as above through Step 1. Cover and refrigerate for up to 24 hours. To serve, continue as directed in Steps 2 and 3.

PER SERVING: 261 cal., 18 g total fat (3 g sat. fat), 147 mg chol., 429 mg sodium, 9 g carbo., 1 g fiber, 16 g pro.
EXCHANGES: ½ Starch, 2 Very Lean Meat, 3 Fat

OFF THE SHELF TIP Don't look for seasoned bread crumbs in the bread section of your supermarket. Instead, try the packaged goods section, near stuffing mixes and mac 'n' cheese.

Rockefeller-Style Crab

EASY

PREP
15 MINUTES

BAKE
30 MINUTES

OVEN
400°F

MAKES
4 SERVINGS

2   12-ounce packages frozen spinach soufflé, thawed
2   6.5-ounce cans refrigerated, pasteurized crabmeat, drained and broken into large flakes
2   cups packaged herb-seasoned stuffing mix
¼   teaspoon bottled hot pepper sauce
2   tablespoons butter, melted

STEP 1 Preheat oven to 400°F. In a large bowl combine thawed spinach soufflé, crabmeat, 1½ cups of the dry stuffing mix, and the hot pepper sauce. Spread in an ungreased 1-quart au gratin dish.

STEP 2 In a small bowl combine remaining ½ cup dry stuffing mix and the melted butter; sprinkle over spinach mixture.

STEP 3 Bake in the preheated oven about 30 minutes or until hot.

PER SERVING: 433 cal., 20 g total fat (7 g sat. fat), 263 mg chol., 1,516 mg sodium, 36 g carbo., 3 g fiber, 27 g pro.
EXCHANGES: ½ Vegetable, 2 Starch, 3 Lean Meat, 2 Fat

OFF THE SHELF TIP Bottled hot pepper sauce is found in the condiment aisle of the supermarket. You can choose from mild to over-the-top hot.

Meatless Meals

Savory Beans & Rice

This quickly assembled slow-cooker dish is a hearty staple of Cajun cuisine—so of course it includes a bit of hot sauce kick. Brown rice is a variety that's processed very little and consequently chock-full of nutritional elements.

PREP
20 MINUTES

STAND
1 HOUR

COOK
9 TO 10 HOURS (LOW)
OR 4 TO 5 HOURS (HIGH)
PLUS 30 MINUTES

MAKES
5 SERVINGS

1¼   **cups dry red beans or dry red kidney beans**
1   **cup chopped onion (1 large)**
¾   **cup sliced celery**
1   **teaspoon bottled minced garlic (2 cloves)**
½   **of a vegetable bouillon cube**
1   **teaspoon dried basil, crushed**
1   **bay leaf**
1¼   **cups water**
1¼   **cups uncooked brown rice**
1   **14.5-ounce can stewed tomatoes, undrained**
1   **4-ounce can diced green chile peppers, drained**
     Few dashes bottled hot pepper sauce

STEP 1   Rinse beans; place in a large saucepan. Add enough water to cover beans by 2 inches. Bring to boiling; reduce heat. Simmer for 10 minutes. Remove from heat. Cover and let stand for 1 hour. (Or place beans in water in a large saucepan. Cover; let soak in a cool place overnight.) Drain and rinse beans.

STEP 2   In a 3½- or 4-quart slow cooker combine beans, onion, celery, garlic, bouillon, basil, and bay leaf. Pour the 1¼ cups water over all.

STEP 3   Cover and cook on low-heat setting for 9 to 10 hours or on high-heat setting for 4 to 5 hours.

STEP 4   Cook brown rice according to package directions; keep warm. Remove

bay leaf from bean mixture; discard. Stir undrained tomatoes, drained chile peppers, and hot pepper sauce into cooked beans. Cover and cook 30 minutes more. Serve bean mixture over hot cooked rice.

PER SERVING: 383 cal., 3 g total fat (0 g sat. fat), 0 mg chol., 406 mg sodium, 74 g carbo., 10 g fiber, 16 g pro.
EXCHANGES: 1 Vegetable, 4½ Starch

OFF THE SHELF TIP Look for canned green chiles in the Mexican section of your supermarket. They come whole and diced as well as mild and hot.

Sweet Beans & Noodles

EASY

START TO FINISH
30 MINUTES

MAKES
4 SERVINGS

8   ounces dried linguine
1½   cups frozen green soybeans
        (shelled edamame)
1   cup purchased shredded carrot
1   10-ounce container refrigerated
        Alfredo pasta sauce
2   teaspoons snipped fresh rosemary

STEP 1   Cook the linguine according to package directions, adding the soybeans and carrot for the last 10 minutes of cooking. Drain and return to pan.

STEP 2   Add Alfredo sauce and rosemary to linguine mixture in pan; toss to combine. Heat through.

PER SERVING: 544 cal., 27 g total fat (1 g sat. fat), 35 mg chol., 280 mg sodium, 57 g carbo., 5 g fiber, 20 g pro.
EXCHANGES: 3½ Starch, 1 Very Lean Meat, 5 Fat

OFF THE SHELF TIP Refrigerated pasta sauce comes in a wide variety of flavors, including Alfredo and tomato-based sauces. They are fabulous convenience products, but note that their shelf life is shorter than their jarred counterparts.

CLEAR YOUR CLUTTERED PANTRY
No doubt there's plenty in there that's collecting dust. Divide what's in your pantry into two boxes, leaving in place, of course items that you're actively using. BOX 1—Toss. Fill it with items you'll never use, expired items, age-old spices. BOX 2—Hmmm. Fill this box with still-good items that you might use if you knew how. Toss box 1 out with the trash; put box 2 where you can peruse its contents if needed. After a month or two, if it still has items in it but you aren't going to use them, donate the items to a shelter.

Black Bean & Corn Quesadillas

EASY

START TO FINISH
20 MINUTES

OVEN
300°F

MAKES
4 SERVINGS

1   8-ounce package shredded Mexican cheese blend (2 cups)

8   8-inch flour tortillas

1½   cups bottled black bean and corn salsa

1   medium avocado, seeded, peeled, and chopped

     Dairy sour cream

STEP 1   Preheat oven to 300°F. Divide cheese evenly among tortillas, sprinkling cheese over half of each tortilla. Top cheese on each tortilla with 1 tablespoon of the salsa. Divide avocado among tortillas. Fold tortillas in half, pressing gently.

STEP 2   Heat a large skillet over medium-high heat for 2 minutes; reduce heat to medium. Cook 2 of the quesadillas for 2 to 3 minutes or until light brown and cheese is melted, turning once. Remove quesadillas from skillet; place on a baking sheet. Keep warm in preheated oven. Repeat with remaining quesadillas, cooking 2 at a time.

STEP 3   Cut quesadillas into wedges. Serve with sour cream and the remaining 1 cup salsa.

PER SERVING: 512 cal., 33 g total fat (14 g sat. fat), 55 mg chol., 940 mg sodium, 38 g carbo., 4 g fiber, 18 g pro.
EXCHANGES: ½ Vegetable, 2 Starch, 2 Medium-Fat Meat, 4 Fat

OFF THE SHELF TIP Flour tortillas come in a wide array of flavors, sizes, and colors. Keep opened bags of tortillas in the refrigerator and watch their expiration date. They can be frozen for up to 3 months.

Chipotle Bean Enchiladas

PREP
25 MINUTES

BAKE
40 MINUTES

OVEN
350°F

MAKES
5 SERVINGS

10   6-inch corn tortillas

1   15-ounce can pinto beans or black beans, rinsed and drained

1   tablespoon chopped chipotle pepper in adobo sauce

1   8-ounce package shredded Mexican cheese blend (2 cups)

2   10-ounce cans enchilada sauce

STEP 1   Preheat oven to 350°F. Grease a 2-quart rectangular baking dish; set aside. Stack the tortillas and wrap tightly in foil. Warm tortillas in the preheated oven for 10 minutes.

STEP 2   Meanwhile, for filling, in a medium bowl combine drained beans, chipotle pepper, 1 cup of the cheese, and ½ cup of the enchilada sauce. Spoon about ¼ cup of the filling onto 1 edge of each tortilla. Starting at the edge with the filling, roll up each tortilla.

STEP 3   Arrange tortillas, seam sides down, in the prepared baking dish. Top with remaining enchilada sauce. Cover with foil.

STEP 4   Bake in the 350° oven about 25 minutes or until heated through. Remove foil. Sprinkle with remaining 1 cup cheese. Bake, uncovered, about 5 minutes or until cheese melts.

PER SERVING: 487 cal., 19 g total fat (8 g sat. fat), 40 mg chol., 1,091 mg sodium, 63 g carbo., 14 g fiber, 23 g pro.
EXCHANGES: 4 Starch, 1½ Lean Meat, 2 Fat

OFF THE SHELF TIP Fetch cans of chipotle peppers in adobo sauce—dried and smoked jalapeño peppers in a tangy sauce of vinegar, pepper, and chiles—from the ethnic section of your supermarket. Take care when chopping them because they contain volatile oils that can burn your skin and eyes.

Cajun Beans on Corn Bread

Beans and tomatoes cook with onion and hot pepper sauce to meld the flavors. The mix mounds on top of corn bread and gets a sprinkle of cheese.

EASY

PREP
10 MINUTES

BAKE
20 MINUTES

MAKES
4 SERVINGS

1	8.5-ounce package corn muffin mix
¾	cup chopped green sweet pepper (1 medium)
1	tablespoon cooking oil
1	15- to 16-ounce can Great Northern beans, rinsed and drained
1	14.5-ounce can diced tomatoes with garlic and onion, undrained
1	teaspoon instant chicken bouillon granules
¼	teaspoon ground black pepper
¼	to ½ teaspoon bottled hot pepper sauce
½	cup shredded cheddar cheese (2 ounces)

STEP 1 Prepare corn muffin mix according to package directions for corn bread. Cool slightly.

STEP 2 Meanwhile, in a medium saucepan cook sweet pepper in hot oil over medium heat just until tender. Add drained beans, undrained tomatoes, bouillon granules, black pepper, and hot pepper sauce. Bring to boiling; reduce heat. Cover and simmer for 10 minutes.

STEP 3 Cut corn bread into 4 portions and place on dinner plates or in shallow bowls. Spoon bean mixture over corn bread. Sprinkle with cheese.

PER SERVING: 485 cal., 17 g total fat (4 g sat. fat), 70 mg chol., 1,563 mg sodium, 68 g carbo., 6 g fiber, 17 g pro.
EXCHANGES: 1 Vegetable, 4 Starch, ½ Medium-Fat Meat, 2 Fat

OFF THE SHELF TIP Find packaged corn muffin mix in the baking aisle of your supermarket. Unopened boxes will last up to a year.

Barley & Green Bean Skillet

1	14-ounce can vegetable broth
⅓	cup water
1¼	cups quick-cooking barley
2	cups frozen cut green beans
1	10.75-ounce can condensed cream of onion soup
½	cup packaged shredded carrot
½	cup milk
½	teaspoon dried thyme, crushed
1	cup shredded sharp cheddar cheese (4 ounces)

OFF THE SHELF TIP Grab a can from the soup section. Just make sure your choice is condensed, not ready-to-serve.

START TO FINISH
30 MINUTES
MAKES
4 SERVINGS

STEP 1 In a large skillet bring broth and the water to boiling. Stir in barley. Return to boiling; reduce heat. Cover and simmer for 5 minutes.

STEP 2 Stir in frozen green beans, soup, carrot, milk, and thyme. Bring to boiling; reduce heat. Cover and simmer for 12 to 15 minutes more or until barley is tender and most of the liquid is absorbed, stirring occasionally. Stir in ½ cup of the cheese.

STEP 3 Sprinkle with remaining ½ cup cheese. Let stand for 2 to 3 minutes or until cheese is melted.

PER SERVING: 394 cal., 15 g total fat (8 g sat. fat), ⊄5 mg chol., 1,193 mg sodium, 52 g carbo., 8 g fiber, 16 g pro.
EXCHANGES: ½ Vegetable, 3½ Starch, 1 Medium-Fat Meat, 1 Fat

Curried Lentils & Spinach

Lentils combine with curry, soup, and spinach to yield a complex and satisfying meal. Hot cooked rice makes a good complement; you could also choose couscous or corn bread.

LOW FAT

PREP
25 MINUTES

COOK
35 MINUTES

MAKES
6 SERVINGS

1   tablespoon butter or margarine
1   cup chopped red sweet pepper (1 large)
1   cup chopped onion (1 large)
1½   teaspoons bottled minced garlic (3 cloves)
2   14-ounce cans vegetable broth
1½   cups dry brown lentils, rinsed and drained
¼   cup water
2   teaspoons curry powder
¼   teaspoon ground black pepper
1   10.75-ounce can condensed tomato soup
1   6-ounce package prewashed baby spinach
2   cups hot cooked rice

OFF THE SHELF TIP Save tons of time by using bottled minced garlic instead of mincing your own. Look for jars near the spices or in the produce section of your supermarket. Be sure to refrigerate after opening.

STEP 1   In a large saucepan melt butter over medium heat. Add sweet pepper, onion, and garlic; cook for 3 to 4 minutes or just until vegetables are tender.

STEP 2   Stir in broth, lentils, water, curry powder, and black pepper. Bring to boiling; reduce heat. Cover and simmer for 30 to 40 minutes or until lentils are tender and most of the liquid is absorbed, stirring occasionally.

STEP 3   Stir in soup; heat through. Gradually stir in spinach until wilted. Serve with hot cooked rice.

PER SERVING: 353 cal., 4 g total fat (2 g sat. fat), 5 mg chol., 895 mg sodium, 63 g carbo., 19 g fiber, 19 g pro.
EXCHANGES: 1 Vegetable, 4 Starch, 1 Very Lean Meat

Ravioli Skillet Lasagna

Cheese-filled ravioli is the quick and easy route to a lasagna-like casserole that's a family pleaser.

START TO FINISH
25 MINUTES

MAKES
4 SERVINGS

RECIPE PICTURED ON PAGE **140.**

2 cups bottled light chunky-style spaghetti sauce
⅓ cup water
1 9-ounce package refrigerated or frozen cheese-filled ravioli
1 egg
1 15-ounce carton ricotta cheese
¼ cup grated Romano or Parmesan cheese (1 ounce)
1 10-ounce package frozen chopped spinach, thawed and well drained
Grated Romano or Parmesan cheese

OFF THE SHELF TIP Refrigerated pasta comes in a wide variety of shapes and flavors, from cheese- and/or meat-filled ravioli to strands of linguine and fettuccine. It is a fabulous convenience product but note that its shelf life is shorter than its dried counterpart.

STEP 1 In a 10-inch skillet combine spaghetti sauce and the water. Bring to boiling. Stir in the ravioli. Cover and cook over medium heat about 5 minutes or until ravioli are nearly tender, stirring once to prevent sticking.

STEP 2 Meanwhile, in a medium bowl beat egg with a fork. Stir in ricotta cheese and the ¼ cup Romano cheese. Dot ravioli with spinach. Spoon ricotta mixture on top of spinach. Cover and cook over low heat about 10 minutes or until ricotta layer is set and pasta is just tender. Sprinkle individual servings with additional Romano cheese.

PER SERVING: 433 cal., 14 g total fat (3 g sat. fat), 131 mg chol., 501 mg sodium, 49 g carbo., 3 g fiber, 36 g pro.
EXCHANGES: 1 Vegetable, 2 Starch, 1 Other Carbo., 3½ Lean Meat

Pasta with Pepper-Cheese Sauce

What pasta shape catches your fancy? Toss it with roasted red peppers and shredded Monterey Jack cheese.

START TO FINISH
25 MINUTES

MAKES
4 TO 6 SERVINGS

8   ounces dried medium shell, mostaccioli, or cut ziti pasta
1   0.9- to 1.25-ounce envelope hollandaise sauce mix
1   7-ounce jar roasted red sweet peppers, drained and chopped
½   cup shredded Monterey Jack cheese with jalapeño chile peppers (2 ounces)

STEP 1 Cook pasta according to package directions; drain well. Return pasta to pan. Cover and keep warm.

STEP 2 Meanwhile, prepare hollandaise sauce according to package directions, except use only 2 tablespoons butter. Stir in roasted sweet peppers. Remove pan from heat. Add cheese to sauce, stirring until cheese melts. Add sauce to pasta in pan; toss to coat.

PER SERVING: 384 cal., 13 g total fat (8 g sat. fat), 36 mg chol., 407 mg sodium, 53 g carbo., 2 g fiber, 13 g pro.
EXCHANGES: ½ Vegetable, 3 Starch, ½ High-Fat Meat, 2 Fat

OFF THE SHELF TIP Roasted red sweet peppers are found in the condiment aisle of your supermarket. They are easy to make at home but why take the time when jars are so easy to snap up?

Linguine with Gorgonzola Sauce

Looking for the perfect simple meal to enjoy with fresh asparagus? Here it is! Light cream and Gorgonzola coat the linguine-asparagus medley sprinkled with toasted nuts.

FAST

START TO FINISH
20 MINUTES

MAKES
4 SERVINGS

1 9-ounce package refrigerated linguine
1 pound fresh asparagus, trimmed and cut into 1-inch pieces, or one 10-ounce package frozen cut asparagus
1 cup half-and-half or light cream
1 cup crumbled Gorgonzola or blue cheese (4 ounces)
¼ teaspoon salt
2 tablespoons chopped walnuts, toasted

STEP 1 Cook linguine and asparagus in same pot according to package directions for the linguine; drain. Return linguine and asparagus to pan.

STEP 2 Meanwhile, for sauce, in a medium saucepan combine half-and-half, ¾ cup of the Gorgonzola cheese, and the salt. Bring to boiling over medium heat; reduce heat. Simmer, uncovered, for 3 minutes, stirring frequently.

STEP 3 Pour sauce over linguine mixture; toss gently to coat. Transfer to a warm serving dish. Sprinkle with the remaining ¼ cup Gorgonzola cheese and the walnuts.

PER SERVING: 399 cal., 20 g total fat (11 g sat. fat), 111 mg chol., 590 mg sodium, 39 g carbo., 3 g fiber, 18 g pro.
EXCHANGES: 1 Vegetable, 2½ Starch, 1 High-Fat Meat, 2 Fat

OFF THE SHELF TIP Refrigerated pasta comes in a wide variety of shapes and flavors from cheese- and/or meat-filled ravioli to strands of linguine and fettuccine. It is a fabulous convenience product but note that its shelf life is shorter than its dried counterpart.

Fettuccine-Vegetable Toss

START TO FINISH
20 MINUTES

MAKES
4 SERVINGS

RECIPE PICTURED ON PAGE 139.

1   9-ounce package refrigerated spinach fettuccine
1   tablespoon olive oil
2   tablespoons chopped green onion (1)
2   cups chopped red and/or yellow tomatoes (4 medium)
½   cup finely chopped carrot (1 medium)
¼   cup oil-packed dried tomato, drained and snipped
½   cup crumbled garlic-and-herb feta cheese, peppercorn feta cheese, or plain feta cheese (2 ounces)

STEP 1   Cook pasta according to package directions; drain well. Return to hot pan; cover and keep warm.

STEP 2   Meanwhile, in a large skillet heat oil over medium heat. Add green onion; cook for 30 seconds. Stir in fresh tomato, carrot, and dried tomato. Cover and cook for 5 minutes, stirring once. Spoon tomato mixture over cooked pasta. Sprinkle with feta cheese; toss gently.

PER SERVING: 311 cal., 11 g total fat (4 g sat. fat), 73 mg chol., 250 mg sodium, 44 g carbo., 2 g fiber, 13 g pro.
EXCHANGES: ½ Vegetable, 3 Starch, 1½ Fat

OFF THE SHELF TIP   Sun-dried tomatoes are typically found in the produce section of the supermarket near the bottled minced garlic. In some stores, look for them in the vegetable aisle.

Saucy Pizza Skillet Dinner

START TO FINISH
30 MINUTES

MAKES
4 SERVINGS

1   6.4-ounce package lasagna dinner mix
3   cups water
1   4-ounce can (drained weight) mushroom stems and pieces, undrained
½   cup chopped green sweet pepper
½   cup sliced, pitted ripe olives (optional)
½   cup shredded mozzarella cheese (2 ounces)

OFF THE SHELF TIP Look for canned mushrooms in the canned vegetable aisle of your supermarket. You can buy them whole or sliced.

STEP 1   If the noodles in the dinner mix are large, break them into bite-size pieces. In a large skillet combine noodles and seasoning from dinner mix, the water, undrained mushrooms, and sweet pepper.

STEP 2   Bring to boiling, stirring occasionally; reduce heat. Cover and simmer about 13 minutes or until pasta is tender. Uncover and cook for 2 to 3 minutes more or until sauce is of desired consistency.

STEP 3   If desired, sprinkle with olives. Top with cheese. Remove from heat; let stand for 1 to 2 minutes or until cheese melts.

PER SERVING: 318 cal., 14 g total fat (5 g sat. fat), 28 mg chol., 1,774 mg sodium, 37 g carbo., 3 g fiber, 14 g pro.
EXCHANGES: ½ Vegetable, 2 Starch, 1 Medium-Fat Meat, 1½ Fat

Mediterranean Alfredo Pizza

This gourmet pizza—topped with creamy Alfredo sauce, fresh spinach, mushrooms, and artichoke hearts—breaks all the rules that pizza must be flavored with tomato-based sauce.

L O W
F A T

PREP
20 MINUTES

BAKE
15 MINUTES

OVEN
425°F

MAKES
6 TO 8 SERVINGS

**RECIPE PICTURED
ON PAGE 143.**

1	16-ounce loaf frozen whole wheat or white bread dough, thawed
⅓	cup refrigerated Alfredo sauce
8	to 10 fresh spinach leaves
1	cup fresh mushrooms, sliced (about 3 ounces)
1	small tomato, thinly sliced
4	canned marinated artichoke hearts, quartered or sliced
1½	teaspoons snipped fresh oregano or ½ teaspoon dried oregano, crushed
1½	cups shredded mozzarella cheese (6 ounces)

STEP 1   Preheat oven to 425°F. On a lightly floured surface, roll bread dough to a 12-inch circle, building edge up slightly. Transfer crust to a greased 12-inch pizza pan or baking sheet.

STEP 2   Spread the crust with Alfredo sauce. Arrange spinach leaves over sauce; sprinkle with mushrooms. Arrange tomato slices and artichoke hearts over mushrooms. Sprinkle with oregano; top with mozzarella cheese. Bake in the preheated oven for 15 to 20 minutes or until cheese is bubbly around edges.

EASY MEDITERRANEAN ALFREDO PIZZA: Substitute one 16-ounce (12-inch) purchased Italian bread shell for the frozen bread dough. Place bread shell on a greased baking sheet. Spread shell with Alfredo sauce and arrange toppings as directed above. Bake in a preheated 400°F oven for 12 to 15 minutes or until crust is golden and toppings are hot.

PER SERVING: 270 cal., 12 g total fat (4 g sat. fat), 28 mg chol., 384 mg sodium, 29 g carbo., 2 g fiber, 11 g pro.
EXCHANGES: ½ Vegetable, 2 Starch, 1 Medium-Fat Meat, ½ Fat

OFF THE SHELF TIP Found in the freezer section, this bread is ready to thaw, shape, and bake. You can find it in whole wheat and white varieties.

Spinach Calzones

This is a splendid way to enjoy your spinach. It's blended with Parmesan, mozzarella, and pizza sauce, then folded into a pizza dough crust for a hot, hearty dinnertime treat.

PREP
30 MINUTES
BAKE
10 MINUTES
OVEN
450°F
MAKES
4 SERVINGS

1	10-ounce package frozen chopped spinach
2	eggs
1	8-ounce can pizza sauce
¼	cup grated Parmesan cheese
1	teaspoon dried basil, crushed
⅛	teaspoon garlic powder
1	10- or 13.8-ounce package refrigerated pizza dough
1	cup shredded mozzarella cheese (4 ounces)
	Cooking oil
1	tablespoon grated Parmesan cheese

STEP 1 Cook spinach according to package directions. Drain, squeezing out excess liquid. In a medium bowl beat eggs with a fork. Stir in spinach, ¼ cup of the pizza sauce, the ¼ cup Parmesan cheese, the basil, and garlic powder.

STEP 2 Preheat oven to 450°F. Grease baking sheet; set aside. Unroll refrigerated pizza dough. On a lightly floured surface, press dough into a 15×10-inch rectangle. Cut into quarters. Divide mozzarella cheese among pizza dough quarters, sprinkling onto one half of each quarter. Spoon spinach mixture evenly over cheese. Fold dough over mixture. Seal edges. Place on prepared baking sheet. Brush with oil. Sprinkle with the 1 tablespoon Parmesan cheese. Cut small slits in top of each calzone.

STEP 3 Bake in preheated oven for 10 to 15 minutes or until golden. Meanwhile, in a small saucepan cook and stir remaining pizza sauce until heated through. Serve warmed pizza sauce with calzones.

PER SERVING: 378 cal., 16 g total fat (6 g sat. fat), 136 mg chol., 1,120 mg sodium, 35 g carbo., 3 g fiber, 22 g pro.
EXCHANGES: 1 Vegetable, 2 Starch, 2 Medium-Fat Meat, 1 Fat

OFF THE SHELF TIP Bottled dressings aren't just good for topping your salads. Grab a bottle from your supermarket and use to marinate meats or vegetables or drizzle over finished dishes for an extra pop of flavor.

Minestrone

START TO FINISH

25 MINUTES

MAKES

8 SERVINGS

3　14-ounce cans chicken broth or vegetable broth

2　14.5-ounce cans stewed tomatoes, undrained

1　15-ounce can white kidney (cannellini) beans, rinsed and drained

1　15-ounce can garbanzo beans (chickpeas), rinsed and drained

1　6-ounce can tomato paste

2　teaspoons dried Italian seasoning, crushed

2　cups frozen mixed vegetables (such as Italian blend)

2　cups fresh spinach leaves, cut into strips

2　cups cooked medium pasta (such as medium shell macaroni or mostaccioli)
　　Finely shredded Parmesan cheese (optional)

STEP 1 In a 4-quart Dutch oven combine broth, undrained tomatoes, white kidney beans, garbanzo beans, tomato paste, and Italian seasoning. Bring to boiling; add mixed vegetables. Reduce heat. Cover and simmer about 10 minutes or until vegetables are tender.

STEP 2 Stir in spinach and cooked pasta; heat through. If desired, sprinkle with Parmesan cheese.

MAKE-AHEAD DIRECTIONS: Prepare Minestrone as directed in Step 1. Cover and refrigerate for up to 24 hours. To serve, reheat soup over medium heat and continue with Step 2.

PER SERVING: 219 cal., 2 g total fat (0 g sat. fat), 2 mg chol., 1,081 mg sodium, 41 g carbo., 8 g fiber, 12 g pro.
EXCHANGES: 2 Vegetable, 2 Starch

OFF THE SHELF TIP Look for packaged spinach that has been prewashed. You'll save the step of rinsing the sand out of the spinach leaves. You'll find it with the packaged salad green mixes.

Mediterranean Couscous with Tofu

Olives take this fast, savory dish to the sunny sea. Serve it on colorful dishes, put your sandals on, and you'll feel the sun with each bite.

LOW FAT **FAST**

START TO FINISH
15 MINUTES
MAKES
4 SERVINGS

1   5.7-ounce package curry-flavored or roasted garlic and olive oil–flavored couscous mix
½   of a 12- to 16-ounce package extra-firm tofu (fresh bean curd), well drained
1   tablespoon olive oil
½   cup sliced, pitted ripe olives or sliced, pitted Greek black olives
½   cup crumbled feta cheese or finely shredded Parmesan cheese (2 ounces)

OFF THE SHELF TIP   When buying tofu, check the label to be certain you are purchasing the correct product. Tofu comes soft, firm, and extra-firm. The firm and extra-firm are better choices for stir-frying and other cooking.

STEP 1   Prepare couscous according to package directions, except omit oil. Meanwhile, cut tofu into ½-inch cubes. Pat tofu dry with paper towels.

STEP 2   In a large skillet heat oil over medium-high heat. Add tofu; stir-fry for 5 to 7 minutes or until tofu is light brown. Stir tofu and olives into couscous. Transfer to a serving dish. Sprinkle with cheese.

PER SERVING: 259 cal., 10 g total fat (4 g sat. fat), 17 mg chol., 763 mg sodium, 33 g carbo., 3 g fiber, 11 g pro.
EXCHANGES: 2 Starch, 1 Medium-Fat Meat, ½ Fat

Asian Noodle Bowl

EASY

START TO FINISH
25 MINUTES

MAKES
4 SERVINGS

8   ounces dried buckwheat soba noodles, udon noodles, or vermicelli noodles

2   cups vegetable broth

½   cup bottled peanut sauce

2   cups frozen Chinese-style stir-fry vegetables with seasonings

½   cup dry roasted peanuts, chopped

STEP 1 Cook the noodles according to package directions. Drain noodles but do not rinse. Set aside. In the same saucepan combine vegetable broth and peanut sauce. Bring to boiling. Stir in frozen vegetables and cooked noodles. Return to boiling; reduce heat. Simmer for 2 to 3 minutes or until vegetables are heated through.

STEP 2 Divide noodles and broth among 4 bowls. Sprinkle with peanuts.

PER SERVING: 403 cal., 15 g total fat (2 g sat. fat), 0 mg chol., 1,326 mg sodium, 59 g carbo., 4 g fiber, 15 g pro.
EXCHANGES: ½ Vegetable, 3 Starch, 1 Other Carbo., 2½ Fat

OFF THE SHELF TIP Look for bottled peanut sauce in the ethnic section of your supermarket. Some stores stock it in the produce section. It makes a fun sauce for dipping egg rolls, wontons, and other Asian appetizers.

Brunch Casserole

Hash brown potatoes, meatless links, and vegetables slow cook to yield a savory casserole to rival the flavor complexity of any egg-and-sausage version.

PREP
15 MINUTES

COOK
5 TO 6 HOURS (LOW) OR
2½ TO 3 HOURS (HIGH)

STAND
15 MINUTES

MAKES
6 TO 8 SERVINGS

Nonstick cooking spray

1   8- to 10-ounce package meatless breakfast links

1   10.75-ounce can condensed cream of potato soup

⅔   cup milk

2   teaspoons Worcestershire or steak sauce

¼   teaspoon ground black pepper

1   28-ounce package loose-pack frozen diced hash brown potatoes with onions and peppers, thawed

1   10-ounce package frozen broccoli, cauliflower, and carrots in cheese sauce, thawed

½   cup shredded cheddar cheese (2 ounces)

STEP 1   Lightly coat a 3½- or 4-quart slow cooker with nonstick cooking spray. Brown sausage according to package directions; cool slightly. Slice links into ½-inch pieces; set aside.

STEP 2   In the slow cooker combine soup, milk, Worcestershire sauce, and pepper. Stir in potatoes, vegetables with cheese sauce, and sausage pieces.

STEP 3   Cover and cook on low-heat setting for 5 to 6 hours or on high-heat setting for 2½ to 3 hours. Turn off cooker. Sprinkle mixture with cheddar cheese. Cover and let stand for 15 minutes before serving.

PER SERVING: 290 cal., 8 g total fat (3 g sat. fat), 15 mg chol., 1,075 mg sodium, 40 g carbo., 6 g fiber, 18 g pro.
EXCHANGES: ½ Vegetable, 2½ Starch, 1½ Lean Meat

OFF THE SHELF TIP Grab a can from the soup section. Just make sure your choice is condensed, not ready-to-serve.

Gardener's Pie

PREP
15 MINUTES

BAKE
45 MINUTES

OVEN
350°F

MAKES
4 SERVINGS

1   **16-ounce package frozen mixed vegetables (any combination), thawed**

1   **11-ounce can condensed cheddar cheese soup**

½   **teaspoon dried thyme, crushed**

1   **20-ounce package refrigerated mashed potatoes**

1   **cup shredded smoked cheddar cheese (4 ounces)**

STEP 1   Preheat oven to 350°F. In a 1½-quart casserole combine vegetables, soup, and thyme. Stir mashed potatoes to soften. Spread mashed potatoes carefully over vegetable mixture to cover surface.

STEP 2   Bake, covered, in the preheated oven for 30 minutes. Uncover and bake about 15 minutes more or until heated through, topping with cheese for the last 5 minutes of baking. Serve in shallow bowls.

PER SERVING: 349 cal., 17 g total fat (8 g sat. fat), 39 mg chol., 1,031 mg sodium, 40 g carbo., 4 g fiber, 15 g pro.
EXCHANGES: 2 Vegetable, 2 Starch, 1 Medium-Fat Meat, 2 Fat

OFF THE SHELF TIP Refrigerated mashed potatoes can be found in the produce section of your supermarket. A few minutes in the microwave or on the stovetop and you're set!

SAMPLE RECIPES Mark recipes that you want to try. Then keep the book with you in the car so that you can fetch ingredients when you're out and about—and wondering what the heck you're going to prepare for dinner!

Side Dishes

Swiss Vegetable Medley

With its nutty flavor, Swiss cheese is a choice complement to mixed veggies. Sour cream joins canned soup to create a creamy element balanced by a crunchy topping.

EASY

PREP
10 MINUTES
BAKE
50 MINUTES
OVEN
350°F
MAKES
6 SERVINGS

1	16-ounce package frozen broccoli, cauliflower, and carrots
1	10.75-ounce can condensed cream of mushroom soup
1	cup shredded Swiss cheese (4 ounces)
⅓	cup dairy sour cream
¼	teaspoon ground black pepper
1	2.8-ounce can french-fried onions

STEP 1 Preheat oven to 350°F. In a large bowl combine the frozen vegetables, soup, ½ cup of the Swiss cheese, the sour cream, and pepper. Stir in half of the french-fried onions. Spoon into a 2-quart square baking dish.

STEP 2 Bake, covered, in the preheated oven for 45 minutes. Sprinkle with the remaining ½ cup cheese and remaining french-fried onions. Bake, uncovered, about 5 minutes more or until heated through.

PER SERVING: 262 cal., 18 g total fat (6 g sat. fat), 25 mg chol., 526 mg sodium, 14 g carbo., 2 g fiber, 10 g pro.
EXCHANGES: 1 Vegetable, ½ Starch, 1 High-Fat Meat, 2 Fat

OFF THE SHELF TIP Grab a can from the soup section. Just make sure your choice is condensed, not ready-to-serve.

Green Bean-Red Pepper Casserole

Red sweet peppers refresh this traditional casserole, which also is updated with an onion-crumb crust.

PREP
20 MINUTES

BAKE
35 MINUTES

OVEN
350°F

MAKES
8 SERVINGS

½   cup finely chopped onion (1 medium)
2   tablespoons butter
⅓   cup fine dry bread crumbs
1   10.75-ounce can condensed cream of mushroom soup
⅓   cup bottled roasted red sweet peppers, chopped
¼   cup slivered almonds, toasted
½   teaspoon salt
⅛   teaspoon ground black pepper
2   16-ounce packages frozen French-cut green beans, thawed and drained

OFF THE SHELF TIP Don't look for dry bread crumbs in the bread section of your supermarket. Instead, try the packaged goods section, near stuffing mixes and mac 'n' cheese.

STEP 1   Preheat oven to 350°F. In a small saucepan cook onion in hot butter over medium heat until tender. Remove from heat. Stir in bread crumbs. Toss to coat. Set aside.

STEP 2   In a large bowl combine soup, red peppers, almonds, salt, and black pepper. Stir in green beans. Transfer to a 2-quart casserole. Sprinkle with crumb mixture.

STEP 3   Bake, uncovered, in the preheated oven for 35 to 40 minutes or until beans are tender.

PER SERVING: 140 cal., 8 g total fat (3 g sat. fat), 9 mg chol., 556 mg sodium, 17 g carbo., 4 g fiber, 4 g pro.
EXCHANGES: 1½ Vegetable, ½ Starch, 1½ Fat

Golden Green Bean Crunch

Chow mein noodles and water chestnuts bring a light, crunchy texture to beans baked in a mushroom sauce.

1   16-ounce package frozen French-cut green beans

1   10.75-ounce can condensed golden mushroom soup

1   8-ounce can sliced water chestnuts, drained (optional)

1   cup chow mein noodles or ½ of a 2.8-ounce can french fried onions (about ¾ cup)

PREP
15 MINUTES
BAKE
30 MINUTES
OVEN
350°F
MAKES
4 TO 6 SERVINGS

STEP 1   Preheat oven to 350°F. Cook frozen beans according to package directions; drain well.

STEP 2   In a 1½-quart casserole combine the green beans, soup, and, if desired, water chestnuts.

STEP 3   Bake, uncovered, in the preheated oven about 25 minutes or until bubbly around edges. Sprinkle with chow mein noodles. Bake about 5 minutes more or until heated through.

PER SERVING: 188 cal., 6 g total fat (1 g sat. fat), 3 mg chol., 719 mg sodium, 27 g carbo., 5 g fiber, 5 g pro.
EXCHANGES: 1 Vegetable, 1½ Starch, 1 Fat

OFF THE SHELF TIP   Look for water chestnuts in the Oriental section of your supermarket. They come whole or sliced; choose sliced for this dish.

STOCK YOUR PANTRY   Once you discover recipes that you like, start stocking the ingredients that you commonly use on your pantry shelves. You'll reduce the number of just-before-dinner shopping trips.

Beer-Simmered Black Beans

Hungry for beans' familiar texture but eager for a new approach? Give these beans a rowdy twist by cooking them with light beer, jalapeño peppers, and cumin.

NO FAT

PREP
10 MINUTES

COOK
8 MINUTES

MAKES
6 SERVINGS

2   15-ounce cans black beans, rinsed and drained
1   cup light beer
2   small fresh jalapeño chile peppers, finely chopped* (optional)
1   teaspoon bottled minced garlic (2 cloves)
1½   teaspoons ground cumin
¼   teaspoon salt

STEP 1 In a large saucepan combine black beans, beer, jalapeño peppers (if desired), garlic, cumin, and salt. Cover and cook over low heat about 8 minutes or until heated through, stirring occasionally.

*NOTE: Because chile peppers contain volatile oils that can burn your skin and eyes, avoid direct contact with them as much as possible. When working with chile peppers, wear plastic or rubber gloves. If your bare hands do touch chile peppers, wash them well with soap and water.

PER SERVING: 127 cal., 0 g total fat (0 g sat. fat), 0 mg chol., 546 mg sodium, 21 g carbo., 6 g fiber, 7 g pro.
EXCHANGES: 1½ Starch, ½ Very-Lean Meat

OFF THE SHELF TIP Save tons of time by using bottled minced garlic instead of mincing your own. Look for jars near the spices or in the produce section of your supermarket. Be sure to refrigerate after opening.

Glazed Brussels Sprouts

START TO FINISH

15 MINUTES

MAKES

3 SERVINGS

RECIPE PICTURED

ON PAGE 134.

1   **10-ounce package frozen Brussels sprouts**
2   **tablespoons mango chutney**
1   **tablespoon butter or margarine**
    Salt
    Ground black pepper

STEP 1 In a medium saucepan cook the Brussels sprouts according to package directions; drain well.

STEP 2 In the same saucepan melt the chutney and butter over medium-low heat. Add Brussels sprouts to chutney mixture in saucepan. Stir to coat. Season to taste with salt and pepper.

PER SERVING: 110 cal., 4 g total fat (3 g sat. fat), 11 mg chol., 159 mg sodium, 17 g carbo., 4 g fiber, 4 g pro.
EXCHANGES: 1 Vegetable, 1 Other Carbo., 1 Fat

OFF THE SHELF TIP Chutneys are on the rise as a favorite condiment. Look for them in the condiment aisle or in some specialty sections of the supermarket. For mango chutney, sometimes it is helpful to cut up any large pieces.

Sweet Saucy Carrots & Pecans

Orange marmalade, butter, and salt meld to glaze a quickly cooked bag of baby carrots. Top with chopped pecans for an elegant, luscious, and delicious side dish.

START TO FINISH
20 MINUTES
MAKES
4 SERVINGS

1	1-pound package peeled baby carrots
2	tablespoons orange marmalade
1	tablespoon butter or margarine
½	teaspoon salt
2	tablespoons pecan pieces, toasted

STEP 1   In a covered large saucepan cook the carrots in a small amount of boiling water for 8 to 10 minutes or until crisp-tender. Drain.

STEP 2   Return carrots to pan. Add orange marmalade, butter, and salt. Stir until carrots are coated. Top with the pecans.

PER SERVING: 124 cal., 6 g total fat (2 g sat. fat), 8 mg chol., 365 mg sodium, 19 g carbo., 4 g fiber, 2 g pro.
EXCHANGES: 2 Vegetable, ½ Other Carbo., 1 Fat

OFF THE SHELF TIP Orange marmalade is not just for toast anymore! Use it in recipes to add a splash of citrus flavor.

Skillet Scalloped Corn

FAST

START TO FINISH
10 MINUTES

MAKES
3 SERVINGS

2   teaspoons butter or margarine
⅓   cup crushed wheat or rye crackers
1   11-ounce can whole kernel corn
        with sweet peppers, drained
2   1-ounce slices process Swiss cheese,
        torn
¼   cup milk
⅛   teaspoon onion powder
        Dash ground black pepper

OFF THE SHELF TIP Whole kernel corn with sweet peppers—found in the canned vegetable aisle of the supermarket—adds two colorful, flavorful ingredients to dishes.

STEP 1   For crumb topping, in a large skillet melt butter over medium heat. Add 1 tablespoon of the crushed crackers to the skillet. Cook and stir until light brown; remove and set aside.

STEP 2   In the same skillet combine the remaining crushed crackers, the corn, cheese, milk, onion powder, and pepper. Cook, stirring frequently, until cheese melts. Transfer to a serving dish; sprinkle with crumb topping.

PER SERVING: 199 cal., 9 g total fat (5 g sat. fat), 25 mg chol., 697 mg sodium, 24 g carbo., 3 g fiber, 8 g pro.
EXCHANGES: 1½ Starch, ½ High-Fat Meat, 1 Fat

Peas & Carrots with Cumin

START TO FINISH
20 MINUTES

MAKES
4 SERVINGS

2	tablespoons cooking oil
1	teaspoon cumin seeds, crushed
½	cup chopped onion (1 medium)
½	teaspoon bottled minced garlic (1 clove)
¼	teaspoon ground coriander
⅛	to ¼ teaspoon crushed red pepper
1½	cups frozen peas
1	16-ounce package crinkle-cut carrots
½	teaspoon salt

STEP 1 In a large nonstick skillet heat oil over medium heat. Add cumin seeds; cook for 10 seconds. Add onion, garlic, coriander, and red pepper. Cook and stir for 4 to 5 minutes or until onion is tender.

STEP 2 Add peas and carrots. Cook and stir for 4 to 6 minutes or until carrots are tender. Stir in salt.

PER SERVING: 131 cal., 8 g total fat (1 g sat. fat), 0 mg chol., 384 mg sodium, 14 g carbo., 4 g fiber, 4 g pro.
EXCHANGES: 2 Vegetable, 1½ Fat

OFF THE SHELF TIP Save time by using packages of sliced or crinkle-cut carrots. Look for them in the produce section of your supermarket. They taste great in salads too.

Gingery Sugar Snap Peas

A light coating of sweet peach preserves, soy sauce, and ginger will tempt even the most finicky eater to enjoy the pleasures of crisp-tender sugar snap peas.

LOW FAT **FAST**

START TO FINISH
15 MINUTES

MAKES
6 SERVINGS

3   cups fresh sugar snap peas or
     frozen sugar snap peas
1   tablespoon butter or margarine
1   tablespoon peach preserves
1   teaspoon soy sauce
     Dash ground ginger
     Dash ground black pepper

STEP 1   Remove strings and tips from fresh sugar snap peas. In a covered medium saucepan cook fresh peas in a small amount of boiling salted water for 2 to 4 minutes or until crisp-tender. (Or cook frozen sugar snap peas according to package directions.) Drain well; set aside.

STEP 2   In the same saucepan melt butter over low heat; stir in preserves, soy sauce, ginger, and pepper. Return sugar snap peas to saucepan, stirring to coat.

PER SERVING: 78 cal., 2 g total fat (1 g sat. fat), 5 mg chol., 85 mg sodium, 11 g carbo., 3 g fiber, 3 g pro.
EXCHANGES: ½ Vegetable, ½ Other Carbo., ½ Fat

OFF THE SHELF TIP Look for peach preserves with the other jams and jellies in your supermarket. You thought these products just paired with bread and peanut butter! They are fabulous for cooking too.

Mexican Potato Cakes

If you're tired of baked or mashed potatoes, then try these mini cakes made crisp with a quick skillet browning. Serve them with shredded cheese and salsa.

START TO FINISH
25 MINUTES

MAKES
6 SERVINGS

1 egg
1 20-ounce package refrigerated shredded hash brown potatoes
1 4-ounce can diced green chile peppers, drained
1 cup finely shredded cheddar cheese (4 ounces)
¼ teaspoon salt
⅛ teaspoon ground black pepper
3 tablespoons cooking oil
Bottled salsa (optional)
Dairy sour cream (optional)

OFF THE SHELF TIP Look for canned green chiles in the Mexican section of your supermarket. They come whole and diced as well as mild and hot.

STEP 1 In a large bowl beat egg with a whisk; stir in potatoes, chile peppers, ½ cup of the cheese, the salt, and black pepper. Form potato mixture into 6 patties (each 4 inches in diameter).

STEP 2 In a 12-inch skillet heat oil over medium to medium-high heat. (Add additional oil during cooking, if necessary.) Cook potato patties in hot oil for 8 to 10 minutes or until brown and crisp, turning once. Sprinkle cakes with remaining ½ cup cheese. Cook about 1 minute more or until cheese is melted. If desired, serve with salsa and sour cream.

PER SERVING: 237 cal., 14 g total fat (5 g sat. fat), 55 mg chol., 339 mg sodium, 20 g carbo., 1 g fiber, 9 g pro.
EXCHANGES: 1 Starch, 1 High-Fat Meat, 1½ Fat

Creamy Mashed Potatoes

Flavored cream cheese transforms instant potato flakes into a full-flavored, soft accompaniment for salmon, steak, or ribs.

2	cups water
¾	to 1 cup milk
2	tablespoons butter or margarine
¼	teaspoon salt
2	cups instant mashed potato flakes
½	of an 8-ounce tub cream cheese spread with chive and onion
	Butter or margarine (optional)
	Snipped chives (optional)

PREP
10 MINUTES

MICROWAVE
5 MINUTES

MAKES
6 SERVINGS

STEP 1 In a 1½-quart microwave-safe casserole combine water, ¾ cup of the milk, the 2 tablespoons butter, and salt. Stir in potato flakes. Microwave, covered, on 100% power (high) for 4 to 5 minutes or until liquid is absorbed.

STEP 2 Stir to rehydrate potatoes. Stir in cream cheese. If necessary, stir in enough of the remaining milk to make desired consistency. Microwave, covered, on high about 1 minute or until heated through. If desired, top with additional butter and chives.

PER SERVING: 173 cal., 11 g total fat (7 g sat. fat), 31 mg chol., 238 mg sodium, 16 g carbo., 1 g fiber, 3 g pro.
EXCHANGES: 1 Starch, 2 Fat

OFF THE SHELF TIP Packaged cream cheese is used in so many ways in convenience cooking. It comes in a variety of sizes and flavors. Whipped cream cheese (called spreadable cream cheese) is often combined with other flavors such as herbs, vegetables, or fruits. Use cream cheese within a week of opening.

Spinach-Scalloped Potatoes

For a flavor-packed dish to accompany roasted meat, combine scalloped potato mix with spinach, bacon, and cheese. Thyme adds a Mediterranean flair.

PREP
20 MINUTES

BAKE
32 MINUTES

STAND
5 MINUTES

OVEN
400°F

MAKES
6 SERVINGS

Nonstick cooking spray
4 slices bacon
½ cup thinly sliced onion (1 medium)
1 10-ounce package frozen chopped spinach, thawed and well drained
1 4.9-ounce package dry scalloped potato mix
Boiling water
Milk
½ teaspoon dried thyme, crushed
1 cup shredded provolone or mozzarella cheese (4 ounces)

STEP 1 Preheat oven to 400°F. Lightly coat a 2-quart rectangular baking dish or oval au gratin dish with nonstick cooking spray; set aside. In a large skillet over medium heat cook bacon until crisp. Remove bacon from skillet, reserving 1 tablespoon drippings in skillet. Drain bacon on paper towels. Crumble bacon; set aside.

STEP 2 In the same skillet cook the onion in the reserved drippings over medium heat for 4 to 5 minutes or until tender. Add spinach; heat through.

STEP 3 In the prepared baking dish combine potatoes and dry sauce mix from package. Stir in boiling water and milk as directed on package (omit margarine or butter). Stir in the crumbled bacon, spinach-onion mixture, and thyme.

STEP 4 Bake, uncovered, in the preheated oven for 30 to 35 minutes or until potatoes are tender. Sprinkle with cheese; bake for 2 to 3 minutes more or until cheese is melted. Let stand for 5 minutes before serving.

PER SERVING: 228 cal., 11 g total fat (6 g sat. fat), 26 mg chol., 785 mg sodium, 21 g carbo., 3 g fiber, 11 g pro.
EXCHANGES: 1 Starch, 1 High-Fat Meat, ½ Vegetable, ½ Fat

OFF THE SHELF TIP Most packages of shredded cheese are 8 ounces, which measures out to 2 cups shredded cheese. If you're simply sprinkling the cheese over a casserole, you can estimate and use about half the package. If you will be stirring the cheese into a sauce or batter, get out the measuring cup.

Sweet Pepper & Onion Bread Pudding

This dish is a luscious, savory concoction that would make a festive accompaniment on a holiday buffet.

PREP
20 MINUTES

BAKE
30 MINUTES

STAND
10 MINUTES

OVEN
350°F

MAKES
8 SERVINGS

8	ounces crusty Italian bread
2	tablespoons butter or margarine, softened
3	eggs, slightly beaten
1½	cups milk
1	12-ounce jar roasted red sweet peppers, well drained and coarsely chopped (about 1½ cups)
½	cup thinly sliced green onion (4)
3	tablespoons snipped fresh oregano or 2 teaspoons dried oregano, crushed
½	to 1 teaspoon bottled hot pepper sauce
¼	teaspoon salt
¼	teaspoon black pepper
1	cup shredded fontina or provolone cheese (4 ounces)

STEP 1 Preheat the oven to 350°F. Cut the bread into 1-inch slices. Spread slices with butter, then tear bread into bite-size pieces. Set aside. Grease eight 6-ounce custard cups or ramekins or one 1½-quart soufflé dish; set aside.

STEP 2 In a large mixing bowl beat together eggs and milk. Stir in roasted peppers, green onion, oregano, hot pepper sauce, salt, and black pepper. Add bread pieces and cheese, stirring well to coat bread.

STEP 3 Divide mixture among the prepared individual custard cups. (Or spoon into prepared soufflé dish.) Press mixture down lightly with the back of a wooden spoon.

STEP 4 Bake, uncovered, in the preheated oven about 30 minutes for the individual custard cups or until tops are puffed and golden brown and a knife inserted near the centers comes out clean. Let stand 10 minutes. (Or bake large soufflé, uncovered, for 40 minutes or until the top is puffed and golden brown and a knife inserted near the center comes out clean. Let stand for 15 to 20 minutes before serving.)

PER SERVING: 220 cal., 11 g total fat (6 g sat. fat), 108 mg chol., 432 mg sodium, 20 g carbo., 2 g fiber, 10 g pro.
EXCHANGES: 1 Lean Meat, 1½ Starch, 1 Fat

OFF THE SHELF TIP Roasted red sweet peppers are found in the condiment aisle of your supermarket. They are easy to make at home, but why take the time when jars are so easy to snap up?

Saffron Rice Baked Tomatoes

L O W
F A T

PREP
30 MINUTES
BAKE
30 MINUTES
OVEN
350°F
MAKES
6 SERVINGS

1	5-ounce package saffron-flavored yellow rice mix
6	ripe large tomatoes (about 3 pounds total)
¼	cup dried mixed fruit bits or golden raisins
¼	cup pine nuts
½	teaspoon dried oregano, crushed

OFF THE SHELF TIP Packaged rice mixes come in a vast array of flavors. They are great as a side dish and are easy to dress up, as demonstrated here.

STEP 1 Preheat oven to 350°F. Prepare rice mix according to package directions, except omit the oil or margarine. Meanwhile, cut a slice off the top of each tomato; reserve the tops. Using a spoon, carefully scoop out the pulp and chop it. Measure 1½ cups of the chopped pulp; set aside. Discard remaining pulp. Place the tomatoes upside down on paper towels to drain.

STEP 2 In a medium bowl combine the cooked rice, the 1½ cups reserved tomato pulp, the fruit bits, pine nuts, and oregano. Spoon the rice mixture into the tomatoes. Cover stuffed tomatoes with the reserved tops. Place in a 2-quart rectangular baking dish. Spoon any remaining rice mixture into the bottom of the baking dish around the tomatoes.

STEP 3 Bake, uncovered, in the preheated oven for 30 to 40 minutes or until tomatoes are tender and rice mixture is heated through.

PER SERVING: 173 cal., 4 g total fat (1 g sat. fat), 0 mg chol., 330 mg sodium, 33 g carbo., 4 g fiber, 6 g pro.
EXCHANGES: 1 Vegetable, 1½ Starch, ½ Fat

East-West Veggies

Corn, beans, red sweet pepper, and celery go Far East with the addition of hoisin sauce.

LOW FAT

START TO FINISH
20 MINUTES

MAKES
6 SERVINGS

1	tablespoon butter or margarine
1	tablespoon olive oil
1	medium onion, cut into thin wedges
6	green onions, cut into 1-inch pieces
3	tablespoons hoisin sauce
1	teaspoon paprika
1	15.25-ounce can whole kernel corn, drained
1	15-ounce can black beans, rinsed and drained
¾	cup chopped celery
½	cup finely chopped red sweet pepper

OFF THE SHELF TIP Look for hoisin sauce in the Oriental section of your supermarket. This sweet and sour sauce is also called "Peking sauce."

STEP 1 In a large skillet heat butter and oil over medium heat. Add onion wedges; cook about 4 minutes or until tender. Stir in green onion, hoisin sauce, and paprika. Cook and stir for 1 minute more.

STEP 2 Add corn, beans, celery, and sweet pepper. Cook and stir until heated through.

PER SERVING: 166 cal., 5 g total fat (2 g sat. fat), 5 mg chol., 574 mg sodium, 28 g carbo., 5 g fiber, 6 g pro.
EXCHANGES: 1½ Starch, 1 Very Lean Meat, ½ Fat

Creamy Lemon Pasta

This refreshing but rich side dish is worth bypassing dessert. Try it with blackened fish, chicken, or pork.

START TO FINISH
15 MINUTES

MAKES
6 SERVINGS

9   ounces refrigerated fettuccine or
     6 ounces dried fettuccine
¾   cup finely shredded Parmesan cheese
     (3 ounces)
½   cup whipping cream
1   teaspoon finely shredded lemon peel
     Salt
     Ground black pepper

STEP 1 Cook pasta according to package directions. Drain well. Add half of the cheese, the whipping cream, and lemon peel. Toss gently to coat.

STEP 2 Transfer to a serving dish. Top with remaining cheese. Season to taste with salt and pepper.

PER SERVING: 245 cal., 12 g total fat (8 g sat. fat), 85 mg chol., 265 mg sodium, 24 g carbo., 1 g fiber, 10 g pro.
EXCHANGES: 1½ Starch, 1 Medium-Fat Meat, 1 Fat

OFF THE SHELF TIP Refrigerated pasta comes in a wide variety of shapes and flavors, from cheese- and/or meat-filled ravioli to strands of linguine and fettuccine. It is a fabulous convenience product, but do note that its shelf life is shorter than its dried counterpart.

PLOT YOUR SHOPPING LISTS
Craft your list to match your favorite grocery store's layout. You'll shop faster and spare yourself doubling back to an earlier-shopped section. As you develop your personal standard fare, craft your own checklist noting frequently used items, then copy it for custom listmaking.

Here are common grocery sections:
■ Bakery ■ Deli ■ Produce, Fruit
■ Produce, Vegetables ■ Meat
■ Dairy ■ Bread, Baked Goods
■ Shelf & Canned Goods ■ Candy
■ Baked ■ Ethnic ■ Baking Aisle
■ Packaged Foods ■ Cereal & Breakfast
■ Snacks ■ Fridge & Freezer Case
■ Oils, Condiments & Seasonings

Savory Couscous

Toss quick-cooking couscous with shredded carrot, sliced mushrooms and onions, and snipped herbs for a side dish that's big on texture. Pale yellow couscous tastes a little heartier than white rice. It's good with heavy meats such as steak.

LOW FAT

START TO FINISH
20 MINUTES

MAKES
8 SERVINGS

RECIPE PICTURED ON PAGE 134.

2	cups water
1½	cups sliced fresh mushrooms
½	cup shredded carrot (1 medium)
⅓	cup thinly sliced green onion
1	tablespoon butter or margarine
2	teaspoons instant chicken bouillon granules
2	teaspoons snipped fresh basil or thyme or ½ teaspoon dried basil or thyme, crushed
1	10-ounce package quick-cooking couscous

STEP 1 In a medium saucepan combine water, mushrooms, carrot, green onion, butter, bouillon granules, and dried herb (if using). Bring to boiling. Stir in uncooked couscous and fresh herb (if using). Remove from heat.

STEP 2 Cover; let stand about 5 minutes or until liquid is absorbed. Fluff with a fork before serving.

PER SERVING: 158 cal., 2 g total fat (1 g sat. fat), 4 mg chol., 241 mg sodium, 29 g carbo., 2 g fiber, 5 g pro.
EXCHANGES: 2 Starch

OFF THE SHELF TIP Bouillon granules—found in the soup aisle of the supermarket—add flavor and depth to recipes. They come in beef and chicken varieties; both also come in low-sodium versions.

Coconut Rice With Snow Peas

PREP
10 MINUTES

COOK
20 MINUTES

STAND
5 MINUTES

MAKES
4 SERVINGS

¾ cup water
⅔ cup unsweetened canned coconut milk
½ cup uncooked long grain white rice
¼ teaspoon salt
1½ cups bias-sliced (2-inch pieces) fresh snow peas or asparagus

STEP 1 In a medium saucepan combine water, coconut milk, uncooked rice, and salt. Bring to boiling; reduce heat. Cover and simmer for 15 minutes.

STEP 2 Place snow peas on top of the rice. Cook, covered, about 5 minutes more or until rice and vegetables are tender. Remove from heat; let stand for 5 minutes.

PER SERVING: 174 cal., 8 g total fat (7 g sat. fat), 0 mg chol., 161 mg sodium, 23 g carbo., 1 g fiber, 3 g pro.
EXCHANGES: ½ Vegetable, 1 Starch, 1½ Fat, ½ Other Carbo.

OFF THE SHELF TIP Look for cans of unsweetened coconut milk in the Oriental section of your supermarket. Don't confuse this product with cream of coconut, which is commonly used in drinks such as a piña colada.

Wild Rice & Spinach Au Gratin

This deeply flavored side dish draws on earthy riches: mushrooms, wild rice, and spinach. When combined with beef broth and some cream cheese, the taste is to die for. Pair with simply cooked beef or pork.

START TO FINISH
35 MINUTES

MAKES
8 SERVINGS

1   6-ounce package long grain and wild rice mix
1   10.5-ounce can condensed beef broth
6   cups thinly sliced fresh mushrooms (1 pound)
2   tablespoons butter
1   10-ounce package frozen chopped spinach, thawed and well drained
1   8-ounce package cream cheese, cut up

STEP 1 Cook the rice mix according to package directions, except use the beef broth for part of the liquid.

STEP 2 Meanwhile, in a large skillet cook mushrooms in hot butter over medium heat until tender. Add spinach and cream cheese; stir to combine and melt cheese. Stir in rice. Heat through.

MAKE-AHEAD DIRECTIONS: Prepare as above. Spread rice-spinach mixture into a 2-quart rectangular baking dish. Cover and refrigerate overnight. To reheat, preheat oven to 350°F. Bake, covered, in the preheated oven for 40 to 45 minutes or until heated through, stirring once. (Or bake, covered, in a preheated 425°F oven for 20 to 25 minutes or until heated through, stirring once.)

PER SERVING: 231 cal., 14 g total fat (8 g sat. fat), 39 mg chol., 620 mg sodium, 20 g carbo., 2 g fiber, 9 g pro.
EXCHANGES: 1 Starch, 3 Fat

OFF THE SHELF TIP Packaged cream cheese is used in so many ways in convenience cooking. It comes in a variety of sizes and flavors. Whipped cream cheese (called spreadable cream cheese) is often combined with other flavors such as herbs, vegetables, or fruits. Use cream cheese within a week of opening.

Fruited Wild Rice Salad

PREP
35 MINUTES

CHILL
4 TO 24 HOURS

MAKES
8 TO 10 SERVINGS

1	6-ounce package long grain and wild rice mix
1	8-ounce can sliced water chestnuts, drained
½	cup chopped celery (1 stalk)
½	cup sliced green onion (4)
½	cup seedless grapes, halved
3	tablespoons olive oil
3	tablespoons lemon juice
¼	teaspoon ground black pepper
1	11-ounce can mandarin orange sections, drained
⅔	cup slivered almonds, toasted

OFF THE SHELF TIP Look for water chestnuts in the Oriental section of your supermarket. They come whole and sliced; chose sliced for this dish.

STEP 1 Prepare rice mix according to package directions, except do not add oil or butter. Cool.

STEP 2 In a large bowl combine rice mixture, drained water chestnuts, celery, green onion, and grapes. For dressing, in a screw-top jar combine oil, lemon juice, and pepper. Cover and shake well to combine. Pour dressing over rice mixture; toss to coat.

STEP 3 Cover and refrigerate at least 4 hours or up to 24 hours. Before serving, gently stir in drained orange sections and almonds.

PER SERVING: 245 cal., 13 g total fat (1 g sat. fat), 0 mg chol., 242 mg sodium, 32 g carbo., 3 g fiber, 6 g pro.
EXCHANGES: 2 Starch, 2 Fat

Taffy Apple Salad

Chopped apple and pineapple are tossed with a cooked sauce, peanuts, marshmallows, and whipped topping for a salty-sweet way to enjoy some fruit.

PREP
25 MINUTES
CHILL
2 HOURS
MAKES
16 SERVINGS

2   8-ounce cans pineapple tidbits (juice pack)
½   cup sugar
1   tablespoon all-purpose flour
1   egg, slightly beaten
1   tablespoon vinegar
½   of an 8-ounce container frozen whipped dessert topping, thawed
3   cups chopped apple (4 medium)
2   cups tiny marshmallows
1   cup Spanish peanuts

OFF THE SHELF TIP   Frozen dessert topping is found near the frozen pies and cakes in the supermarket. It comes in regular, light, and fat-free versions.

STEP 1   Drain pineapple tidbits, reserving juice (should have about ¾ cup juice). Cover pineapple tidbits and refrigerate.

STEP 2   In a small saucepan stir together the reserved pineapple juice, the sugar, flour, egg, and vinegar. Cook and stir over medium heat until thickened and bubbly. Cook and stir for 1 minute more. Transfer mixture to a large bowl; cover surface with plastic wrap and refrigerate for at least 2 hours or until thoroughly chilled.

STEP 3   Fold whipped topping into the chilled mixture. Fold the pineapple tidbits, apple, marshmallows, and peanuts into whipped topping mixture. Serve immediately. (Or cover and refrigerate for up to 24 hours.)

PER SERVING: 153 cal., 6 g total fat (2 g sat. fat), 13 mg chol., 9 mg sodium, 23 g carbo., 1 g fiber, 3 g pro.
EXCHANGES: ½ Fruit, 1 Other Carbo., 1 Fat

Ginger Ale Salad

A double-ginger whammy of crystallized ginger and ginger ale makes this refreshing fruit- and nut-studded gelatin mold a star of the buffet. This retro salad is worth a try, and another, and another.

N O
F A T

PREP
20 MINUTES
CHILL
6½ HOURS
MAKES
12 SERVINGS

1 6-ounce package lemon-flavored gelatin
1 cup water
2 cups ginger ale
2 cups assorted chopped fruit (such as drained canned pineapple {do not use fresh pineapple}, fresh strawberries, fresh or canned peaches, fresh or canned pears, fresh apple, or fresh grapes)
½ cup chopped celery (1 stalk) or toasted nuts
2 tablespoons finely chopped crystallized ginger

OFF THE SHELF TIP Head for the baking aisle to find packages of gelatin in a vast array of flavors.

STEP 1   In a medium saucepan combine gelatin and water; heat and stir until gelatin dissolves. Stir in ginger ale. Refrigerate about 30 minutes or until partially set (the consistency of unbeaten egg whites). Fold in fruit, celery, and crystallized ginger.

STEP 2   Pour into a 6-cup mold. Cover; refrigerate about 6 hours or until firm. Unmold salad onto a serving plate.

PER SERVING: 100 cal., 0 g total fat (0 g sat. fat), 0 mg chol., 46 mg sodium, 25 g carbo., 0 g fiber, 1 g pro.
EXCHANGES: 1½ Other Carbo.

Mango-Spinach Salad

Soft, sultry mangoes and peppery spinach make lively salad partners. Pine nuts and sunflower seeds add a soft crunch.

FAST

START TO FINISH
15 MINUTES
MAKES
4 SERVINGS

6	cups fresh baby spinach or baby mixed greens
⅛	teaspoon salt
⅛	teaspoon ground black pepper
½	cup bottled Dijon-lime dressing or light Italian dressing
1	26-ounce jar refrigerated mango slices, well drained
⅓	cup pine nuts, toasted, or shelled sunflower seeds
¼	cup thinly sliced green onion (2)

STEP 1 Place spinach in a large bowl. Sprinkle with salt and pepper. Drizzle with dressing; toss lightly to coat.

STEP 2 Divide spinach mixture evenly among 4 salad plates. Arrange mango slices on the spinach. Sprinkle with pine nuts and green onion. Serve immediately.

PER SERVING: 348 cal., 21 g total fat (2 g sat. fat), 0 mg chol., 264 mg sodium, 41 g carbo., 1 g fiber, 5 g pro.
EXCHANGES: 1½ Vegetable, 1 Fruit, 1 Other Carbo., 4 Fat

OFF THE SHELF TIP Look for refrigerated mango slices in the produce section of the supermarket. With them you will also find refrigerated papaya, pineapple, and other tropical fruits—perfect for a side dish or as a topper on a salad.

Desserts

Chocolate Hazelnut Ice Cream Sauce

Finish a fine day with a special sauce treat: Warm chocolate-hazelnut sauce on the stove and stir in cream and coffee crystals. Drizzle it over ordinary ice cream or cake for an extraordinary combination.

FAST

START TO FINISH

10 MINUTES

MAKES

ABOUT ¾ CUP SAUCE

½   cup chocolate-hazelnut spread
¼   cup half-and-half or light cream
1   teaspoon instant coffee crystals (optional)
¼   cup hazelnuts, toasted and coarsely chopped
     Vanilla, coffee, or other favorite ice cream

STEP 1   In a small saucepan combine chocolate-hazelnut spread, half-and-half, and, if desired, coffee crystals. Heat over low heat until spread is melted, whisking until smooth. Stir in nuts. Serve warm over ice cream.

PER 2 TABLESPOONS SAUCE: 155 cal., 11 g total fat (1 g sat. fat), 4 mg chol., 24 mg sodium, 14 g carbo., 1 g fiber, 2 g pro.
EXCHANGES: 1 Other Carbo., 2 Fat

OFF THE SHELF TIP Chocolate-hazelnut spread is found near the peanut butter in most supermarkets. Use it in recipes, but don't forget how great it tastes on toast and ice cream or with just an—oops—accidental swipe of the finger right out of the jar.

Apricot-Orange Sauce

FAST

START TO FINISH
15 MINUTES

MAKES
2 CUPS SAUCE

1   **21-ounce can apricot pie filling**
1   **cup mixed dried fruit bits**
¾   **cup orange juice**
½   **cup chopped pecans, toasted**
1   **tablespoon orange liqueur (optional)**
      Pound cake or vanilla ice cream

STEP 1   For sauce, in a medium sauce-pan combine pie filling, fruit bits, and orange juice; cook and stir until warm. Stir in pecans and, if desired, liqueur.

STEP 2   Serve warm sauce over pound cake or ice cream.

PER 2 TABLESPOONS SAUCE: 93 cal., 2 g total fat (0 g sat. fat), 0 mg chol., 8 mg sodium, 17 g carbo., 1 g fiber, 1 g pro.
EXCHANGES: 1 Other Carbo., ½ Fat

OFF THE SHELF TIP Pie filling is a versatile ingredient in all kinds of recipes. Look for it in its many flavors in the baking aisle of the supermarket.

Raspberry-Cranberry Sauce

Sweet frozen raspberries join cranberries for a perfectly complementary berry union that makes a gorgeous ruby red sauce to drizzle over pound cake, brownies, ice cream, or pancakes. Spike it with kirsch or brandy if you like.

START TO FINISH
15 MINUTES

MAKES
2 CUPS SAUCE

2   tablespoons sugar
1   tablespoon cornstarch
½   of a 16-ounce can whole cranberry
     sauce
1   10-ounce package frozen red
     raspberries (in syrup), thawed
2   tablespoons kirsch or brandy
     (optional)
     Pound cake, unfrosted brownies,
     or vanilla ice cream

STEP 1   In a medium saucepan combine sugar and cornstarch. Stir in cranberry sauce and raspberries. Cook and stir over medium heat until thickened and bubbly. Cook and stir for 2 minutes more. Remove from heat. If desired, stir in kirsch.

STEP 2   Serve warm sauce over pound cake, brownies, or ice cream.

PER 2 TABLESPOONS SAUCE: 57 cal., 0 g total fat (0 g sat. fat), 0 mg chol., 8 mg sodium, 14 g carbo., 1 g fiber, 0 g pro.
EXCHANGES: 1 Other Carbo.

OFF THE SHELF TIP Kirsch is a cherry-flavored brandy typically used in fondue and cherries jubilee.

Berry Compote

You can serve this berry-layered thick sauce warm or chilled, with ice cream or cake, or as a side dish on a holiday buffet.

PREP
10 MINUTES

COOK
8 TO 10 HOURS (LOW) OR
4 TO 5 HOURS (HIGH)

STAND
10 MINUTES

MAKES
10 SERVINGS

2½ cups cranberry-raspberry drink or cranberry juice
1 7-ounce package mixed dried fruit, cut into 1-inch pieces
⅔ cup dried cranberries or raisins
⅓ cup packed brown sugar
3 inches stick cinnamon
1 12-ounce package loose-pack frozen red raspberries

STEP 1 In a 3½- or 4-quart slow cooker combine the cranberry-raspberry drink, mixed dried fruit, dried cranberries, brown sugar, and stick cinnamon.

STEP 2 Cover and cook on low-heat setting for 8 to 10 hours or on high-heat setting for 4 to 5 hours. Stir in frozen raspberries; let stand 10 minutes. Discard cinnamon stick.

PER SERVING: 149 cal., 0 g total fat (0 g sat. fat), 0 mg chol., 16 mg sodium, 38 g carbo., 3 g fiber, 1 g pro.
EXCHANGES: 1½ Fruit, 1 Other Carbo.

OFF THE SHELF TIP Dried fruits possess stronger, more intense flavors than their fresh counterparts. Nearly every fruit is available in its dried form and is most commonly packaged in bags or boxes.

Butterscotch Fondue

Don't let chocolate be the only sweet dipper at your table. Slow-cook this rich confection and spike it with rum, if you like, then scoop up with fruit, cake, or brownie cubes.

SLOW COOKER

PREP
10 MINUTES

COOK
3 HOURS (LOW)

MAKES
ABOUT 5¼ CUPS

2   14-ounce cans sweetened condensed milk
2   cups packed brown sugar
1   cup butter, melted
⅔   cup light corn syrup
1   teaspoon vanilla
¼   cup rum or milk
     Apple slices, whole strawberries, cubed sponge cake, and/or cubed brownies

STEP 1   In a 3½- or 4-quart slow cooker stir together the sweetened condensed milk, brown sugar, butter, corn syrup, and vanilla.

STEP 2   Cover and cook on low-heat setting for 3 hours (do not cook on high-heat setting). Whisk in rum until smooth. Keep warm on low-heat setting for up to 2 hours, stirring occasionally.

STEP 3   Serve with apple slices, strawberries, sponge cake, and/or brownies.

PER ¼ CUP FONDUE: 317 cal., 13 g total fat (8 g sat. fat), 38 mg chol., 163 mg sodium, 49 g carbo., 0 g fiber, 3 g pro.
EXCHANGES: 3 Other Carbo., 3 Fat

OFF THE SHELF TIP Head to the baking aisle of the supermarket for sweetened condensed milk. Store unopened cans up to six months. Once opened, use the milk within 5 days.

Rocky Road Squares

This decadent no-bake dessert is the simple union of just five pantry ingredients.

1   10-ounce package tiny marshmallows
1   12-ounce jar dry-roasted peanuts
1   14-ounce can sweetened condensed milk
1   12-ounce package semisweet chocolate pieces (2 cups)
2   tablespoons butter or margarine

PREP
20 MINUTES
CHILL
2 HOURS
MAKES
48 SQUARES

OFF THE SHELF TIP Head to the baking aisle for packages of tiny (and regular) marshmallows. They are a great snack eaten right out of the bag and are essential to any campfire—what would it be without s'mores?

STEP 1   In an extra-large bowl combine marshmallows and peanuts; set aside. Line a 13×9×2-inch baking pan with foil, extending foil beyond edges of pan; grease the foil.

STEP 2   In a medium saucepan combine sweetened condensed milk, chocolate pieces, and butter. Cook and stir over medium-low heat until chocolate is melted. Pour over the marshmallow mixture. Stir just until combined. Spread into prepared pan.

STEP 3   Refrigerate for 2 hours or until set. Cut into squares. Store, covered, in the refrigerator.

PER SQUARE: 121 cal., 6 g total fat (2 g sat. fat), 4 mg chol., 76 mg sodium, 15 g carbo., 1 g fiber, 3 g pro.
EXCHANGES: 1 Starch, 1 Fat

Salted Peanut Bars

PREP
25 MINUTES

CHILL
1 HOUR

MAKES
60 PIECES

Nonstick cooking spray

4 cups dry-roasted or honey-roasted peanuts

1 10.5-ounce package tiny marshmallows

½ cup butter

1 14-ounce can (1⅓ cups) sweetened condensed milk

1 10-ounce package peanut butter-flavor pieces

½ cup creamy peanut butter

OFF THE SHELF TIP Head to the baking aisle of the supermarket for sweetened condensed milk. Store unopened cans up to six months. Once opened, use the milk within 5 days.

STEP 1 Line a 13×9×2-inch baking pan with heavy foil, extending foil beyond edges of pan. Coat foil with nonstick cooking spray. Spread half of the peanuts evenly in the prepared pan.

STEP 2 In a large saucepan combine marshmallows and butter; heat and stir over medium-low heat until melted. Stir in sweetened condensed milk, peanut butter pieces, and peanut butter until smooth. Quickly pour peanut butter mixture over peanuts in pan. Sprinkle remaining peanuts on top. Gently press peanuts into peanut butter mixture.

STEP 3 Refrigerate about 1 hour or until firm; cut into pieces. Store, covered, in refrigerator.

PER PIECE: 144 cal., 10 g total fat (3 g sat. fat), 7 mg chol., 128 mg sodium, 12 g carbo., 1 g fiber, 4 g pro.
EXCHANGES: 1 Other Carbo., 2 Fat

Orange-Pumpkin Custard

Allspice, cinnamon, and orange peel add light zip to this creamy slow-cooker custard.

SLOW COOKER

PREP
15 MINUTES
COOK
4 HOURS (LOW)
STAND
20 MINUTES
MAKES
6 SERVINGS

2	eggs, slightly beaten
1	cup canned pumpkin
½	cup sugar
½	teaspoon ground cinnamon
½	teaspoon finely shredded orange peel
¼	teaspoon ground allspice
1	12-ounce can (1½ cups) evaporated milk
	Whipped cream (optional)
	Chopped pecans, toasted (optional)

STEP 1 In a large bowl combine eggs, pumpkin, sugar, cinnamon, orange peel, and allspice. Stir in evaporated milk. Pour into a 1-quart soufflé dish. Cover the dish tightly with foil.

STEP 2 Tear off two 20×6-inch pieces of heavy foil. Fold each piece in thirds lengthwise. Crisscross the strips and place the soufflé dish in the center. Bring up foil strips, lift the ends of the strips, and transfer the dish and foil to a 4- to 6-quart slow cooker. (Leave foil strips under dish.) Pour warm water into the cooker around the dish to a depth of 1½ inches.

STEP 3 Cover and cook on low-heat setting (do not cook on high-heat setting) about 4 hours or until a knife inserted near the center comes out clean.

STEP 4 Using the foil strips, carefully lift the dish out of the cooker. Let stand for 20 minutes. Serve warm or chilled. If desired, top each serving with whipped cream and toasted pecans.

PER SERVING: 186 cal., 7 g total fat (3 g sat. fat), 89 mg chol., 90 mg sodium, 26 g carbo., 1 g fiber, 7 g pro.
EXCHANGES: ½ Milk, 1½ Other Carbo., 1 Fat

OFF THE SHELF TIP It's not just for pie anymore! Head to the baking aisle for canned pumpkin.

Apricot-Almond Torte

Fruity filling is slipped between a solid cookie bottom and lattice cookie top. This torte is beautiful and tasty.

1   18-ounce roll refrigerated sugar cookie dough
½   of a 12-ounce can apricot cake and pastry filling
¼   cup sliced almonds, toasted
2   tablespoons all-purpose flour
1   egg yolk
1   tablespoon water

PREP
25 MINUTES
BAKE
45 MINUTES
OVEN
325°F
MAKES
12 SERVINGS

STEP 1 Preheat oven to 325°F. Grease a 9- to 10-inch tart pan with a removable bottom. Pat two-thirds of the cookie dough into the bottom of the prepared pan. Spread with apricot filling; sprinkle with toasted almonds.

STEP 2 On a lightly floured surface, knead the flour into the remaining cookie dough. Roll to a 9- or 10-inch circle; cut into ½-inch strips. Lay strips across the filling to form a lattice pattern. In a small bowl stir together egg yolk and the water; brush over dough strips.

STEP 3 Bake in the preheated oven for 45 to 50 minutes or until golden. Cool on a wire rack.

PER SERVING: 239 cal., 11 g total fat (2 g sat. fat), 30 mg chol., 188 mg sodium, 33 g carbo., 1 g fiber, 3 g pro.
EXCHANGES: 2 Other Carbo., 2½ Fat

OFF THE SHELF TIP Head to your grocer's cooler for refrigerated cookie dough. Find a variety of flavors: sugar, chocolate chip, peanut butter, chocolate chunk, white chocolate macadamia nut, to name a few.

Extreme Chocolate Pie

PREP
25 MINUTES
BAKE
20 MINUTES
COOL
1 HOUR
CHILL
4 TO 24 HOURS
OVEN
350°F
MAKES
10 SERVINGS

1   **8-ounce package brownie mix**
1   **cup sugar**
¾   **cup butter**
6   **ounces unsweetened chocolate, melted and cooled**
1   **teaspoon vanilla**
¾   **cup refrigerated or frozen egg product, thawed, or ¾ cup pasteurized eggs**
1   **1.45-ounce bar dark sweet chocolate, coarsely chopped**
1   **recipe Chocolate Whipped Cream (optional)**

STEP 1   Preheat oven to 350°F. Grease a 9-inch pie plate; set aside. For crust, prepare brownie mix according to package directions. Spread in the bottom of the prepared pie plate. Bake in the preheated oven for 20 to 25 minutes or until a wooden toothpick inserted in center comes out clean. Cool on wire rack for 1 hour.

STEP 2   For filling, in a medium mixing bowl beat sugar and butter with an electric mixer on medium speed about 4 minutes or until fluffy. Stir in the melted chocolate and the vanilla. Gradually add egg product, beating on low speed until combined. Beat on medium to high speed about 1 minute or until light and fluffy, scraping side of bowl constantly.

STEP 3   Spoon filling over baked brownie in pie plate. Cover and refrigerate for at least 4 hours or up to 24 hours.

STEP 4   To serve, sprinkle with chopped chocolate bar. If desired, serve with Chocolate Whipped Cream.

PER SERVING: 428 cal., 29 g total fat (16 g sat. fat), 61 mg chol., 285 mg sodium, 45 g carbo., 3 g fiber, 5 g pro.
EXCHANGES: 3 Other Carbo., 5½ Fat

CHOCOLATE WHIPPED CREAM: In a chilled small mixing bowl combine ½ cup whipping cream, 1 tablespoon sugar, and 1½ teaspoons unsweetened cocoa powder. Beat with chilled beaters of an electric mixer on medium speed until soft peaks form (tips curl).

OFF THE SHELF TIP   Look in the baking aisle near the chocolate chips for unsweetened chocolate. Remember that it is great in cooking but terribly bitter eaten out of hand.

Lemon Cream Tart

You could call this lemon lush. Let each bite linger—soft, nutty crust beneath creamy, rich, citrusy goodness. Don't talk, just eat!

PREP
30 MINUTES

BAKE
35 MINUTES

COOL
1 HOUR

CHILL
2 TO 24 HOURS

OVEN
350°F

MAKES
12 TO 16 SERVINGS

1   16.5-ounce package lemon bar mix
½   cup finely chopped macadamia nuts
1   8-ounce package cream cheese, softened
½   teaspoon vanilla
1   teaspoon finely shredded lemon peel
1   8-ounce carton dairy sour cream
1   tablespoon sugar
½   teaspoon vanilla
1½   to 2 cups fresh berries (blueberries, raspberries, and/or blackberries)
        Fresh mint leaves, cut into long thin strips (optional)

STEP 1   Preheat oven to 350°F. Prepare lemon filling mixture according to package directions for lemon bar mix; set aside. Press packaged crust mixture into the bottom of a 10-inch springform pan or a 9×9×2-inch baking pan. Sprinkle macadamia nuts evenly over crust; press gently into crust. Bake in the preheated oven about 10 minutes or until light brown. Cool on a wire rack.

STEP 2   Meanwhile, in a medium mixing bowl combine cream cheese and ½ teaspoon vanilla; beat with an electric mixer on medium to high speed until smooth. Add lemon filling mixture; beat until combined. Stir in lemon peel. Pour cream cheese mixture evenly over the crust in the pan.

STEP 3   Bake in the 350° oven about 25 minutes more or until set. Cool on wire rack for 1 hour. Cover and refrigerate for at least 2 hours or up to 24 hours.

STEP 4   Just before serving, in a small bowl stir together sour cream, sugar, and ½ teaspoon vanilla. Spread sour cream mixture over tart. Sprinkle fresh berries and, if desired, mint evenly over tart.

PER SERVING: 190 cal., 16 g total fat (8 g sat. fat), 82 mg chol., 109 mg sodium, 7 g carbo., 5 g fiber, 4 g pro.
EXCHANGES: ½ Other Carbo., 3½ Fat

OFF THE SHELF TIP Packaged cream cheese is used in so many ways in convenience cooking. It comes in a variety of sizes and flavors. Whipped cream cheese (called spreadable cream cheese) is often combined with other flavors such as herbs, vegetables, or fruits. Use cream cheese within a week of opening.

Peanut Butter S'more Tarts

PREP
15 MINUTES

CHILL
2 TO 24 HOURS

STAND
30 MINUTES

MAKES
6 TARTS

1 cup semisweet chocolate pieces (6 ounces)
½ cup peanut butter
1½ cups tiny marshmallows
½ cup chopped peanuts
1 4-ounce package (6) graham cracker tart shells

STEP 1 In a small saucepan melt the chocolate pieces over low heat, stirring constantly. Remove from heat. Stir in peanut butter until smooth. Stir in marshmallows and peanuts. Spoon into tart shells.

STEP 2 Cover and refrigerate for at least 2 hours or up to 24 hours. Let stand at room temperature for 30 minutes before serving.

PER TART: 505 cal., 31 g total fat (8 g sat. fat), 0 mg chol., 257 mg sodium, 42 g carbo., 7 g fiber, 10 g pro.
EXCHANGES: 2½ Other Carbo., 1½ High-Fat Meat, 4½ Fat

OFF THE SHELF TIP Graham cracker tart shells are found in the baking aisle; they don't need to be refrigerated.

Banana Split Trifles

Soft purchased cookies and ice cream stand in for the traditional cake and pudding in this quick-to-compose trifle. Make it in a glass bowl to give diners a full view of all the tempting ingredients.

FAST

START TO FINISH
15 MINUTES

MAKES
4 SERVINGS

2   to 3 cups tin roof sundae, chocolate chunk, or vanilla ice cream

4   soft-style oatmeal or chocolate chip cookies (each about 3 inches in diameter), crumbled

⅔   cup hot fudge ice cream topping and/or strawberry preserves

½   cup whipped cream

2   small bananas, halved lengthwise and sliced into 1- to 2-inch pieces

STEP 1   In a medium bowl use a wooden spoon to stir ice cream until softened. In each of 4 parfait glasses or other tall glasses layer cookie crumbs, softened ice cream, and hot fudge topping and/or preserves, layering ingredients to the top of the glasses.

STEP 2   Top trifles with whipped cream and banana slices. Serve immediately or cover and freeze until serving time or up to 1 hour.

PER SERVING: 524 cal., 23 g total fat (12 g sat. fat), 48 mg chol., 161 mg sodium, 73 g carbo., 3 g fiber, 6 g pro.
EXCHANGES: ½ Fruit, 4½ Other Carbo., 5 Fat

OFF THE SHELF TIP You'll find ice cream in the freezer case, of course! Buy it in pints, half gallons, or by the bucket.

Peach & Tropical Fruit Cobbler

SLOW COOKER

PREP
10 MINUTES
COOK
2½ HOURS (HIGH)
COOL
45 MINUTES
MAKES
10 SERVINGS

Nonstick cooking spray
2   21-ounce cans peach pie filling
1   15.25-ounce can tropical fruit salad undrained
1   13.9-ounce package cinnamon swirl snack cake mix
½   cup chopped pecans, toasted
4½   cups vanilla ice cream

OFF THE SHELF TIP Pie filling is a versatile ingredient in all kinds of recipes. Look for it in its many flavors in the baking aisle of the supermarket.

STEP 1 Lightly coat the inside of a 3½- or 4-quart slow cooker with nonstick cooking spray. In the prepared cooker combine the pie filling and undrained fruit salad.

STEP 2 Cover and cook on high-heat setting for 1½ hours (do not cook on low setting) or until fruit mixture is hot and bubbly; stir fruit mixture.

STEP 3 Prepare snack cake mix batter according to package directions; stir in pecans. Spoon cake batter over fruit mixture. Cover and cook for 1 hour more on high-heat setting or until a wooden toothpick inserted near center of cake comes out clean. Remove liner from cooker, if possible, or turn off cooker. Let stand, uncovered, for 45 to 60 minutes to cool slightly before serving.

STEP 4 To serve, spoon warm cobbler into dessert dishes. Top with ice cream.

PER SERVING: 497 cal., 19 g total fat (8 g sat. fat), 61 mg chol., 309 mg sodium, 77 g carbo., 2 g fiber, 6 g pro.
EXCHANGES: ½ Fruit, 4½ Other Carbo., 4 Fat

Cherry Cheese Turnovers

This treat's big on taste but light on calories and fat. Slip cherries and cream cheese into phyllo pockets for a rich flavor burst in a light, flaky pastry.

PREP
30 MINUTES
BAKE
12 MINUTES
OVEN
350°F
MAKES
12 TURNOVERS

½	cup dried tart cherries
3	tablespoons frozen apple juice concentrate, thawed
¼	teaspoon ground cinnamon
¼	of an 8-ounce package (2 ounces) reduced-fat cream cheese (Neufchâtel)
2	tablespoons granulated sugar
2	tablespoons refrigerated or frozen egg product, thawed
8	sheets frozen phyllo dough (9×14-inch rectangles), thawed Nonstick cooking spray
¼	cup graham cracker crumbs
3	tablespoons granulated sugar Powdered sugar

STEP 1 For filling, in a small saucepan combine cherries, apple juice concentrate, and cinnamon. Bring to boiling; reduce heat. Cover and simmer about 5 minutes or until liquid is absorbed. Remove from heat. In a small mixing bowl beat cream cheese and the 2 tablespoons granulated sugar with an electric mixer on medium speed until fluffy. Beat in egg product. Gently stir in the cherry mixture. Set aside.

STEP 2 Preheat oven to 350°F. Lightly coat 1 sheet of the phyllo dough with nonstick cooking spray. (To keep remaining sheets of phyllo dough from drying out, cover with plastic wrap.) Sprinkle with about 1½ teaspoons of the graham cracker crumbs and about 1 teaspoon granulated sugar. Repeat layers again, coating just the top side of the second phyllo sheet. Cut phyllo stack lengthwise into 3 strips. Place 1 well-rounded teaspoon of the filling about 1 inch from the end of each strip. Bring a corner of the phyllo over the filling so the short edge lines up with the long edge. Continue folding the triangular shape along the strip until the end is reached. Repeat with the remaining strips.

STEP 3 Repeat with the remaining phyllo dough, graham cracker crumbs, granulated sugar, and filling. Place turnovers on a baking sheet. Lightly coat with cooking spray.

STEP 4 Bake in the preheated oven for 12 to 15 minutes or until light brown and crisp. Transfer to a wire rack and let cool. Sprinkle with powdered sugar.

PER TURNOVER: 100 cal., 3 g total fat (2 g sat. fat), 7 mg chol., 90 mg sodium, 17 g carbo., 0 g fiber, 2 g pro.
EXCHANGES: 1 Other Carbo., ½ Fat

OFF THE SHELF TIP Look in the frozen section of the supermarket for phyllo dough. When working with it, be sure to keep the sheets you aren't using covered with plastic wrap; the fragile pastry sheets tend to dry out quickly.

Raisin Pudding Cake

Spice cake mix, raisins, and pecans in the slow cooker produce a warm pudding cake that's a treat on its own or with a scoop of vanilla ice cream.

SLOW COOKER

PREP
15 MINUTES

COOK
2½ HOURS (HIGH)

STAND
45 MINUTES

MAKES
8 TO 10 SERVINGS

1	package 2-layer-size spice cake mix
⅔	cup milk
1	cup raisins
½	cup chopped pecans
1½	cups water
½	cup packed brown sugar
½	cup butter or margarine
1	teaspoon vanilla
	Vanilla ice cream (optional)

STEP 1 For batter, in a large bowl stir together cake mix and milk with a wooden spoon until smooth. Stir in raisins and pecans (batter will be thick); set aside.

STEP 2 In a small saucepan combine water, brown sugar, and butter; bring to boiling. Remove from heat. Stir in vanilla. Pour into a 3½- or 4-quart slow cooker with removeable liner. Carefully drop large spoonfuls of batter into sugar mixture.

STEP 3 Cover and cook on high-heat setting for 2½ hours (do not cook on low-heat setting). The center may appear moist but will set up upon standing. Remove liner from cooker; let stand for 45 minutes to cool slightly before serving. Serve warm. If desired, top with ice cream.

PER SERVING: 527 cal., 22 g total fat (10 g sat. fat), 34 mg chol., 548 mg sodium, 82 g carbo., 1 g fiber, 4 g pro.
EXCHANGES: 1 Fruit, 4½ Other Carbo., 4½ Fat

OFF THE SHELF TIP You'll find all sorts of salted and unsalted nuts in the baking aisle near the chips. Look for packages of pieces and already chopped nuts.

Chocolate-Covered Strawberry Cakes

PREP
30 MINUTES
STAND
30 MINUTES
MAKES
18 MINI CAKES

RECIPE PICTURED ON PAGE 144.

1   10¾-ounce frozen loaf pound cake
3   tablespoons strawberry jam
½   cup semisweet chocolate pieces
½   of a 16-ounce can chocolate frosting (about 1 cup)
1   tablespoon strawberry liqueur or amaretto
18   fresh medium strawberries

STEP 1 Cut cake into ½-inch slices using a serrated knife. (You should have 12 slices.) Spread one side of half of the slices with strawberry jam. Top each of the jam-covered slices with a plain cake slice, making a sandwich. Cut each sandwich diagonally to form 3 triangles. You should end up with 18 mini sandwiches.

STEP 2 For icing, cook and stir chocolate pieces over low heat until melted. Add frosting, stirring to combine. Stir in liqueur. Heat and stir for 1 to 2 minutes more or until mixture is melted enough to coat cakes. Remove from heat.

STEP 3 Insert a 2- or 3-prong long-handle fork into the side of the bottom slice of one cake. Holding the cake over the saucepan of icing, spoon on enough icing to cover the sides and top. Place the frosted cake on a wire rack. Repeat with remaining cakes, reheating icing, if necessary. Let stand for 30 minutes or until icing sets.

STEP 4 Before serving, transfer cakes to a serving platter and place a strawberry on top of each serving.

PER MINI CAKE: 167 cal., 7 g total fat (3 g sat. fat), 19 mg chol., 106 mg sodium, 23 g carbo., 1 g fiber, 1 g pro.
EXCHANGES: 1½ Other Carbo., 1½ Fat

OFF THE SHELF TIP Canned frosting finds its home in the baking aisle of the supermarket. The number of flavors available is amazing.

Bananas Suzette over Pound Cake

Gently spiced and fruited, sauteed bananas transform a scoop of ice cream and slice of pound cake into a lovely, dressy dessert.

FAST

START TO FINISH
15 MINUTES

MAKES
4 SERVINGS

1   **tablespoon butter or margarine**
½   **of a 10¾-ounce package frozen pound cake, thawed and cut into 4 slices**
2   **ripe, firm medium bananas**
3   **tablespoons sugar**
2   **tablespoons orange-flavored liqueur or orange juice**
2   **tablespoons orange juice**
1   **tablespoon butter or margarine**
⅛   **teaspoon ground nutmeg**
1   **cup vanilla ice cream**

STEP 1   In a medium skillet melt 1 tablespoon butter over medium heat. Add pound cake slices; cook for 1 to 2 minutes or until brown, turning once. Remove from skillet; set aside.

STEP 2 Peel bananas; bias-slice each banana into 8 pieces. In the same skillet combine sugar, liqueur, orange juice, and 1 tablespoon butter. Cook about 1 minute or until butter melts and sugar begins to dissolve. Add the bananas; cook for 2 to 4 minutes more or just until bananas are tender, stirring once. Stir in nutmeg.

STEP 3   To serve, place each pound cake slice on a dessert plate. Top each with a small scoop of vanilla ice cream. Spoon bananas and sauce over ice cream and pound cake slices.

PER SERVING: 394 cal., 18 g total fat (11 g sat. fat), 74 mg chol., 229 mg sodium, 53 g carbo., 2 g fiber, 4 g pro.
EXCHANGES: ½ Milk, 1 Fruit, 2 Other Carbo., 3½ Fat

OFF THE SHELF TIP Frozen pound cake is dense and buttery and is found—you guessed it—in the frozen aisle of the supermarket. Keep an extra one on hand for a fast-to-fix dessert. Top slices with ice cream and drizzle with your favorite topping.

Snow Angel Cake

FAST

START TO FINISH
15 MINUTES

MAKES
12 SERVINGS

1	purchased angel food cake
2	ounces white chocolate baking squares or ⅓ cup white baking pieces
1	8-ounce container frozen whipped dessert topping, thawed
¼	cup coconut

STEP 1   Place cake on a serving plate; set aside.

STEP 2   In a small saucepan melt white baking squares over low heat, stirring occasionally. Remove from heat.

STEP 3   Frost cake with whipped topping. Sprinkle with coconut. Drizzle with melted white baking bars.

PER SERVING: 152 cal., 6 g total fat (5 g sat. fat), 1 mg chol., 190 mg sodium, 22 g carbo., 1 g fiber, 2 g pro.
EXCHANGES: 1½ Other Carbo., 1 Fat

OFF THE SHELF TIP   Frozen dessert topping is found near the frozen pies and cakes in the supermarket. It comes in regular, light, and fat-free versions. **TOO BUSY TO THINK ABOUT DINNER?**   Follow this 3-stepper—in advance—to save your sanity on busy days. 1. Choose one or two meals that you can make in 20 minutes or less, using only pantry items. 2. Stock those items in your pantry. 3. Post the recipes inside the pantry door.
    On those days when your head's spinning, open the pantry and follow the instructions you wrote for yourself. You're so smart.

Chocolate Chip Ice Cream Cake

Hollow out an angel food cake, then stuff it with an ice cream–cream cheese blend for a unique fudge- or strawberry-topped dessert.

PREP
20 MINUTES
FREEZE
6 TO 24 HOURS
MAKES
10 TO 12 SERVINGS

1   **3-ounce package cream cheese, softened**
1   **tablespoon sugar**
1½   **cups chocolate chip, strawberry, or vanilla ice cream**
1   **8- or 9-inch purchased angel food cake (15 or 16 ounces)**
⅓   **cup sliced fresh strawberries**
⅓   **cup chocolate fudge or strawberry ice cream topping**

STEP 1   For filling, in a small bowl stir together cream cheese and sugar. In a medium bowl use a wooden spoon to stir ice cream just until it begins to soften; fold cream cheese mixture into ice cream. Place in freezer while preparing the cake.

STEP 2   Use a serrated knife to cut off the top ½ inch of the cake; set aside. Hold the knife parallel to the center hole of the cake and cut around the hole, leaving about ¾-inch thickness of cake around the hole. Cut around the outer edge of the cake, leaving an outer cake wall about ¾ inch thick. Use a spoon to remove center of cake, leaving about a ¾-inch-thick base. (Reserve scooped-out cake for another use.)

STEP 3   Spoon filling into hollowed cake. Arrange sliced strawberries on the filling. Replace the top of the cake. Cover and freeze for at least 6 hours or up to 24 hours.

STEP 4   To serve, in a small saucepan heat ice cream topping until drizzling consistency; drizzle over cake. Slice cake with a serrated knife.

PER SERVING: 219 cal., 7 g total fat (4 g sat. fat), 18 mg chol., 265 mg sodium, 37 g carbo., 0 g fiber, 5 g pro.
EXCHANGES: 2½ Other Carbo., 1½ Fat

OFF THE SHELF TIP   Packaged cream cheese is used in so many ways in convenience cooking. It comes in a variety of sizes and flavors. Whipped cream cheese (called spreadable cream cheese) is often combined with other flavors such as herbs, vegetables, or fruits. Use cream cheese within a week of opening.

Boldfaced page references indicate photographs.

A

Appetizers. *See also* Dips and spreads
Black Bean Nachos, 23
Buffalo Chicken Wings, 20
Cajun Peanuts, 16
Chicken & Rice-Filled Spring Rolls, 21
Coconut Shrimp with Mango Ginger Dip, 22
Cranberry-Sauced Franks, 18
Cucumber-Cheese Bites, 26
Five-Spice Pecans, 15
Glazed Ham Balls & Smokies, 19
Spinach-Stuffed Mushrooms, 25
Sweet 'n' Sour Ham Balls, 17
Toasted Ravioli, 24

Apples
Cranberry Chicken, 116
Taffy Apple Salad, 226

Apricots
Apricot-Almond Torte, 238
Apricot-Glazed Pork Roast, 88, **137**
Apricot-Orange Sauce, 231
Apricot Turkey Steaks, 126

Artichokes
Easy Mediterranean Alfredo Pizza, 198
Hot Artichoke & Roasted Pepper Dip, 8, **142**
Mediterranean Alfredo Pizza, **143**, 198
Shrimp-Artichoke Skillet, 175

Asparagus
Chicken and Rice-Filled Spring Rolls, 21
Lemon Chicken with Asparagus, 114
Linguine with Gorgonzola Sauce, 195

B

Bacon-Corn Chowder, 39
Banana Split Trifles, 242
Bananas Suzette over Pound Cake, 247
Barley & Green Bean Skillet, 191
Barley-Tomato Soup with Garden Vegetables, 55
Beans. *See also* Green beans
Beer-Simmered Black Beans, 209
Black Bean & Corn Quesadillas, 188
Black Bean Nachos, 23
Black Bean & Sausage Posole, 38, **132**
Cajun Beans on Corn Bread, 190
Chili with Polenta, 31
Chipotle Bean Enchiladas, 189
Chunky Chicken Chili, 46
Curried Lentils & Spinach, 192
East-West Veggies, 220
Fish with Black Bean Sauce, 158
Garbanzo Bean Dip, 7
Margarita Fajitas with Sub-Lime
Salsa, 110, **130**
Mexican Stromboli, 154
Minestrone, 200
Quick Pork-Bean Soup, 37

Savory Beans & Rice, 186
Spicy Shrimp & Noodle Soup, 51, **132**
Sweet Beans & Noodles, 187
Taco Chili, 32
Tamale Pie, 70
Texas Two-Step Stew, 35
Three-Bean Chili, 56
Turkey-Bean Soup, 47
White & Green Chili, 33

Beef
Asian-Style Meatballs, 68
Barbecue Beef Calzones, 79
Beef & Broccoli with Plum Sauce, 60, **136**
Beef Bunburgers, 72
Beef Burgundy, 77
Beef Ragout, 82
Beef Roast with Vegetables, 81
Chili-Sauced Burgers & Spaghetti, 73
Chili with Polenta, 31
Chipotle Brisket Sandwich, 78
Dijon-Pepper Steak, 62
Easy Beef & Noodle Soup, 30
Flank Steak Sandwiches, 64
French Onion & Beef Soup, 28
Hamburger Stroganoff, 74
Mexican-Style Hash, 80
Peppery Steak with Bordelaise Sauce, 58
Pot Roast with Chipotle-Fruit Sauce, 63
Reuben Chowder, 34
Reuben Loaf, 84
Roast Beef & Mashed Potato Stacks, 76
Roasted Vegetable & Pastrami Panini, 83
Saucy Steak, 65
Sausage-Cavatelli Skillet, 99
Spiced Beef Brisket, 67
Steaks with Horseradish Cream Sauce, 61
Steak with Mushrooms, 66
Stroganoff-Sauced Beef Roast, 75, **138**
Stroganoff-Style Beef with Broccoli, 59
Stroganoff-Style Meatballs, 69
Sweet & Sour Beef Stew, 29
Taco Chili, 32
Taco Pizza, 71
Tamale Pie, 70
White & Green Chili, 33

Berries. *See also* Cranberries; Raspberries
Berry Compote, 233
Chocolate-Covered Strawberry
Cakes, **144**, 246
Lemon Cream Tart, 240
Bread Pudding, Sweet Pepper & Onion, 218

Broccoli
Beef & Broccoli with Plum Sauce, 60, **136**
Broccoli Chowder, 52
Broccoli-Salmon Pasta, 174
Broccoli-Swiss Soup, 53
Orange-Sauced Fish with Broccoli, 165

Stroganoff-Style Beef with Broccoli, 59
Tofu-Mushroom Noodle Soup, 54
Turkey Manicotti with Chive Cream
Sauce, **141**, 149
Brussels Sprouts, Glazed, **134**, 210

Burgers
Beef Bunburgers, 72
Chili-Sauced Burgers & Spaghetti, 73
Lamb Burgers with Feta & Mint, 102
Butterscotch Fondue, 234

C

Cakes
Chocolate Chip Ice Cream Cake, 249
Chocolate-Covered Strawberry
Cakes, **144**, 246
Raisin Pudding Cake, 245
Snow Angel Cake, 248
Calzones, Barbecue Beef, 79
Calzones, Spinach, 199

Carrots
Peas & Carrots with Cumin, 213
Sweet Saucy Carrots & Pecans, 211
Cashew Chicken, 108

Cheese
Baked Parmesan Chicken, 111
Barbecue Beef Calzones, 79
Black Bean & Corn Quesadillas, 188
Black Bean Nachos, 23
Blue Cheese Walnut Spread, 13
Broccoli Chowder, 52
Broccoli-Swiss Soup, 53
Cheesy Chops & Corn Bread Dressing, 92
Cherry Cheese Turnovers, 244
Chipotle Bean Enchiladas, 189
Chipotle Chicken Enchiladas, 122
Chipotle con Queso Dip, 12
Country-Style Stuffed Peppers, 98
Creamy Lemon Pasta, 221
Cucumber-Cheese Bites, 26
Easy Chicken Turnovers, 124
Easy Mediterranean Alfredo Pizza, 198
Fettuccine-Vegetable Toss, **139**, 196
Gardener's Pie, 204
Hawaiian-Style Barbecue Pizza, 120
Hot Artichoke & Roasted Pepper Dip, 8, **142**
Lamb Burgers with Feta & Mint, 102
Linguine with Gorgonzola Sauce, 195
Mediterranean Alfredo Pizza, **143**, 198
Mexican Potato Cakes, 215
Mexican Stromboli, 154
Mexican Turkey Pie, 128
Mock Monte Cristo Sandwiches, 152
No-Fail Swiss Fondue, 10
Parmesan Baked Fish, 160
Pasta with Pepper-Cheese Sauce, 194
Pastry-Wrapped Chicken, 112

Ravioli Skillet Lasagna, **140**, 193
Reuben Chowder, 34
Reuben Loaf, 84
Roasted Vegetable & Pastrami Panini, 83
Salmon with Feta & Pasta, 159
Saucy Pizza Skillet Dinner, 197
Skillet Scalloped Corn, 212
Smoky Chipotle Fondue, 11
South-of-the-Border Snapper, 168
Spinach Calzones, 199
Spinach-Scalloped Potatoes, 217
Swiss Vegetable Medley, 206
Taco Pizza, 71
Tamale Pie, 70
Turkey Manicotti with Chive Cream
    Sauce, **141**, 149
Turkey-Potato Bake, 151
Turkey Strudel, 150
Cherry Cheese Turnovers, 244

Chicken
Baked Parmesan Chicken, 111
Buffalo Chicken Wings, 20
Cashew Chicken, 108
Chicken & Pasta Salad with Tomatoes, 123
Chicken & Rice-Filled Spring Rolls, 21
Chicken & Vegetables Alfredo with Rice, 119
Chicken Breasts in Herbed Tomato Sauce, 118
Chicken Tortilla Soup, 44
Chicken-Vegetable Soup, 43
Chicken with Buttermilk Gravy, 117
Chicken with Noodles, 121
Chipotle Chicken Enchiladas, 122
Chunky Chicken Chili, 46
Cranberry Chicken, 116
Creamy Chicken & Vegetable Stew, 45
Creamy Chicken Noodle Soup, 42
Curried Chicken & Corn Chowder, 41
Dijon Chicken & Mushrooms, 115
Easy Chicken Turnovers, 124
Hawaiian-Style Barbecue Pizza, 120
Lemon Chicken with Asparagus, 114
Margarita Fajitas with Sub-Lime
    Salsa, 110, **130**
Mexican Stromboli, 154
Orange Chicken & Fried Rice, 113
Pastry-Wrapped Chicken, 112
Plum Wonderful Chicken, 107, **129**
Quick Asian Chicken Soup, 40
Quick Thai Chicken, 109, **131**
Saucy Cranberry Chicken, 106, **130**

Chickpeas
Garbanzo Bean Dip, 7
Minestrone, 200
Three-Bean Chili, 56

Chile peppers
Beer-Simmered Black Beans, 209
Chipotle Brisket Sandwich, 78

Chipotle Chicken Enchiladas, 122
Chipotle con Queso Dip, 12
Margarita Fajitas with Sub-Lime
    Salsa, 110, **130**
Mexican Potato Cakes, 215
Mexican Turkey Pie, 128
Peppery Pork Sandwiches, 90
Pot Roast with Chipotle-Fruit Sauce, 63
Smoky Chipotle Fondue, 11
Tamale Pie, 70
Three-Bean Chili, 56

Chili
Chili with Polenta, 31
Chunky Chicken Chili, 46
Taco Chili, 32
Three-Bean Chili, 56
White & Green Chili, 33

Chocolate
Chocolate Chip Ice Cream Cake, 249
Chocolate-Covered Strawberry
    Cakes, **144**, 246
Chocolate Hazelnut Ice Cream Sauce, 230
Chocolate Whipped Cream, 239
Extreme Chocolate Pie, 239
Peanut Butter S'more Tarts, 241
Rocky Road Squares, 235
Snow Angel Cake, 248

Chowder
Broccoli Chowder, 52
Clam Chowder, 50
Corn-Bacon Chowder, 39
Curried Chicken & Corn Chowder, 41
Reuben Chowder, 34
Sausage-Corn Chowder, 36
Seafood Chowder, 48
Clam Chowder, 50
Cobbler, Peach & Tropical Fruit, 243

Coconut
Coconut Shrimp with Mango Ginger Dip, 22
Snow Angel Cake, 248
Cod, Beer-Battered, 157

Corn
Black Bean & Corn Quesadillas, 188
Chicken Tortilla Soup, 44
Corn-Bacon Chowder, 39
Curried Chicken & Corn Chowder, 41
East-West Veggies, 220
Mexican-Style Hash, 80
Saucy Shrimp over Polenta, 179
Sausage-Corn Chowder, 36
Skillet Scalloped Corn, 212
Taco Chili, 32
Texas Two-Step Stew, 35

Couscous
Mediterranean Couscous with Tofu, 201
Orange-Sauced Fish with Broccoli, 165
Savory Couscous, **134**, 222

Crab
Crab Cakes with Red Pepper Relish, 183
Crab-Tomato Bisque, 49
Hot Crab Spread, 14
Rockefeller-Style Crab, 184

Cranberries
Berry Compote, 233
Cranberry Chicken, 116
Cranberry-Sauced Franks, 18
Lamb Chops with Cranberry Relish, 101
Raspberry-Cranberry Sauce, 232
Saucy Cranberry Chicken, 106, **130**
Turkey Steaks with Cranberry-Orange
    Sauce, 147
Cucumber-Cheese Bites, 26
Curried Chicken & Corn Chowder, 41
Curried Lentils & Spinach, 192
Custard, Orange-Pumpkin, 237

D
Desserts. *See also* Cakes
Apricot-Almond Torte, 238
Apricot-Orange Sauce, 231
Banana Split Trifles, 242
Bananas Suzette over Pound Cake, 247
Berry Compote, 233
Butterscotch Fondue, 234
Cherry Cheese Turnovers, 244
Chocolate Hazelnut Ice Cream Sauce, 230
Extreme Chocolate Pie, 239
Lemon Cream Tart, 240
Orange-Pumpkin Custard, 237
Peach & Tropical Fruit Cobbler, 243
Peanut Butter S'more Tarts, 241
Raspberry-Cranberry Sauce, 232
Rocky Road Squares, 235
Sweet Peanut Bars, 236

Dips & spreads
Blue Cheese Walnut Spread, 13
Chipotle con Queso Dip, 12
Creamy Spinach Dip, 9
French Onion Dip, 6
Garbanzo Bean Dip, 7
Hot Artichoke & Roasted Pepper Dip, 8, **142**
Hot Crab Spread, 14
No-Fail Swiss Fondue, 10
Smoky Chipotle Fondue, 11

E
Enchiladas, Chipotle Bean, 189
Enchiladas, Chipotle Chicken, 122

F
Fajitas, Margarita, with Sub-Lime Salsa, 110, **130**
Fish. *See also* Salmon
Beer-Battered Cod, 157
Creamy Tuna Mac, 172

Easy Baked Fish, 170
Fish Fillets with Yogurt Dressing, 156
Fish Stew, 162
Fish with Black Bean Sauce, 158
Lime-Poached Mahi Mahi, 164
Orange-Sauced Fish with Broccoli, 165
Parmesan Baked Fish, 160
Seafood Chowder, 48
Sesame-Coated Tilapia Salad, 166
Snapper Veracruz, 167
South-of-the-Border Snapper, 168
Sweet Mustard Halibut, 169
Tuna Spinach Braid, **135**, 171
Five-Spice Powder, Homemade, 89
Fondue
Butterscotch Fondue, 234
No-Fail Swiss Fondue, 10
Smoky Chipotle Fondue, 11
Fruit. *See also* specific fruits
Fruited Wild Rice Salad, 225
Fruit Salsa, 100
Ginger Ale Salad, 227
Peach & Tropical Fruit Cobbler, 243
Pot Roast with Chipotle-Fruit Sauce, 63

G
Ginger Ale Salad, 227
Green beans
Barley & Green Bean Skillet, 191
Beef Ragout, 82
Golden Green Bean Crunch, 208
Greek-Style Lamb Skillet, 104, **133**
Green Bean-Red Pepper Casserole, 207

H
Halibut, Sweet Mustard, 169
Ham
Glazed Ham Balls & Smokies, 19
Mock Monte Cristo Sandwiches, 152
Peach-Mustard Glazed Ham, 100
Sweet 'n' Sour Ham Balls, 17
Hash, Mexican-Style, 80
Hazelnut Chocolate Ice Cream Sauce, 230

L
Lamb
Greek-Style Lamb Skillet, 104, **133**
Lamb Burgers with Feta & Mint, 102
Lamb Chops with Cranberry Relish, 101
Saucy Lamb Meatballs, 103
Lemon Cream Tart, 240
Lentils & Spinach, Curried, 192

M
Mahi Mahi, Lime-Poached, 164
Mango-Spinach Salad, 228
Maple-Mustard-Sauced Turkey Thighs, 125

Maple-Pecan Glazed Pork Chops, 91
Meatballs
Asian-Style Meatballs, 68
Saucy Lamb Meatballs, 103
Stroganoff-Style Meatballs, 69
Sweet 'n' Sour Ham Balls, 17
Meatless dishes
Asian Noodle Bowl, 202
Barley & Green Bean Skillet, 191
Black Bean & Corn Quesadillas, 188
Brunch Casserole, 203
Cajun Beans on Corn Bread, 190
Chipotle Bean Enchiladas, 189
Curried Lentils & Spinach, 192
Easy Mediterranean Alfredo Pizza, 198
Fettuccine-Vegetable Toss, **139**, 196
Gardener's Pie, 204
Linguine with Gorgonzola Sauce, 195
Mediterranean Alfredo Pizza, **143**, 198
Mediterranean Couscous with Tofu, 201
Minestrone, 200
Pasta with Pepper-Cheese Sauce, 194
Ravioli Skillet Lasagna, **140**, 193
Saucy Pizza Skillet Dinner, 197
Savory Beans & Rice, 186
Spinach Calzones, 199
Sweet Beans & Noodles, 187
Mushrooms
Beef Burgandy, 77
Dijon Chicken & Mushrooms, 115
Flank Steak Sandwiches, 64
Hamburger Stroganoff, 74
Peppery Steak with Bordelaise Sauce, 58
Savory Couscous, **134**, 222
Spinach-Stuffed Mushrooms, 25
Steak with Mushrooms, 66
Stroganoff-Sauced Beef Roast, 75, **138**
Tofu-Mushroom Noodle Soup, 54
Wild Rice & Spinach au Gratin, 224

N
Nachos, Black Bean, 23
Noodles
Asian Noodle Bowl, 202
Beef Burgandy, 77
Beef Ragout, 82
Chicken with Noodles, 121
Creamy Chicken Noodle Soup, 42
Easy Beef & Noodle Soup, 30
Five-Spice Turkey Stir-Fry, 127
Hamburger Stroganoff, 74
Shrimp Alfredo, 176
Spicy Shrimp & Noodle Soup, 51, **132**
Stroganoff-Sauced Beef Roast, 75, **138**
Stroganoff-Style Beef with Broccoli, 59
Sweet Beans & Noodles, 187
Thai Shrimp & Sesame Noodles, 181

Tofu-Mushroom Noodle Soup, 54
Turkey-Vegetable Goulash, 153
Nuts. *See also* Peanuts; Pecans
Blue Cheese Walnut Spread, 13
Cashew Chicken, 108
Chocolate Hazelnut Ice Cream Sauce, 230
Fruited Wild Rice Salad, 225

O
Onions
French Onion & Beef Soup, 28
French Onion Dip, 6

P
Pasta. *See also* Noodles
Broccoli-Salmon Pasta, 174
Chicken & Pasta Salad with Tomatoes, 123
Chili-Sauced Burgers & Spaghetti, 73
Creamy Lemon Pasta, 221
Creamy Tuna Mac, 172
Fettuccine-Vegetable Toss, **139**, 196
Greek-Style Lamb Skillet, 104, **133**
Linguine with Gorgonzola Sauce, 195
Minestrone, 200
Pasta with Pepper-Cheese Sauce, 194
Ravioli Skillet Lasagna, **140**, 193
Salmon with Feta & Pasta, 159
Saucy Pizza Skillet Dinner, 197
Sausage-Cavatelli Skillet, 99
Shrimp Alfredo, 176
Shrimply Divine Pasta, **140**, 178
Sweet Beans & Noodles, 187
Thai Shrimp & Sesame Noodles, 181
Toasted Ravioli, 24
Turkey Manicotti with Chive Cream
Sauce, **141**, 149
Pastrami & Roasted Vegetable Panini, 83
Peach & Tropical Fruit Cobbler, 243
Peach-Mustard Glazed Ham, 100
Peanut butter
Peanut Butter S'more Tarts, 241
Quick Thai Chicken, 109, **131**
Sweet Peanut Bars, 236
Peanuts
Asian Noodle Bowl, 202
Cajun Peanuts, 16
Peanut Butter S'more Tarts, 241
Rocky Road Squares, 235
Sweet Peanut Bars, 236
Taffy Apple Salad, 226
Peas
Chicken with Noodles, 121
Coconut Rice with Snow Peas, 223
Creamy Tuna Mac, 172
Gingery Sugar Snap Peas, 214
Peas & Carrots with Cumin, 213
Spanish-Style Rice with Seafood, 180

Pecans
    Five-Spice Pecans, 15
    Maple-Pecan Glazed Pork Chops, 91
    Nutty Turkey Tenderloins, 145
    Sweet Saucy Carrots & Pecans, 211
Peppers. *See also* Chile peppers
    Country-Style Stuffed Peppers, 98
    Green Bean-Red Pepper Casserole, 207
    Herb-Crusted Salmon with Roasted
      Pepper Cream, 163
    Hot Artichoke & Roasted Pepper Dip, 8, **142**
    Pasta with Pepper-Cheese Sauce, 194
    Red Pepper Relish, 183
    Sweet Pepper & Onion Bread Pudding, 218
    Taco Pizza, 71
Pie, Extreme Chocolate, 239
Pizza. *See also* Calzones
    Easy Mediterranean Alfredo Pizza, 198
    Hawaiian-Style Barbecue Pizza, 120
    Mediterranean Alfredo Pizza, *143*, 198
    Taco Pizza, 71
Polenta, Chili with, 31
Polenta, Saucy Shrimp over, 179
Pork. *See also* Ham; Pork sausages
    Apricot-Glazed Pork Roast, 88, **137**
    Balsamic & Garlic Pork, 87
    Barbecued Ribs & Kraut, 97
    Barbecue Pork Ribs, 96
    Cheesy Chops & Corn Bread Dressing, 92
    Corn-Bacon Chowder, 39
    Glazed Ham Balls & Smokies, 19
    Maple-Pecan Glazed Pork Chops, 91
    Oriental Pork Sandwiches, 89
    Peppery Pork Sandwiches, 90
    Pork & Slaw Barbecue Rolls, 86
    Pork Chops Dijon, 95
    Pork Chops with Orange-Dijon Sauce, 94
    Pork Chops with Raspberries, 93, **136**
    Quick Pork-Bean Soup, 37
    Shredded Pork Sandwiches, 85, **142**
    Sweet 'n' Sour Ham Balls, 17
    White & Green Chili, 33
Pork sausages
    Black Bean & Sausage Posole, 38, **132**
    Country-Style Stuffed Peppers, 98
    Cranberry-Sauced Franks, 18
    Glazed Ham Balls & Smokies, 19
    Sausage-Cavatelli Skillet, 99
    Taco Pizza, 71
    Tamale Pie, 70
    Texas Two-Step Stew, 35
Potatoes
    Barbecued Ribs & Kraut, 97
    Brunch Casserole, 203
    Clam Chowder, 50
    Creamy Mashed Potatoes, 216
    Gardener's Pie, 204

Maple-Mustard-Sauced Turkey Thighs, 125
Mexican Potato Cakes, 215
Mexican-Style Hash, 80
Roast Beef & Mashed Potato Stacks, 76
Sausage-Corn Chowder, 36
Seafood Chowder, 48
Spinach-Scalloped Potatoes, 217
Turkey-Potato Bake, 151
Potpie, Dijon-Turkey, 148
Pudding, Bread, Sweet Pepper & Onion, 218
Pumpkin-Orange Custard, 237

Q
Quesadillas, Black Bean & Corn, 188

R
Raisin Pudding Cake, 245
Raspberries
    Berry Compote, 233
    Pork Chops with Raspberries, 93, **136**
    Raspberry-Cranberry Sauce, 232
Ravioli, Toasted, 24
Ravioli Skillet Lasagna, **140**, 193
Relish, Red Pepper, 183
Rice
    Cajun Shrimp & Rice, 182
    Chicken & Rice-Filled Spring Rolls, 21
    Chicken & Vegetables Alfredo with Rice, 119
    Coconut Rice with Snow Peas, 223
    Fruited Wild Rice Salad, 225
    Orange Chicken & Fried Rice, 113
    Saffron Rice Baked Tomatoes, 219
    Savory Beans & Rice, 186
    Shrimp over Rice, 177
    Spanish-Style Rice with Seafood, 180
    Texas Two-Step Stew, 35
    Wild Rice & Spinach au Gratin, 224

S
Salads
    Chicken & Pasta Salad with Tomatoes, 123
    Fruited Wild Rice Salad, 225
    Ginger Ale Salad, 227
    Mango-Spinach Salad, 228
    Sesame-Coated Tilapia Salad, 166
    Taffy Apple Salad, 226
Salmon
    Broccoli-Salmon Pasta, 174
    Browned Butter Salmon, 161
    Herb-Crusted Salmon with Roasted Pepper
      Cream, 163
    Salmon-Sour Cream Turnovers, 173
    Salmon with Feta & Pasta, 159
Sandwiches. *See also* Burgers
    Chipotle Brisket Sandwich, 78
    Flank Steak Sandwiches, 64
    Mexican Stromboli, 154

Mock Monte Cristo Sandwiches, 152
Oriental Pork Sandwiches, 89
Peppery Pork Sandwiches, 90
Pork & Slaw Barbecue Rolls, 86
Roasted Vegetable & Pastrami Panini, 83
Shredded Pork Sandwiches, 85, **142**
Sauces
    Apricot-Orange Sauce, 231
    Chocolate Hazelnut Ice Cream Sauce, 230
    Honey Mustard Sauce, 112
    Raspberry-Cranberry Sauce, 232
Sauerkraut
    Barbecued Ribs & Kraut, 97
    Reuben Chowder, 34
    Reuben Loaf, 84
Sausages. *See also* Pork sausages
    Black Bean & Sausage Posole, 38, **132**
    Sausage-Cavatelli Skillet, 99
    Sausage-Corn Chowder, 36
    Turkey-Bean Soup, 47
Seafood. *See* Fish; Shellfish
Shellfish. *See also* Crab; Shrimp
    Clam Chowder, 50
Shrimp
    Cajun Shrimp & Rice, 182
    Coconut Shrimp with Mango Ginger Dip, 22
    Saucy Shrimp over Polenta, 179
    Shrimp Alfredo, 176
    Shrimp-Artichoke Skillet, 175
    Shrimply Divine Pasta, *140*, 178
    Shrimp over Rice, 177
    Spanish-Style Rice with Seafood, 180
    Spicy Shrimp & Noodle Soup, 51, **132**
    Thai Shrimp & Sesame Noodles, 181
Snapper, South-of-the-Border, 168
Snapper Veracruz, 167
Soups. *See also* Chowder; Stews
    Black Bean & Sausage Posole, 38, **132**
    Broccoli-Swiss Soup, 53
    Chicken Tortilla Soup, 44
    Chicken-Vegetable Soup, 43
    Crab-Tomato Bisque, 49
    Creamy Chicken Noodle Soup, 42
    Easy Beef & Noodle Soup, 30
    French Onion & Beef Soup, 28
    Minestrone, 200
    Quick Asian Chicken Soup, 40
    Quick Pork-Bean Soup, 37
    Spicy Shrimp & Noodle Soup, 51, **132**
    Tofu-Mushroom Noodle Soup, 54
    Tomato-Barley Soup with Garden Vegetables, 55
    Turkey-Bean Soup, 47
Soybeans
    Sweet Beans & Noodles, 187
Spinach
    Creamy Spinach Dip, 9
    Curried Lentils & Spinach, 192

Mango-Spinach Salad, 228
Ravioli Skillet Lasagna, **140**, 193
Rockefeller-Style Crab, 184
Spinach Calzones, 199
Spinach-Scalloped Potatoes, 217
Spinach-Stuffed Mushrooms, 25
Tuna Spinach Braid, **135**, 171
Wild Rice & Spinach au Gratin, 224
Spreads. *See also* Dips and spreads
Squash
Orange-Pumpkin Custard, 237
Three-Bean Chili, 56
Tomato-Barley Soup with Garden
Vegetables, 55
Stews. *See also* Chili
Beef Burgundy, 77
Beef Ragout, 82
Creamy Chicken & Vegetable Stew, 45
Fish Stew, 162
Sweet & Sour Beef Stew, 29
Texas Two-Step Stew, 35
Strawberry Cakes, Chocolate-
Covered, **144**, 246
Strudel, Turkey, 150

T
Taco Chili, 32
Taco Pizza, 71
Tamale Pie, 70
Tarts
Apricot-Almond Torte, 238
Lemon Cream Tart, 240
Peanut Butter S'more Tarts, 241
Tilapia Salad, Sesame-Coated, 166
Tofu, Mediterranean Couscous with, 201
Tofu-Mushroom Noodle Soup, 54
Tomatoes
Chicken & Pasta Salad with Tomatoes, 123
Crab-Tomato Bisque, 49
Saffron Rice Baked Tomatoes, 219
Snapper Veracruz, 167
Tomato-Barley Soup with Garden
Vegetables, 55
Tortillas
Black Bean & Corn Quesadillas, 188
Black Bean Nachos, 23
Chicken Tortilla Soup, 44
Chipotle Bean Enchiladas, 189
Chipotle Chicken Enchiladas, 122
Margarita Fajitas with Sub-Lime
Salsa, 110, **130**
Tuna Mac, Creamy, 172
Tuna Spinach Braid, **135**, 171
Turkey
Apricot Turkey Steaks, 126
Dijon-Turkey Potpie, 148
Five-Spice Turkey Stir-Fry, 127

Maple-Mustard-Sauced Turkey Thighs, 125
Mexican Stromboli, 154
Mexican Turkey Pie, 128
Mock Monte Cristo Sandwiches, 152
Nutty Turkey Tenderloins, 145
Sausage-Corn Chowder, 36
Turkey-Bean Soup, 47
Turkey Manicotti with Chive Cream
Sauce, **141**, 149
Turkey-Potato Bake, 151
Turkey Steaks with Cranberry-Orange
Sauce, 147
Turkey Strudel, 150
Turkey Tenderloin with Bean & Corn
Salsa, 146
Turkey-Vegetable Goulash, 153

V
Vegetables. *See also* specific vegetables
Asian Noodle Bowl, 202
Beef Roast with Vegetables, 81
Brunch Casserole, 203
Chicken & Vegetables Alfredo with Rice, 119
Chicken-Vegetable Soup, 43
Creamy Chicken Noodle Soup, 42
Creamy Chicken & Vegetable Stew, 45
Dijon-Turkey Potpie, 148
East-West Veggies, 220
Easy Chicken Turnovers, 124
Fettuccine-Vegetable Toss, **139**, 196
Fish Stew, 162
Five-Spice Turkey Stir-Fry, 127
Gardener's Pie, 204
Minestrone, 200
Quick Asian Chicken Soup, 40
Roasted Vegetable & Pastrami Panini, 83
Sweet & Sour Beef Stew, 29
Swiss Vegetable Medley, 206
Tomato-Barley Soup with Garden
Vegetables, 55
Turkey-Vegetable Goulash, 153

W
Walnut Blue Cheese Spread, 13
Whipped Cream, Chocolate, 239
Wild Rice & Spinach au Gratin, 224
Wild Rice Salad, Fruited, 225

Metric Information

The charts on this page provide a guide for converting measurements from the U.S. customary system, used throughout this book, to the metric system.

Product Differences

Most of the ingredients called for in the recipes in this book are available in most countries. However, some are known by different names. Here are some common American ingredients and their possible counterparts:

- Sugar (white) is granulated, fine granulated, or castor sugar.
- Powdered sugar is icing sugar.
- All-purpose flour is enriched, bleached or unbleached white household flour. When self-rising flour is used in place of all-purpose flour in a recipe that calls for leavening, omit the leavening agent (baking soda or baking powder) and salt.
- Light-colored corn syrup is golden syrup.
- Cornstarch is cornflour.
- Baking soda is bicarbonate of soda.
- Vanilla or vanilla extract is vanilla essence.
- Bell peppers are capsicums.
- Golden raisins are sultanas.

Volume & Weight

The United States traditionally uses cup measures for liquid and solid ingredients. The chart below shows the approximate imperial and metric equivalents. If you are accustomed to weighing solid ingredients, the following approximate equivalents will be helpful.

- 1 cup butter, castor sugar, or rice = 8 ounces = $1/2$ pound = 250 grams
- 1 cup flour = 4 ounces = $1/4$ pound = 125 grams
- 1 cup icing sugar = 5 ounces = 150 grams

Canadian and U.S. volume for a cup measure is 8 fluid ounces (237 ml), but the standard metric equivalent is 250 ml.

1 British imperial cup is 10 fluid ounces.

In Australia, 1 tablespoon equals 20 ml, and there are 4 teaspoons in the Australian tablespoon.

Spoon measures are used for smaller amounts of ingredients. Although the size of the tablespoon varies slightly in different countries, for practical purposes and for recipes in this book, a straight substitution is all that's necessary. Measurements made using cups or spoons should be level unless stated otherwise.

Common Weight Range Replacements

Imperial / U.S.	Metric
$1/2$ ounce	15 g
1 ounce	25 g or 30 g
4 ounces ($1/4$ pound)	115 g or 125 g
8 ounces ($1/2$ pound)	225 g or 250 g
16 ounces (1 pound)	450 g or 500 g
$1 1/4$ pounds	625 g
$1 1/2$ pounds	750 g
2 pounds or $2 1/4$ pounds	1,000 g or 1 Kg

Oven Temperature Equivalents

Fahrenheit Setting	Celsius Setting*	Gas Setting
300°F	150°C	Gas Mark 2 (very low)
325°F	160°C	Gas Mark 3 (low)
350°F	180°C	Gas Mark 4 (moderate)
375°F	190°C	Gas Mark 5 (moderate)
400°F	200°C	Gas Mark 6 (hot)
425°F	220°C	Gas Mark 7 (hot)
450°F	230°C	Gas Mark 8 (very hot)
475°F	240°C	Gas Mark 9 (very hot)
500°F	260°C	Gas Mark 10 (extremely hot)
Broil	Broil	Grill

*Electric and gas ovens may be calibrated using celsius. However, for an electric oven, increase celsius setting 10 to 20 degrees when cooking above 160°C. For convection or forced air ovens (gas or electric) lower the temperature setting 25°F/10°C when cooking at all heat levels.

Baking Pan Sizes

Imperial / U.S.	Metric
9×1$1/2$-inch round cake pan	22- or 23×4-cm (1.5 L)
9×1$1/2$-inch pie plate	22- or 23×4-cm (1 L)
8×8×2-inch square cake pan	20×5-cm (2 L)
9×9×2-inch square cake pan	22- or 23×4.5-cm (2.5 L)
11×7×1$1/2$-inch baking pan	28×17×4-cm (2 L)
2-quart rectangular baking pan	30×19×4.5-cm (3 L)
13×9×2-inch baking pan	34×22×4.5-cm (3.5 L)
15×10×1-inch jelly roll pan	40×25×2-cm
9×5×3-inch loaf pan	23×13×8-cm (2 L)
2-quart casserole	2 L

U.S. / Standard Metric Equivalents

$1/8$ teaspoon	= 0.5 ml
$1/4$ teaspoon	= 1 ml
$1/2$ teaspoon	= 2 ml
1 teaspoon	= 5 ml
1 tablespoon	= 15 ml
2 tablespoons	= 25 ml
$1/4$ cup = 2 fluid ounces	= 50 ml
$1/3$ cup = 3 fluid ounces	= 75 ml
$1/2$ cup = 4 fluid ounces	= 125 ml
$2/3$ cup = 5 fluid ounces	= 150 ml
$3/4$ cup = 6 fluid ounces	= 175 ml
1 cup = 8 fluid ounces	= 250 ml
2 cups = 1 pint	= 500 ml
1 quart	= 1 litre